THE BATTLE OF ROCROI 1643

Clash of Seventeenth Century Superpowers

Alberto Raúl Esteban Ribas

'This is the Century of the Soldier', Fulvio Testi, Poet, 1641

Helion & Company

Helion & Company Limited
Unit 8 Amherst Business Centre
Budbrooke Road
Warwick
CV34 5WE
England
Tel. 01926 499 619
Email: info@helion.co.uk
Website: www.helion.co.uk
Twitter: @helionbooks
Visit our blog http://blog.helion.co.uk/

Published by Helion & Company 2022
Designed and typeset by Mach 3 Solutions Ltd (www.mach3solutions.co.uk)
Cover designed by Paul Hewitt, Battlefield Design (www.battlefield-design.co.uk)

ISBN 978-1-915113-97-9

British Library Cataloguing-in-Publication Data.
A catalogue record for this book is available from the British Library.

For details of other military history titles published by Helion & Company Limited contact the above
address or visit our website: http://www.helion.co.uk.

We always welcome receiving book proposals from prospective authors.

The Series Editor would like to thank Michal Paradowski for his help in the making of this book.

Contents

1

Introduction

The Battle of Rocroi, fought on 19 May 1643, has always attracted a strong interest, mainly from French historians but then closely followed by change to their British counterparts. Curiously, it was not until the end of the nineteenth century that Spanish historians began to take an interest in the battle.

The explanation for such a paradox lies in the fact that, for the French, Rocroi represents a great victory, celebrated for three important reasons. First, it represented a great success for the French army, after the defeat at Honnecourt, 26 May 1642, and the end of the Spanish campaign in France. Second, it was the first success of the brilliant career of Louis de Bourbon, Duc d'Enghien, later Prince de Condé and known to history as *le Grand Condé*. Third, it meant the entrenchment in power of the Regent Anne of Austria – and her new first minister, Jules Mazarin, by birth an Italian named Giulio Raimondo Mazzarino. As a culmination of all this, French propaganda raised the battle of Rocroi to the myth that on that day the Spanish tercios lost their invincibility and France rose to become the dominant European power for the rest of the century.

International military historians have accepted this vision, and for decades, the battle was always explained and analysed from the French point of view. For its part, Spanish historiography, self-conscious after centuries of decadence, accepted that point of view and assumed that at Rocroi the tercios had been overwhelmingly defeated.

However, it is noteworthy that, even with abundant primary sources from both sides, the French version, that of the victors, triumphed. Thus accepting not only the facts explained from their point of view, but also accepting facts that are either improbable or directly false – the massacre of the Spanish soldiers before their surrender for example.

Following the words of Stéphane Thion in *Rocroi 1643: The Victory of Youth*,[1] "Thus, there exist today two battles of Rocroi: the one found in Spanish works and the one found in numerous French works."

The primary sources for the study of the battle, those that are most relevant and profusely analysed, are the following:

For the French accounts, issue No. 65, dated May 27 1643, of *La Gazzete*, edited by Théopraste Renaudot; the manuscript *Relation des Campagnes de*

---

1   Stéphane Thion, *Rocroi 1643: The Victory of Youth*. Paris, Histoire & Collections, 2013. (Thion's book exists in both French and English editions – Ed).

Rocroy et de Friburg, the Memoirs of the Barón de Sirot and a letter from François de Montbas.

On the Spanish side, we have *Relación de los Sucesos de las Armas de S. M. C. el Rey D. Felipe IV Nuestro Señor, Gobernadas por el Excelentísimo Sr. D. Francisco de Melo, de la Campaña del Año de 1643* (Relation of the Campaign of 1643) by Juan Antonio Vincart, Melo's secretary. In addition, the letters sent by Melo himself and by the Duque de Albuquerque, as well as an anonymous letter *Relation written by a person who it was found in the battle that took place in Rocroix*, attributed supposedly to a member of Governor Melo's retinue or escort during the battle.

Peter Wilson was the first non-Spanish author to question the course of the battle[2], and at the same time, to attribute the fame of this battle to French propaganda. In Spanish historiography, there was a review of the traditional historical approaches; going from detailing the heroic acts of arms of the defeated Spanish, to questioning the true role of this battle in Spanish military history and questioning whether it actually marked the beginning of a decline.

---

2   Peter Wilson, *Europe's Tragedy. A History of the Thirty Years War.* Harvard: Belknap Press, 2011.

2

Background

The war between Spain and France that began in 1635 has its immediate origin in the Thirty Years' War (1618–1648), but we can trace its causes back to the century before, with the struggle between France and Spain for the control of Italy.

Thus, at the end of the fifteenth century, the Valois France invaded the Italian Peninsula with the intention of establishing its domination either directly or through the submission of the various states of the fragmented peninsula. This threatened the Kingdom of Naples, which had been conquered by Alfonso V of Aragon in 1442, and was ruled by a cadet branch of the Aragonese Trastámara.

French expansionism pushed the Aragonese King Fernando V, "the Catholic", Pope Alexander VI and Maximilian of Austria to form a League against Charles VIII. The League defeated the French at the Battle of Fornovo on July 6 1495.

A truce between France and Aragon in 1500, with the distribution of the lands of Naples and Sicily between the two powers, seemed to resolve the conflict. However, the partisan interpretation of the two contenders for the territorial limits of the peace treaty caused the outbreak of hostilities again in 1502. It was during this war that the figure of the Spanish General Gonzalo Fernández de Córdoba, called 'the Great Captain', shone for his skills on the battlefield and also for the creation of the concept of modern infantry – no longer simply an adjunct to medieval horse, but an arm of its own equipped with both firearms and polearms.

Between 1494 and 1559, Spain and France faced each other in nine wars for dominance of Italy, but they also fought on other fronts – Spain, France and Flanders. After several decades of almost uninterrupted war, the Spanish armies defeated the French at San Quentin, 10 August 1557, and Gravelines, 13 July 1558. It was at that point that France signed the Peace of Cateau-Cambrésis, by which she renounced her claim and rights over the Italian territories and the two protagonists returned the conquered places along the border of Flanders to each other.

With the victory, Spain was not only confirmed as the dominant power in Europe but it was also strengthened politically and territorially. In contrast, France was plunged into a long-running instability – Henri II died in a tournament in 1559 to be succeeded by his sons Francis II (1559–1560), Charles IX (1560–1574), Henri III (1574–1589). On the Henry III's death, Henri III of Navarre, married to the Valois Princess Margaret, ascended the throne of France as Henri IV, establishing a new dynasty – the Bourbons.

However, Henri of Navarre was a Protestant and the Catholic nobility opposed his reign. Supported by Spain, this nobility formed 'The Catholic League' and thus Spain encouraged the continuing instability of its constant rival. France bled through the internal conflict of eight bloody civil wars, collectively known as the Wars of Religion, from 1562–1598.

Henri IV, imposing himself with blood and fire, restored order in France and laid the foundations for it to begin a cycle of expansion. He also aided England and The Netherlands in their wars against Spain, in clear revenge for Felipe II's opposition to his accession to the throne. However, the assassination of Henri IV on 14 May 1610 by the Catholic fanatic François Ravaillac, cut short the Country's expansion. The new King, Louis XIII, had a character completely opposite to that of his father and was prone to lethargy. However, he had to militarily confront the conspiracies of his own mother, the regent Marie de Medici (1619–1620) and internal wars against the Huguenots supported by England and The Netherlands from 1621–1629.

It is in this new context of crisis, in 1624, that the figure of Armand Jean du Plessis, Cardinal de Richelieu, emerged in French politics, when he was appointed a member of the Royal Council. The Cardinal gained the trust and respect of the monarch, and while it seems that they did not have a personal friendship, they did forge a good relationship of close collaboration and service. Richelieu's political action was aimed at achieving two objectives: the centralisation of power in favour of the King and the fight against the House of Habsburg, which ruled Spain and the Holy Roman Empire.

At an international level, France and The Netherlands signed the Treaty of Compiègne on 10 June 1624, by which France contributed 480,000 thalers so that The United Provinces could resume hostilities against Spain after the end of the Twelve Years' Truce in 1621, this aid would be followed by other subsidies over a period of three years.

Portrait of Cardinal Richelieu (1585–1642), Philippe de Champagne (1602–1674), painted between 1633 and 1640. Richelieu was ordained a bishop in 1607 at the age of 22, he entered politics and was appointed Ministre des Affaires Étrangères (Minister of Foreign Affairs) in 1616; was appointed Cardinal in 1622, and Principal Ministre d'État (Principal Minister of State, effectively 'Prime Minister') of King Louis XIII in 1624. As 'Prime Minister' of France, he consolidated the power of the monarchy by fighting the various internal factions, counteracting the power of the nobility, and turned France into a strongly centralised state. Foreign policy, on the other hand, focused on countering the power of the Austro-Spanish Habsburgs. (Musée de la Ville de Strasbourg. Public Domain via Wikipedia Commons)

Intensifying the pressure against the Spanish Habsburgs, Richelieu turned his attention to the Italian situation. Italy was a military base and a source of economic resources for Spain. In the period 1629 to 1631 French troops entered Italy to intervene in the Mantuan War of Succession and Savoy became a French ally, after several decades of collaboration with Spain.

However, when Denmark was defeated in the Thirty Years' War in 1629, France signed the Treaty of Barwalde with Sweden on 23 January 1631. This was a military, commercial and political alliance between the two states, with the common goal of defeating the Habsburgs. With this action, Richelieu continued his policy of offering support to any power that was willing to fight the Habsburgs, but without any direct involvement since he considered that it was still too soon for French troops to come into direct conflict with the renowned Spanish tercios.

The Treaty of Barwalde established that Sweden undertook to deliver to France riggings, artillery pieces, masts, hemp, copper and in general all the materials necessary for shipbuilding, and also to maintain an army of 30,000 foot and 6,000 horse in Germany to fight against the Holy Roman Empire. France, for its part, agreed to pay 400,000 Reichstaler annually for 5 years.

Along the same aggressive lines, in June 1633 France invaded Lorraine, an ally of Spain, expelling both Duc Charles II and his younger brother Nicholas Francis, who had later ascended to the throne to try to appease the expansionist French.

The Swedes' aura of invincibility faded with the death of King Gustav II Adolph at the Battle of Lützen on 16 November 1632. The Swedes and the German Protestants were left without their beloved leader, almost causing the collapse of their cause. Richelieu could not afford a political and military victory for the Habsburgs, so he promoted the creation of the Heilbronn League on 23 April 1633.

The negotiations were difficult: the German Protestant states wanted to disassociate themselves from the Swedish pre-eminence, which had given ample evidence of its desire to create its own empire in Germany. France, for its part, wanted to set itself up as the protector of those states and direct military action to wear down the Habsburgs, while Sweden wanted to continue its military leadership and consolidate its territorial presence in the Baltic Sea. League members agreed to finance a 78,000 strong army, but put up less than a third of the money needed. In addition, Saxony and Brandenburg-Prussia initially supported but then did not join the League.

On the Catholic side, at the end of 1633 The Emperor, Ferdinand II, had assumed that Catholicism could not be re-imposed by force in Germany, and tried to persuade the Protestant German principalities to return to Imperial obedience while maintaining freedom of worship.

Throughout 1633 and 1634 a number of campaigns took place in Germany, with the fates swinging from one side to another. But after the Spanish Army of Ferdinand of Austria, Cardinal-Infante of Spain, joined with that of his cousin Ferdinand of Habsburg, King of Hungary and Imperial heir, their combined armies defeated a Swedish-German army, under the command of Gustav Horn and Bernhard of Saxe-Weimar, at Nördlingen on 6 and 7 September 1634. The defeat dealt a very heavy blow to French and Swedish interests.

Soldiers playing dice on a drum. Jacques Callot (1592-1635), after 1625. Note the sausage-like 'snapsack' in front of the drum and the soldiers looting in the background. (Rijksmuseum, Amsterdam)

With the Lutheran states of Denmark-Norway and Hesse-Darmstadt acting as mediators, in November 1634 the Imperial heir agreed to a general pacification with Elector Johann Georg I, of Saxony. The Catholic victory at Nördlingen had convinced many Protestant states that it was impossible to resist the Catholic offensive, and most States of The Empire signed the Peace of Prague in 1635, which dissolved both The Catholic League and the League of Heilbronn.

Sweden was alone, with its finances in tatters, its army dispersed, poorly paid and distant from its supply bases, and appeared unable to withstand the Imperial onslaught. With its ally seemingly about to falter France was forced, even if not yet ready, to enter directly into the war to prevent the collapse of the Protestant allies. On 19 May 1635 France declared war on Spain, invoking as a *casus belli* the arrest of the Elector of Trier by Spanish troops two months earlier.

Before embarking on war however, Richelieu orchestrated a network of alliances:

> On 8 February 1635 the Treaty of Paris was signed between France and The Netherlands, by which if Spain were defeated, the two would divide Spanish Flanders: Artois, Flanders, Hainaut, Namur and Luxembourg would go to France and the remaining territories to The Netherlands.
>
> France signed the Treaty of Compiègne with Sweden on 28 April 1635, agreeing that France would claim Alsace and the right bank of the Rhine when the Spanish and Imperials were expelled.
>
> On 11 July of the same year, the Treaty of Rivoli was signed between France and Savoy to divide the Duchy of Milan.

The Treaty of Saint Germain was signed between France and Bernhard of Saxe-Weimar on 26 October. By this Treaty the latter undertook to maintain an army of 12,000 foot and 6,000 horse to conquer Alsace, with France agreeing to provide the finance to pay for the army.

France had enormous resources and the military budget in 1635 amounted to 16.5 million thalers, so it could maintain a number of operational armies. In their Treaty hiring the services of Bernhard of Saxe-Weimar and his veteran army, France agreed to an annual payment of 1.6 million thalers. In addition, France raised several armies of its own with which to attack Flanders, Italy and Spain. Its strategic central position allowed reinforcements to be moved from one theatre of operations to another, safely and through its own territory. By contrast, Spain had to embark its troops for Italy and then march from there along 'the Spanish Road' to reach Flanders, or alternately move them the whole way to Flanders along the dangerous sea routes.

However, despite its economy and the size of its armies, France did not have military experience comparable to the Spanish.

Upon the outbreak of the war, French maritime traffic was almost immediately attacked by Spanish and Flemish privateers based at Dunkirk. In the period 1635–1638, more than 2,000 French ships were seized. Similar attacks happened against the Dutch merchant fleet – in August 1635 the Spanish annihilated the Dutch fishing fleet in the vicinity of the Shetland Islands.

In 1635, immediately that France entered the war, they and the Dutch launched offensives against Spanish Flanders. The French and Dutch armies attacked Flanders from the east and west, putting the Cardinal-Infante in trouble and under pressure. These actions were poorly coordinated however, and he defeated the two armies separately, thanks to the lines of fortifications and his veteran troops.

Having stopped the double offensive of 1635, the Cardinal-Infante planned an offensive campaign for 1636. In the spring, he organised the defence of East Flanders to prevent a Dutch attack, and in July launched an offensive against France, capturing La Capelle, Le Catelet and Corbie. Richelieu, 'pour encouragez les autres', ordered the execution of the commanders of these garrisons.

The Spanish Army was only 120 kilometres from Paris and the Cardinal-Infante sent a number of parties of scouts on deep raids that even reached Pontoise, 50km from the French capital. Panic spread in the Louvre, because simultaneously an Imperial Army, under the command of the veteran General Mathias Gallas, was advancing towards Dijon intent on conquering Burgundy. However, the Swedish victory at Wittstock on 4 October 4 1636 forced an Imperial retreat and the Spanish Army, feeling its supply lines from Flanders too extended and vulnerable, retreated to the frontier.

The following years did not see any major French victories until 1638, when the first was achieved in the Alsatian campaign led by Bernhard of Saxe-Weimar: the conquest of the important town of Breisach. Bernhard, however, did not surrender the town to his French ally, but retained it under his personal control, since he was anxious to increase his power as Duke of

Franconia. His death, on July 18 1639, meant the loss of a great strategist, but also the disappearance of an unstable and expensive ally, with France gaining control of his army.

As of 1639, the diversity and distance of the various fronts meant that Spain did not have sufficient human and economic resources to maintain offensives everywhere, so Flanders, from where Paris could be directly threatened, was prioritised. A powerful fleet was organised, of around a hundred ships of all kinds, transporting 6,000 foot and another 8,000 sailors and marine infantry all intended for Flanders – some sources put the total number of men on board at more than 20,000. However, on 21 October 1639, at The Downs off the east coast of Kent, the Spanish fleet, under Admiral Antonio de Oquendo, clashed with the Dutch fleet of the Admiral Maarten Harpertszoon Tromp. The Spanish fleet lost the battle with 14 ships captured, 51 ships destroyed and 7,000 dead, at a cost of only 1 Dutch ship sunk and a hundred dead. The Spanish however, claimed to have destroyed 10 ships and caused 1,000 enemy casualties.

The year 1640 did not go well for Felipe IV either: with rebellions in Catalonia and Portugal breaking out simultaneously – it was the most serious crisis experienced by the Spanish Habsburg Monarchy.

The Principality of Catalonia was a territory that had been at the forefront of the war since 1637, as the spearhead of Spain against France's southern border. As in other territories, the permanent presence of troops caused discontent and problems among the civilian population. The uprising originated from the existing tension due to the presence of the Royal army.

In May 1640, some soldiers, short of food and money, sacked some towns in the province of Gerona and the peasants attacked the soldiers, in other localities the revolt broke out due to the high taxes. The local authorities sided with their compatriots and demanded that the Madrid Court withdraw the troops. Violence increased amongst the rural populations, and on 7 June 1640, many of the rebels entered Barcelona, taking advantage of the fact that labourers were needed for the summer harvest. Once inside the capital, a socio-political riot broke out, in which the lower classes attacked the aristocracy. The rebels murdered the Governor, who was also a Catalan, and other Royal officials.

The Conde-Duque de Olivares organised a military response, recruiting an army in a hurry, which would join the forces defending Roussillon, whose mission was to advance south, in a converging attack to recapture Barcelona. To maintain resistance, the rebels asked Cardinal Richelieu for help. Richelieu agreed to send an army in exchange for the Catalans appointing Louis XIII as Count of Barcelona and Lord of Catalonia. Within weeks a French army entered Barcelona, just in time to defeat the Spanish Royal army at the Battle of Barcelona on 26 January 1641 and forcing the Spanish Army to retreat to Tarragona. Thus began the long conflict called *Guerra de los Segadores* (the Reapers' War) which did not end until 1652.

In December 1640, Portugal also rose in revolt. Since its annexation to Spain in 1580, part of the Portuguese nobility and common people had been dissatisfied with the high taxes and the demand for troops to defend Flanders and the colonial empire. In contrast, the higher Portuguese Aristocracy held important positions in the administration of the Spanish Empire. The future King, João de Braganza, had even held positions, and his wife, Luisa de Guzmán, was Spanish and a sister of the Duque de Medina Sidonia. Francisco de Melo, also of the House of Braganza, was Governor and Captain-General of the Spanish Tercios of Flanders. When in the course of the war against The United Provinces, the Dutch attacked Portuguese colonies in Brazil, the Portuguese feelings of abandonment and their grievances against the Spanish were exacerbated further.

To quell the Catalan revolt, Felipe IV requested troops and money from the other Spanish territories. In Portugal, some nobles, annoyed because they felt neglected, grouped themselves around the Duque de Braganza, who was proclaimed King on 1 December as João IV. This began a long conflict that would not finally end until 1668, with the recognition of Portuguese independence.

Thus Spain now had a war on two fronts in Europe, in Flanders and in Italy, and another two in the Iberian Peninsula itself, in Catalonia and in Portugal. In Flanders, throughout the period 1637 to 1641, the Cardinal-Infante had to face the combined pressure of both the French and Dutch. However, he was receiving barely enough money and troops necessary to maintain his position, since the Madrid Court had not only to send troops to Italy, Roussillon, Catalonia and Portugal, but also to maintain garrisons in the cities of their extensive colonies in America, Africa and Asia.

Given that the campaigns of 1640 and 1641 were failures for the Spanish armies in the Iberian Peninsula, the Cardinal-Infante tried to relieve the pressure on the Iberian theatre of operations, and in August 1641 opened the siege of Aire-sur-la-Lys, which had fallen into French hands a month earlier. The siege lasted for seven months, during the course of which, the Cardinal-Infante fell ill and died in Brussels on 9 November 1641. Although today it is believed that his death was caused by exhaustion coupled with a stomach ulcer, at the time, there was speculation and rumours that pointed to a possible poisoning as the cause of his death.

The government of Flanders fell provisionally to the Portuguese Francisco de Melo. The *Valido* Olivares commissioned the new Governor-General to undertake a campaign from Flanders as soon as possible in order to distract the French from Catalonia, a front that was considered priority. Melo meticulously organised the preparations and pre-empted the Dutch and French, who had not yet prepared their armies. Melo's army invaded France in mid-April 1642, taking Lens on 19 April, and La Bassé on 20 May.

The two French armies guarding the border separated: The Comte d'Harcourt, with 17,000 men, headed towards Boulogne, while The Duc de Guiche, with 10,000 men, marched towards Champagne. Melo learned of the French plans and decided to concentrate against Guiche, who entrenched his troops on a hill next to the village of Honnecourt-sur-Escaut, near the Scheldt River. On 26 May the Spanish launched several attacks against the French line, breaking their flanks and forcing the surrender of the centre. De Guiche's army was destroyed: 3,200 dead, 500 wounded and 3,400 prisoners, losing 10 guns, 50 standards and colours and all their baggage. Melo took about 500 casualties, dead and wounded. The Spanish victory was total, but Melo's prudence and lack of ambition did not let him exploit it and he did not want to advance further into France.

In the French Court, however, there was fear of an "imminent" Spanish advance, and they remembered that the armies of Charles V and Felipe II had previously invaded France, as had that of the Cardinal-Infante in 1636. The topography of northern France, the forests north of the Somme and the river itself, were not impenetrable; and the fortified cities of Amiens, Péronne and Saint-Quentin, had fallen into Spanish hands in the past and could easily do so again. The other invasion route, through the Ardennes and Thiérache, following the course of the Oise, taking Guise, Noyon and Compiègne, led directly to Paris.

Melo, however, did not want to tempt fate and was exceedingly cautious, and made no attempt to take another important city or seek another pitched battle. In addition, the Dutch army was mustered and Melo wanted to protect the north of Flanders. By contrast, this passivity caused the French to launch an offensive that allowed them to conquer Perpignan and its region of Roussillon, and to repel Spanish attempts to recapture Lérida, where the Spanish lost 5,000 dead, wounded and prisoners.

These military defeats caused King Felipe IV to blame his bad fortune on his favourite Olivares, who in January 1643 was ordered into exile from Court and to retire to his possessions for life. It was a consolation for Olivares to know that in December 1642 Cardinal Richelieu, his archenemy, had died without being able to conceive that Olivares would be removed from power and exiled.

The new French 'Prime Minister', Cardinal Mazarin, planned an offensive campaign for 1643, with the coordinated actions of up to four field armies. The Army of Picardy, commanded by the Duc d'Enghien, destined for the invasion of the provinces of Hainaut and the Artois. The Army of Champagne, under the command of *Maréchal* de Guiche, to defend Paris and serve as a reserve. The Army of Burgundy, under the orders of *Maréchal* La Milleraye, was to attack Franche-Comté. In addition, there was the Army of Catalonia, within the Iberian Peninsula, charged with the task of pressing towards the interior of Spain.

Cardinal Jules Mazarin (1602–1661), by Pierre Mignard I (1612–1695) painted between 1658 and 1660. Mazarin's life was a succession of adventures that did not presage that he would devote himself to either religious life or French politics; as a young man he was very studious, but also an inveterate gambler. Initially he was to be a lawyer or a military officer, but Pope Urban VIII took notice of him and entrusted him with diplomatic posts, which he carried out with great skill. He was sent to Paris as an emissary, where he developed a good working relationship with Richelieu. He became the French agent in Rome and finally Richelieu succeeded in having him made a Cardinal in 1638. Thereafter Mazarin settled permanently in France, becoming a protégé of Richelieu, whom he succeeded in 1642. Mazarin's succession to the post of 'Prime Minister' of Louis XIII, however, was neither automatic nor immediate. It was the Regent Anne who appointed him to the post and as effective Head of the Government, after getting rid of his rivals De Noyers and De Chavigny. (Condé Museum, PE 314. Public Domain through Wikipaedia Commons)

The map shows how the Spanish Netherlands were vulnerable to attack from the North by The United Provinces, and from the South by France. Additionally, to the east they are open to invasion by armies from or through 'Germany'. The territories of the Bishopric of Liège and the Duchy of Luxembourg were allies of the Spain but, because of conventions, could be traversed by Dutch or French armies.

Taking into account the French mobilisation, for the campaign of 1643 Melo was ordered to attack the French as soon as possible, fearing that they would initiate a major offensive in Catalonia. However, the political news coming from France invited a certain optimism in Spain – Richelieu, the political genius, was dead; King Louis XIII was dying; the future King Louis XIV was only four years old and the Regent Anne of Austria, sister of King Felipe IV, was supported only by the new Minister Cardinal Mazarin; and much of the higher aristocracy were impatient to recover the power lost under Richelieu. If a victory was achieved in Flanders, and the campaigns of the Cardinal-Infante and that of Honnecourt both presented an excellent precedent, it was thought in Madrid that the French would ask for a peace to be able to concentrate on their internal situation.

3

The Opposing Armies

The French Army

For a comprehensive overview of the French army during the reign of Louis XIII, I would recommend *Richelieu's Army: War, Government and Society in France, 1624–1642*.[1] For the French participation in the long European conflict, *French armies of the Thirty Years' War*.[2] And for the army during Louis XIV's long reign the best work is *Giant of the Grand Siècle. The French Army, 1610–1715*.[3] For this study of Rocroi, I will focus only on the tactical and organisational aspect of the French army at the end of Louis XIII's reign, since Louis XIV was only a boy of four.

Foot

In 1479 King Louis XI had created the *Bandes Françaises*, inspired by the Swiss pike companies, whose fighting model was adopted by many armies in Europe. In France, this organisational model for foot was initially known as the *Bandes de Picardie*, and they were the first permanent military units paid for by the monarchy. In 1480, Louis XI signed a contract with the Swiss cantons to provide him with 6,000 mercenaries, who trained the levies he had recruited in France, mainly in the Picardy area. In 1483, the new French bands were put in charge of guarding the northern French border against the Army of the Emperor Maximilian. From 1494 onwards, the bands took part in successive Italian campaigns.

More companies were recruited in the style of the original bands, the new ones being known as *Bandes de Piémont*, or popularly *Bandes au-delà des Monts* (the bands beyond the mountains), while the Bands of Picardy were the *Bandesendeçà des Monts* (the bands on this side of the mountains).

---

1   David Parrott: *Richelieu's Army. War, Government and Society in France, 1624–42.* Cambridge University Press, Cambridge 2001.

2   Stéphane Thion: *French Armies of the Thirty Years' War.* LRT Editions, Auzielle 2008.

3   John A. Lynn: *Giant of the Grand Siècle : The French Army, 1610–1715.* Cambridge University Press, Cambridge 2009.

Various other detachments were also raised, the *Bandes de Champagne, Bandes de Normandie, Bandes de Bretagne,* and these served as the backbone of the armies of the French Monarchy in the Italian wars, until their disbandment by a Royal Order on 1 August 1563, although they were actually operational for a few more years.

Like most European armies in the early and mid–sixteenth century, the Roman military tradition inspired the organisation of the French armies and the way they fought. The reading of classics by Livy, Tacitus, et cetera by French treatise writers and military men inspired the organisation of their army. This is why, in 1534, François I issued an Ordinance for the Foot, which sought to create a permanent military institution that evolved and stayed up-to-date. Seven provincial foot units called *Légions Nationales* (National Legions), each of 6,000 men, were created. The *Légions* were commanded by a colonel, and organised into six companies of 1,000 men, each commanded by a captain, assisted by two lieutenants, two ensigns and six sergeants. Each company was divided into 10 *centeniers* (100 man "centuries") of 80 pikemen and 20 arquebusiers. However, the practical experience with these units was not positive: in 1536 the Légion de le Dauphin was disbanded for insubordination. In 1543, during the siege of Luxembourg, 1,500 men deserted, and in 1557 they mutinied at Metz but the mutiny was put down by the marshal of Vielle-Ville, François de Scépeaux.

François I also created the rank of *Colonel-Général de l'Infanterie Française* (Colonel-Général of the French Infantry), as an operational command below the Constable and the Maréchals de France. In 1581, Jean-Louis de Nogaret de La Valette d'Épernon, 1er Duc d'Épernon, was appointed Colonel-Général: he was as such considered colonel of all foot regiments and therefore his signature appeared on all officer appointments.

The decades of war with the Spanish in Italy, in Flanders, and against The Catholic League, in which the Spanish had been victorious, led the French to adopt customs and habits of the Spanish Army model. For example, in 1560 François de Guise created three regiments modelled on the Spanish tercio.

After the failure in the creation of the *Légions* and based on a core of veterans of European campaigns, three "permanent" regiments were created; these were named Picardie, Piémont and Champagne. The Huguenot leader Henri of Navarre had raised a regiment of Guards from his most experienced men and when he ascended to the throne, under the name of Henri IV, that regiment was renamed Navarre. These four regiments formed what came to be called *Les Vieux Corps* (the old Corps).

Under Henri IV, around 1602, Maximilien de Béthune, Duc de Sully, reorganised the French foot into permanent regiments and temporary regiments that were raised only in time of war. By 1616, both the regiments of *Les Vieux* and the two regiments of Guards (the French and the Swiss) carried the *Drapeau Blanc* (the White Flag), symbolising the authority of the Colonel-Général of the foot. This privilege was later extended to more foot regiments. In the original regiments, both of the *Garde* and of *Les Vieux,* the *Colonel-Général* had his own company, commanded by a lieutenant-colonel, which carried the *Drapeau Blanc.*

In 1616, the permanent Régiment de Normandie was formed, becoming considered part of the *Les Vieux.* In 1620, the permanent regiments of the

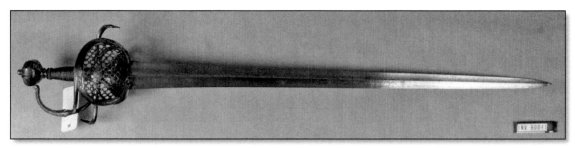

Cavalry sword, 1630. Total length of 1.12 metre and blade a length of 0.91 metre, with a blade width of 53mm at the hilt, overall weight of 1.25kg. The blade is double-edged, and although wide at the hilt, it tapers towards the tip. On both sides it is adorned with engraved ornaments and on the outside with an image of Bernhard de Saxe-Weimar in a medallion frame. Inside, in addition to the ornaments, there is a portrait of Gustav II Adolph within the same type of frame as the portrait outside. However, on the sheet it bears the inscription "ME FECIT SOLINGEN 1652" (I was manufactured in Solingen in 1652). All this suggests that the hilt and bowl of the sword were manufactured around 1630 and belonged to an officer of one of the regiments of Bernhard de Saxe-Weimar, when he was in the service of Sweden. The blade was repaired in 1652. (Armémuseum, AM.060041)

Vieux Corps (Champagne, Picardie, Piémont, Normandie and Navarre) were grouped together with the regiments of the Guard (Gardes Françaises and Gardes Suisses) and thereafter the two Guards regiments were considered part of *Les Vieux*. Six permanents regiments, which were initially named after their Colonel (Chappes, Rambures, Bourg-l'Espinasse, Sault, Vaubecourt and Beaumont), henceforward became known as *Les Petits Vieux* (The Little Old [ones]). Some years later in 1635, Richelieu formed the régiment de La Marine, to which the Cardinal granted the rank as the sixth regiment of the *Les Vieux*.

With France's direct involvement in the Thirty Years' War, although it had also intervened in Italy, it became necessary to increase the number of regiments of foot. The wealth of the French coffers, as well as France's high population, did not slow down the growth, at least initially, of these temporary regiments, recruited for a single campaign or for a couple of years of service and disbanded at the end of the reason for their raising. A staff company was usually left 'in service' and was garrisoned in a town during the winter, to be reactivated and recruited to a new regiment for the following campaign. Unlike the *Vieux* and the *Petit Vieux Corps*, these temporary regiments initially bore the name of their "Mestre de Camp".

In 1635, when France entered the war against Spain, it had about 100,000 foot in 135 regiments, and 18,000 horse; by the end of that year, the army had increased to 150,000 foot and 30,000 horse. France was a rich and populous state, thus Louis XIII and Louis XIV had no trouble recruiting soldiers for the various theatres of war. Moreover, the Country's strategic location in the centre of Europe allowed it to send reinforcements to different fronts using inland waterways: troops could be sent from Paris to Catalonia, Italy, Germany or Flanders without the threat of being attacked on the march, or having to rely on having a fleet, as in Spain's case.

As France became more amenable to Dutch military doctrine, from the 1620s onwards regiments of foot on campaign began to be divided into battalions, a unit of 500 to 600 foot, assuming that the formation was no more than ten men deep. From the 1630s onwards, the battalions sometimes consisted of 700 to 900 or even 1,000 men.

There were generally two battalions per regiment, but the number depended on the troops available. As regiments lost men during a campaign, battalions might be formed from companies of different regiments.

One-third of the troops were pikemen, who formed in the centre of the battalion, and who could be formed six to eight ranks deep; two-thirds were musketeers, who formed equally either side of the pikes, or to the front. A battalion of 800 men, 6 ranks deep, had a frontage of 135 men, assuming that there is a pace of 3 feet for each soldier. When closed up for battle the frontage will reduce by a third. Generally each pike squadron had a detachment of 45 musketeers on each side.

Like the Spanish arquebusier *mangas*, the French detached units of musketeers to operate independently often in detachments of 50 men: these were known as *enfants perdus* (literally "lost children"). Their main function was to act as skirmishers, preceding the foot detachments on the march, and in battle acting as a protective screen, or serving as a mobile reserve, ready to go anywhere on the battlefield.

When detachments of musketeers were formed for specific missions or were interspersed in the horse, these groupings were known as *mousquetaires commandes* (commanded musketeers), and formed units of 100 to 500 men. This practice of combining foot with horse began in the mid–sixteenth century, in the Huguenot armies of Gaspar de Coligny and Henri of Navarre, but became widespread across Europe with the tactical innovations of Gustav II Adolph of Sweden.

In 1635, Richelieu established the battalion as an official subdivision of the regiment. In practice, administratively, units were counted by regiments and companies, while the battalion remained a tactical and therefore a temporary formation. Theoretically, in combat a battalion was deployed in ten ranks with pikes in the centre on a 20 man front and musketeers in the wings, 5 ranks of musketeers on each side following the Dutch model. Later, as French military doctrine evolved the battalion was often formed in six ranks deep or sometimes eight ranks deep for inexperienced units.

The military successes of Gustav II Adolph and the subsequent incorporation of the German units of Bernhard of Saxe-Weimar caused Swedish military doctrine to take root in the French army from the second half of the 1630s onwards. In some battles, the French generals adopted the concept of a "brigade" to group battalions on the battlefield; these generally consisted of two to four battalions, with an exclusively tactical and not permanent purpose. At the Battle of Honnecourt for example, the regiments of Piémont and Rambures formed the Brigade Rantzau.

Both horse and foot of the French army used the company as the basic organisational unit. A peculiarity of the standard French company was that it was smaller than those of other armies – varying from 50 to 200 men. By 1610, regiments of foot usually numbered 20 companies of 100 men each; however, the number of companies varied over the years and the temporary regiments maintained different numbers – sometimes 30 companies, sometimes 15, sometimes 12 or 10.

In 1635, Cardinal Richelieu reformed the foot so that all regiments had the same establishment: 20 companies of 53 men each, totalling a strength of 1,060 men per regiment, although exceptionally, the regiments with the *Drapeau Blanc* had 30 companies. Each company comprised a captain, a lieutenant, an ensign, two sergeants, three corporals, five *anspessades* and some *appointees* (men who, for their long service or demonstrated courage, received higher pay) in total, 40 men – 60 percent musketeers and 40 percent pikemen. There were units, however, that were comprised exclusively of musketeers, such as the Régiment de Cardinal La Valette. Both the corporals and the *anspessades* had the armament of their rank and file.

In the French army, the pike was 14 feet long, similar to the Spanish pike; pikemen wore helmets, but the best helmets (morions, burgonets or cabassets) with back and breasts, were reserved for those in the front line, for corporals and for *anspessades*. As the 1640s approached, pikemen began to reduce the amount of armour they wore, although Régiments Suisse were renowned for having retained heavier armour longer than any other units.

As for shot, as in Sweden, arquebuses gradually disappeared as muskets became lighter and in 1622 the arquebus was officially replaced in the French army by the musket. Initially the musket used a forked rest, but by the 1630s it had become light enough to be used without. Musketeers generally wore a hat, but on rare occasions a morion; generally they wore a cassock, and it was uncommon for them to wear a buff coat.

During the years after 1635, the theoretical strength of the companies varied: 53 men during the period 1635 to 1637; 75 men in 1638 and 1639; 60 men during 1640 to 1642 and 70 men per company in 1643 and 1644.

On 10 October 1642 Louis XIII issued an Ordinance for the Foot, in which he established a strength of 56 men for all French companies, except the so-called "royal" ones, with 150 men. Moreover, each company, in theory, had 1/3 pikemen and 2/3 musketeers. In practice however, by the 1630s in the veteran companies there was already a ratio of two-thirds pikemen and one-third musketeers, but in newly raised companies, the ratio could be the other way round – two-thirds pikemen and one-third musketeers. Soldiers of both arms carried a sword.

The regimental organisation of 20 companies became usual, but was not uniform across all regiments. At the beginning of the 1643 campaign, the French army had 166 regiments of foot, of which 141 were French and 25 foreign. The French regiments comprised: one regiment of French Guards, 15 regiments of 30 companies, 107 regiments of 20

French high ranking officer, c1630. 'Fight for Saint Martin on Île de Ré' Jacques Callot, 1629-1631. By 1643 the falling ruff would have probably been replacd by a more traditional collar and the sleeves of the Officer's coat may have lost the exaggerated 'slashes', all this may depending on the personal tastes of the officer of course. Overall however the senior French Officers at Rocroi would have looked very little different to the one shown here. (Rijksmuseum, Amsterdam. Public Domain)

companies, one regiment of 18 companies, one regiment of 15 companies, six regiments of 12 companies and ten regiments of 10 companies. The composition of each company varied between 50, 80 and 200 troops – the companies of Guards usually had their full complement of 200 men.

Generally, the permanent (*entretenu*) regiments numbered 30 companies, while the non-permanent regiments, those disbanded at the end of the campaign, numbered 20 companies. In January 1643 Louis XIII stated that in many regiments of 30 companies the number of troops was so small that he had decided to maintain only 20 companies and to disband the rest, whose personnel were incorporated into the remaining companies.

On the battlefield, a regiment of 30 companies formed into two battalions of 800–900 men, and a regiment of 20 companies formed a battalion of 1,000–1,200 men; regiments with 10 and 12 companies were often paired together to form a battalion.

In terms of tactics, French armies deployed in two to three lines, in a 'diamond-like' arrangement: the first line was made up of two groups of two battalions; the second line had three groups of two battalions; and if there was a third line, it had two groups of two battalions. The horse was placed in the wings, generally equally distributed on the two flanks, also in a 'diamond shape', one unit in front, two in the second line, and another squadron closing the formation in the third line.

At battalion deployment level, there were various formations – *le croix*, *l'echiquier*, *le cinquain*, et cetera, but the most common was *le croix* (the cross): it is the closest order because the rearguard troops are in direct line behind the vanguard.

If necessary, there were still intervals of almost 80 metres between each battalion of the second line to allow the first line to fall back through it, thus the army's lines were deployed in a checkerboard form.

In the French army, the location of marching troops was paralleled by their deployment on the battlefield: a marching army was divided into three corps: *avant-garde* (vanguard), *bataille* (centre), and *arrière-garde* (rearguard). On the battlefield, the usual form of deployment was in three lines: the first was called the vanguard; the second line, formed by the centre, was about the same strength as the vanguard; and the third, the rearguard, if it was about the same strength as the others or the reserve if it was much weaker.

The foot formed in the centre of the deployment, with the horse protecting both flanks, and with the artillery deployed in the front line of the foot. The field artillery was usually falconets, small calibre falcons, although larger pieces were also used.

Régiment des Gardes Française (The French Guard Regiment)

This regiment held precedence over all other units; its origins date back to the reign of Charles IX, with a complement of ten companies, each of fifty men. During the reigns of his successors, the regiment increased its number of companies and the number of men in each company. At the time of the declaration of war on Spain (1635), sources indicate that there was a total of 30 companies, with 300 men per company; the numbers were later reduced to 200 men per company.

In December 1642, King Louis XIII created thirty elite companies, nick-named *Royaux,* each consisting of 300 men, which took the names of their captains: d'Enghien, Nemours, La Trémoille, Liancourt, et cetera. The cost of each company was 4,500 livres and eight of them took part in the battle of Rocroi.

Only the units of the Royal Guard had a uniform in modern terms, while in the rest of the units the clothing was usually provided by the soldier. Frequently however the State directly, or the general of the army, contracted the supply of clothing for their troops, generally at the beginning of a campaign. This was not primarily in order to provide a single uniform for their men, but to provide them with warm clothing for the campaign.

Régiments Étrangers (Foreign Regiments)

France had a long tradition of recruiting mercenaries – mainly Swiss and Germans – to increase the size of its armies. By 1640, the foreign regiments totalled 41,000 men, divided as follows: seven Swiss regiments, totalling 83 companies at an average of 200 men each; four Irish regiments, with 50 companies of 100 men each; four Scottish regiments, totalling 62 companies, at an average of 100 men each; eight German regiments, with 107 companies of 100 men each; one Liégeois regiment, totalling 20 companies, at an average of 100 men each; and one Italian regiment, with 10 companies of 50 men each.

Special notice should be taken of the units of Bernhard of Saxe-Weimar's, which entered direct French service in 1636. The units numbered 12,000 foot and 6,000 horse, theoretically making a

BERNHARDVS D.G. Dux Saxoniæ, Iuliæ Cliviæ et Mont: Landgravi, Thuringiæ Marchio Misniæ cõ: Marc et Ravensperg Dom. Rauenstein etc:

C. Danck exc.

Bernhard of Saxe-Weimar, by Matthäus Merian (1593-1650) Bernhard was the eleventh son of Herzog Johann II of Saxony-Weimar and Dorothy Mary of Anhalt. He received a careful education and was a very religious man, professing a fervent Protestant faith that led him to enlist at the age of 18, and participating in the battles of Wiesloch (1622), Wimpfen (1622) and Stadtlohn (1623). He later took part in the campaigns of Christian IV of Denmark, and after the landing of Gustav II Adolph in Pomerania, he put himself at his service. As a reward for his courage he rose to command an independent army and was subsequently created Herzog of Franconia. He later became the military leader of the League of Heilbronn, serving in France. Richelieu promised to provide Bernhard with four million livres a year in grants during the war to support an army of 12,000 foot and 6,000 horse with the necessary artillery. In a secret article he was granted Alsace, on condition that he did not expel Catholics. Between 1635 and 1638 Bernhard fought for the Protestant cause, but also to consolidate his own personal power in Alsace. Bernhard died on 18 July 1639 in Neuenburgam Rhein, while preparing for a new campaign against the imperialists. The suspicion that he died of poison that could have been administered to him at the request of Richelieu is not proven. Sweden, France and The Holy Roman Empire fought for Bernhard's legacy. (Peace Palace Library. Public Domain through Wikipaedia Commons) total of 2,000 men in each regiment of foot and 1,000 in each regiment of horse. The cost of this army was of 4 million *livres* per year, to be paid in quarterly instalments. However, Saxe-Weimar's army turned out to be only 4,000 foot and 2,000 horse and additional men had to be recruited to make the contingent effective.

Régiment des Gardes Suisses (The Regiment of Swiss Guards)

Traditionally, French kings had relied on the service of Swiss mercenaries; however, in 1567, Louis Pfiffer's Swiss regiment distinguished itself in the service of King Charles IX, being awarded the distinction of being the King's regiment of Swiss Guards. Since then, this unit had men of excellent physical quality and courage. Its strength was 12 companies of 200 men each.

In January 1635, the *Gardes Écossaises* was raised, with 30 companies of 150 men.

Horse

The once mighty medieval French horse had been defeated on successive occasions by infantry: English, Burgundian, Swiss and Spanish. During the sixteenth century, the decline of the late medieval type of heavy horse became evident, despite the clear improvement in the way they fought. These horse resisted disappearing completely however, due to the political entanglement that persisted both in France and in other countries, namely the struggle between the centralising monarchy and the territorial nobility. The latter was reluctant to lose its privileges, which were associated with the right to have companies of armed men, generally made up of its vassals, loyal to the nobleman and not to the King.

Precisely because the sovereign wanted loyalty and obedience to the Crown and not to a subject a new kind of chivalry would make its way throughout the sixteenth century, free of feudal ties and dependent only on the monarch.

From the mid–fifteenth century onwards, France tended to consolidate onto a central power structure, a struggle that led to various noble revolts, aggravated by the religious conflict between Catholicism and Protestantism. All of this resulted in a semi-permanent climate of civil war from the second half of the sixteenth century onwards, ending with the revolt of the Fronde from 1648 to 1653. In Spain, on the other hand, the last noble revolt was the Castilian Civil War from 1474 to 1479 against the Catholic Monarchs, and the *Guerra de las Comunidades de Castilla* ('Revolt of the Communities of Castile') against Charles V in 1520 and 1521.

In France, after the civil wars, King Henri IV reformed the horse in 1600. He created the *Maison du Roi* (King's Household), made up of four companies of Guards (a company of chevau-légers, a company of gendarmes, a company of 100 arquebusiers and carabins, and a Scottish company). There were also 19 companies of gendarmes and chevau-légers, with 25 to 30 men in each. The Gendarmerie Companies were of two types: the companies of Princes of the Royal Blood, and the Companies of the Gentlemen, drawn from the higher nobility. At the time, the companies of chevau-légers, armed with arquebuses, were reinforced by small parties of horse armed with carabins. While in 1603 there had been 1,500 horse of all types, in 1609 there were 8,500.

In 1620, only a part of the Gendarmerie still retained full armour, and even this was being progressively lightened, with three-quarter armour, and a burgonet often replacing the characteristic closed helmet. Weapons comprised a sword and two horse pistols; the gendarmes formed in formations six ranks deep. Also in 1620 the companies of chevau-légers replaced their arquebuses with carbines. The chevau-légers wore a morion or, more frequently, a burgonet, and a back and breast over a buff coat; they also carried a sword and two pistols.

French horse in the first half of the seventeenth century were of three types: gendarmes, light horse and dragoons. While the first two were the result of the evolution from medieval cavalry, the third was an evolution from the infantryman with a horse and a firearm to a mounted infantryman able to operate either on foot or on horseback, depending on the needs of combat. For this reason, the dragoons in their early days, must have felt a certain contempt for horse. It was not for nothing that they were considered mounted infantry, not horse, and a good part of the first dragoon units were made up of infantry.

Dragoons first appeared in the French army during the reign of Henri II, the concept being attributed to Charles de Cossé, Comte de Brissac and *Maréchal* de France, who commanded the French army from 1550 to 1559, and their origin was in the French campaign in Piémont in the 1550s. Given their success, the Duque de Alba, after fighting the French in Italy, adopted the idea into the Spanish Army; and when he left Italy for Flanders in 1567, Spanish mounted arquebusiers entered combat in the Eighty Years' War.

The combat unit was the squadron, composed of 120 to 150 horse. One or more *cornettes* (companies) were grouped together to form a squadron. The officers of a squadron were a captain, a lieutenant, a sub-lieutenant (sous-lieutenant), a guidon (for the gendarmerie) or a cornette (for the chevau-légers), four quartermasters, three brigadiers and three trumpeters. The 'eldest' (senior) of the captains commanded the squadron. On campaign, however, the number of troops fell drastically due to deaths, wounded and desertions, and there are records of squadrons with only 50 troops. In 1634 the light horse was reorganised, creating 98 squadrons of 100 men each. In combat, each of these squadrons deployed 20 men abreast and five ranks deep. In battle, these companies were sometimes grouped into one large squadron, between 400–500 men, as a higher number would be difficult to govern.

Richelieu, aware of the power held by the nobility, wanted to subjugate them to the central Government in Paris, and to this end tried to limit the military power of the great nobles by granting privileges to those nobles who dispensed with their feudal military contingents and preferred to pay a financial contribution to the King in order not to serve in the army, as opposed to those who actually did so with their contingents.

Richelieu drew many of Sweden's former allies into the French orbit, as France feared the Swedes would try again to rebuild their German "Empire". These mercenaries were experienced and tested in hundreds of combats. Moreover, the service of such troops did not entail the costs of French conscription, training, armaments and clothing – or the problems of conscription with the civilian population. Following the entry into the

French army's ranks of numerous foreign corps (most notably the horse of Bernhard of Saxe-Weimar, who entered French service in 1635 – his regiments were to be known as Bernadines, Swedes or Weymarians) the influence was so strong that regimental organisation was introduced into the French horse

In May 1635, Richelieu, influenced by Swedish military doctrine and the Bernadines, reorganised the horse into regiments: twelve regiments of French horse (Canillac, Cardinal-Duc, Chaulnes, d'Enghien, Le Ferron, Guiche, Matignon, La Meilleraye, Nanteuil, Sauveboeuf, Sourdis and Treillis), three regiments of foreign horse (Savoy, Piémont and one German) and two regiments of carbines were established. By the end of 1635, eight more regiments had been recruited. These regiments were made up of two or three squadrons each of two companies.

Six dragoon regiments were also formed from the carbine or arquebusier companies (Cardinal, Alègre, Brûlon, Bemieules, Mahé and Saint-Rémy regiments), but in 1643 only one survived, the *Fusiliers à Cheval de Son Eminence*. On 1 August 1643 the regiment was renamed *Fusiliers à Cheval du Roy*, but retained the classic dragoon role of being mounted infantry and, when appropriate, dismounted and fought on foot.

In July 1636, the organisation reverted to the previous model of independent companies of horse, as the regimental did not give the expected results. The new units consisted of 3 companies of 55 men, with a captain, a lieutenant, a cornette, a quartermaster, two brigadiers, one trumpet and 48 horse.

In addition, Richelieu definitively established that, in exchange for financial compensation, the nobles were exempted from their military obligations, i.e. recruiting and maintaining horse companies. With these resources, Richelieu could pay regiments that would only be loyal to the Crown, and at the same time eliminate any noble armed force that might be a potential enemy in the future.

In 1638, Richelieu ordered the re-establishment of the regimental unit and 36 French regiments of horse were created, each was composed of 8 companies of chevau-légers and 1 company of carabins. The regiments could be divided into 2 squadrons, each of 4 companies. There were also 25 regiments of foreign horse, mainly from Weimarian units. In addition, there were the non-regimented gendarmerie companies and the *Maison du Roi* (the four companies of *Gardes du Corps*, the *Gendarmes* and *Chevau-Légers* of the Guard, and the single company of the *Mousquetaires du Roi*, the King's Musketeers made famous by Alexandre Dumas). The gendarmerie companies remained independent and non-regimented, and were to serve as guards to the General of each army.

As France intensified its war effort, the number of horse regiments grew with regiments raised in Lotharingia and Hungary and new French units. In addition, six dragoon regiments were created as specialised units for scouting.

In battle, the French squadron was 8 to 10 men in front, and 3 to 6 ranks deep, while the depth was 6 to 12 ranks for German regiments. Depending on the terrain, the size and age of the horse, and the weight of the rider, eighteenth century studies indicate that a horse could walk at a speed between 5.8 and 7.7km/h, could trot at between 7.8 and 13km/h and canter at 13.3 to 19km/h. In the seventeenth century the horse charged at a gallop only for the last 40 to 50 metres – both to avoid tiring out the horses before the clash, and to avoid disordering the formation. Breaking into a gallop too soon meant that some horses would be overtaken and others would be left behind, losing the cohesion necessary to clash with the enemy line. In combat, the horse would advance at a trot, the front line would fire their pistols and then make the charge with the sword.

By 1638 each company of gendarmes and of chevau-légers comprised a captain, a lieutenant, a trumpeter, a quartermaster, two brigadiers, and fifty-four men, totalling 60 per company. Dragoon squadrons were commanded by the senior captain, and had twelve officers, six brigadiers, three trumpeters and one hundred and forty-four horse. But the theoretical strength of the companies of horse, including officers, varied from one hundred men

between 1635 and 1637, to sixty men between 1639 and 1642, to seventy men in 1643 and 1644, fifty men from 1645 to 1646, and forty-four men between 1647 and 1648.

Thus, in 1642, the companies of gendarmes and chevau-légers had 60 troops, including officers, while the companies of carabins had 50 men, including officers.

From 1635 /1636, the equipment of the French horseman became lighter, in imitation of the Swedish and Weimarian horse, and so an order was issued whereby, as a minimum, horse were to keep the breastplate. In 1642 a horseman's armament was to be a breastplate, a pot, a sword and two pistols. The light horse protected

Illustration from Military art on Horseback. Instruction of the principles and Foundations of the Horse (Art Militaire à Cheval. Instruction des Principles et Fondements de la Cavallerie) by Johann Jacobi Wallhausen, 1616. Wallhausen was born around 1580 in Wallhausen, near Bad Kreuznach in the Rhineland, but little is known about his life. He probably became a soldier in The Netherlands, then entered the service of the City of Gdańsk, where he became Colonel sergeant. By contract signed in February 1617 with John VII of Nassau-Siegen, he became the head of the Siegen war school, the first in Europe. Like many authors of the early seventeenth century, he considered the "gendarme" (gens d'armes, heavy horse) to be the elite of the horse and the lance as the most effective of the offensive weapons. He was very reluctant to use portable firearms deemed unworthy of a true gentleman. In this illustration are shown the four types of horse proposed by Wallhausen: the gendarme – with a heavy medieval lance, the cuirassier – armed with pistols, the arquebusiers – with arquebuses, and the dragoons – armed with both arquebuses and pikes, to fight on horseback or on foot.

themselves with a cuirass worn over a buff coat, or a buff coat only, and a helmet or wide-brimmed hat. The gendarme companies were equipped with back and breast, tassetts, a vambrace, a pot, a sword and two pistols, and they were paid for two horses. Only the Guard units had a standardised uniform, while in the rest of the horse, the troopers bought their own clothing and were thus dressed differently.

Artillery

With the consolidation of the French monarchy after the 100 Years' War and the later wars against Burgundy, the stability of the Country meant that the Royal coffers could call on enormous resources. As a result, the French monarchy was able to rely on a highly skilled artillery train and master gunners; and, as in other countries, such as Spain under the Catholic Monarchs, the enormous cost of production and maintenance of artillery was only affordable by the monarchy and not by the feudal lords, further strengthening Royal power.

At the beginning of the seventeenth century, the French artillery had six types of artillery: the cannon, the long culverin, the bastard cannon, the medium cannon, the falcon and the falconet. At the organisational level, there was the rank of *Grand Maitre de l'Artillerie* (Grand Master of the Artillery), one lieutenant-general, 3 general controllers, and at the provincial level, 18 commissioners who were responsible for ensuring that the artillery was in good condition.

The incorporation of the Bernadine units and the experience of senior French officers who had served in the Swedish army, transferred some tactical innovations to the French army: light guns in the front line of the battlefield and howitzers in the siege lines.

But, compared to the other combatant armies of the Thirty Years' War, in the initial stages of French participation (1635–1645), the French used less artillery on the battlefield and French gunners were less skilled than Spanish or Imperialists. Historians have put forward various explanations to try to explain this French artillery weaknesses, such as the lack of capacity to cast cannons – there were no workshops with either the expertise or the appropriate equipment, so artillery pieces had to be imported mainly from The Netherlands or Scandinavia. Another problem was that artillery was mainly destined for fortresses and ships, following Richelieu's directives. A third reason was the relative predilection of French doctrine for large guns, both for siege and battle, which took longer to manufacture, were more expensive and more difficult to transport.

War Effort

The main way of joining the French army, like the Spanish, was by voluntary enlistment – it was only further into the reign of Louis XIV, from the 1670s onwards, that conscription was widely used, and that due to the huge need for manpower for the military that French expansionism required. (Although conscription had certainly existed in the earlier years of Louis XIV's reign.)

Generally in this period from 1620–1660, military recruitment was a Royal monopoly, although it functioned in different ways. In any case, all troops were assumed to be volunteers for service, as in the Spanish Army. From the documentation preserved in the archives, however, in modern terms it can be said that the rules concerning recruitment were exceedingly vague: thus, Le Tellier's rules of 1643 placed more emphasis on the economic aspect, the cost of new recruits, than on stipulating the conditions of military service, the obligations and rights, or simply the years of service -which was understood to be for life.

Many of the soldiers were supplied by officers who sought recruits from their home district, or if they were nobles, from their own lands: the method known as "manorial recruiting". But many recruits came from the cities, where recruiting officers flaunted their wealth gained from years of service, luring recruits with promises of glory and wealth. Sometimes the methods of recruitment were much more expedient, and the common people referred to these practices as "robbery" – forcing or abducting young men for military service.

Recruiting a company cost a great deal of money; although it was agreed that the service was at the cost of the Royal finances, the captain of the company had to advance a lot of money: salary, joining bounty, board and lodging, equipment and arms, until they were inducted into the Royal service, after passing muster with the Royal officials.

The state was responsible for arming, equipping and feeding the soldiers once they had passed the muster to be fit for service. The cost of recruiting the troops and getting them to the point of muster also fell to the state, but often this cost was born in advance by the captain recruiting the company, the amount to be reimbursed once the unit was officially in the King's service; although there were often delays in these payments, and the officers kept the soldiers at their own expense until they received the money. In return, if the captain presented his company at full strength, he received a gratuity (sometimes 600 *livres*, sometimes 300); but for each missing soldier, an amount was deducted from that gratuity. By 1643, the cost of an infantryman was 18 *livres* per month, 34 *livres* for a horseman.

Throughout the first two decades of the seventeenth century, Dutch military influence crept into French military thinking, mainly at the theoretical level. At the practical level, the French made a mixture of their own military tradition, such as the changes introduced by Henri IV, especially in the horse, and observation of the innovations of their Dutch allies and their Spanish enemies.

Recruits joining the French army were trained by senior comrades with proven combat experience – the *anspessades* and the *appointes*.

However, after the entry into the war against Spain, the massive increase in recruits and the lack of time to train them – given the need to send them to the war front as soon as possible – meant that the high command increasingly relied on a core of veterans (*vieux soldats*). These units not only formed the backbone of the armies, but sometimes also some of the companies were detached from their original regiments to form newly raised regiments, but with some of these companies as a cadre, both to instruct the recruits and to give them some *esprit de corps*.

The Spanish Army

Foot

The Spanish Tercios

When discussing the Spanish Army, historiography is based around the notion of the tercio, which was the organisational unit of Spanish foot. The tercio was officially created based on three orders: the decree from Emperor Charles V to Pedro Álvarez de Toledo y Zúñiga, Viceroy of Naples of 23 October 1534, the Genoa Ordinance of 15 November 1536 and the Instruction of Alfonso de Ávalos Aquino y Sanseverino, Marqués de Vast, to the Tercio de Lombardía in August 1538. In 1587 the Governor-General of Flanders Alessandro Farnese (1545–1592), Duque de Parma, completed the Tercios' legal corpus with the promulgation of two Ordinances concerning the ranks of Auditor General and Provost, as being responsible for military accounting and justice.

The exact origin of the word "tercio" is not known. The first time it is used in an official document is in the Genoa Ordinance of 1536. Spanish sources sometimes claim that it may have come from the name of a Roman legion that had garrisoned Hispania (*Legio Tertia*, which in fact was never in Spain). Other scholars explain that its name is because in the Ordinances of 1497 there were three different groups of weapons -pikemen, crossbowmen and arquebusiers. While yet a third explanation states that it also comes from Latin *tertia*, referring to the third part of the personnel of a Roman legion. It is true that the theoretical number of men in a tercio was 3,000 divided into 10 companies of 300 men, while a complete Roman legion according to Titus Livius, had 6,000 Roman and 3,000 auxiliary soldiers, totalling 9,000 men, of which a third part would indeed be 3,000.

In his study the veteran *Maestre de Campo* (literally "Field Master", the Commander of a tercio) Sancho de Londoño wrote:

> The Tercios, although instituted in imitation of such legions, can be compared in a small way with them, that the number is half less, and though formerly there were three thousand soldiers, by whom they were called Tercio, and not Legions, as ancients say, even if they do not have more than a thousand men; formerly in every tercio there were twelve companies, though often there are more in some, and in others less than 12.[4]

But the origin of the tercios goes back to the establishment of a permanent professional army in Spain, conceived during the War of Granada (1482–1492). Fernando II of Aragon and Isabel I of Castile, known as their Most Catholic Majesties, reorganised the Royal hosts and the noble troops, both having medieval roots, to provide themselves with a permanent and

---

4   *El Discurso Sobre la Forma de Reduzir la Disciplina Militar, a Meyor y Antiguo Estado,* (Madrid 1589). (Discourse on how to Reduce Military Discipline to Better and Former State)

well-organised force. Units called *batallas* (battles), consisting of 500 men, with an amalgamation of soldiers with various weapons: primitive arque-buses, crossbows, pikes, halberds, and sword and buckler (called, in Spanish, *rodeleros*). Each battle was divided into 10 'squads' of 50 men, commanded by a *Jefe de Pelotón* (literally "platoon chief"). The union of several battles formed a division.

In 1493 an Ordinance was promulgated, standardising all troops in a basic unit called a *capitanía* (captaincy) similar to a company, of 500 men: commanded by a captain, his second was a lieutenant, who was also respon-sible for defending the unit's colours; each captaincy was divided into groups, led by a sergeant. Over time, it was found that apart from a perma-nent tactical structure (the *capitanías*), a greater organisational unit was needed: and so came the *coronelía* (colonelship) commanded by a Colonel, which were instituted by Fernando II in 1502, following the recommenda-tions of the Gonzalo de Ayora (1466–1538), to provide a permanent higher structure to the *capitanías*.

These reforms were applied, most especially by Gonzalo Fernández de Córdoba (1453–1515), known as the "Great Captain", in the campaigns in Italy. Indeed, for the first Spanish expeditionary force to Naples, 1495 to 1497, the army was divided in *capitanías* of 500 men (200 pikemen, 200 sword and buckler men and 100 arquebusiers). However in 1504, de Córdoba organised his force based on the new Ordinances. The *coronelías* were theoretically composed of 6,000 men, grouped into 12 *capitanías*, but in practice, they ranged from 12 to 16 *capitanías*; and in the expedition to Oran (1509), the *coronelías* were formed by between 8 and 16 *capitanías*.

After the conquest of Naples by de Córdoba, Spanish military doctrine changed thanks to his practical contributions on the battlefield. These included the consolida-tion of an army, mobilised permanently throughout the year, and the ability to act at great distances from the Iberian Peninsula. The foot taking precedence over heavy horse (now the foot would be the backbone of the army, passing to the horse to perform secondary tasks), and forced to coordinate with foot. And the inclusion of the service of foreigners to compensate for the numer-ical weaknesses of the Spanish contingent. However, current Anglo-Saxon historiog-raphy, in its study of the so-called Military Revolution, has ignored or downplayed the innovations and actions of de Córdoba.

The conflict in Italy was resumed by the Emperor Charles V of the Holy Roman Empire and Charles I of Spain (1500–1558), and it was through the "laboratory" of the Italian Wars that the Spanish learned a number of important lessons in mobilising their armed forces. Traditional models of

Trumpeter of Horse, c1642-1645.
Diverses Exercices de Cavalerie: Stefano della Bella (Paris, Israel Henriet c1645). The long coat, was commonly worn by trumpeters of horse during the 1640s and some time before this became the fashionable cut for men's coats. Also notable is the large amount of lace on the sleeves and around the lower edge of the coat. (Rijksmuseum, Amsterdam. Public Domain)

military mobilisation used in the wars against the Arabs (the *Reconquista*) did not work for offensive wars in distant places. In addition, they became more aware of the need for a large, highly trained and highly motivated permanent armed force with the ability to navigate any military scenario, and for extended periods of time – not just for a campaign or for a year, but for many years if necessary.

In Italy the best units were allocated to fight French expansionism; and when there were no battles, the soldiers remained within the Italian fortresses to protect them. The Spanish garrisons in Italy, known as the *Presidios*, constituted the strategic reserve of soldiers of the Spanish Monarchy. They were all highly trained troops who had gained experience in fighting against the French, against the Turks or against the North African pirates, and thanks to this experience, their training and their professionalism, they were available and able to perform in any theatre of operations.

To organise the units in the *Presidios*, in 1534 and 1536 new Ordinances were drafted and it was in this context that the first tercios, known as the *Tercios Viejos* (Old Tercios), were created in 1534. The units quartered at the Italian fortresses: one in the Kingdom of Sicily, another in the Duchy of Milan (or the Kingdom of Lombardy) and another in the Kingdom of Naples. In 1536 the Tercio de Cerdeña (Tercio of Sardinia) and the Tercio de Galeras, which was the first Marine unit in modern history, were created. The other units that were created later were known as *Tercios Nuevos* (New Tercios), or simply Tercios.

The *tercio* was an administrative unit that, at the same time, could be constituted as a combat unit. Each tercio had a certain number of companies, which could either be serving in the same territory, be garrisoned in several cities, or could fight on different fronts, far from each other.

In 1534, the tercios had ten companies with 300 men each, eight of these were of pikemen and two were of arquebusiers. The tercio had its own staff, with the military's commanding functions of the unit, as well as the administration and payment of salaries. This staff was made up of 29 members, the commander of the tercio held the rank of *Maestre de Campo* ("Field Master", the 'General' of the tercio), his second in command was the *Sargento Mayor* (sergeant-major).

Both types of companies had the same number of men and the same *prima plana* (officers and staff) which comprised 11 men: 1 *capitán* (captain) and his page, 1 *alférez* (second lieutenant, as second in command of the company and in charge of protecting the flag), 1 sergeant, 1 standard-bearer, 2 drummers and 1 flautist, 1 chaplain, 1 quartermaster and 1 barber (acting as a doctor).

The pikemen companies consisted of the previous 11 members, 135 *corseletes* (literally 'corselets'; pikemen wearing back and breast), 44 *picas secas* (unarmoured or 'light' pikemen), 90 arquebusiers and 20 musketeers. The arquebusiers companies also had 11 members of the *prima plana*, 35 *picas secas,* 239 arquebusiers and 15 musketeers.

The Spanish companies were also divided into squads of 25 men under the command of an officer known as a *Cabo de Escuadra* (squad corporal). Additionally, and somewhat informally, the soldiers were grouped into *camaradas* (comrades), groups of 6 to 12 men who shared food, lodging, et cetera, this social structure was felt very important for morale and *"esprit de corps"*. The organisational model of the tercios rooted in Italy was spread throughout Spanish domains.

Thirty years later, in 1567, to quell the incipient rebellion in The Netherlands, the third Duque de Alba, Fernando Álvarez de Toledo y Pimentel (1507–1580), known as the *Duque de Hierro* (Iron Duke), left Milan for Flanders at the head of the four Spanish tercios which had been quartered in Italy (Sardinia, Sicily, Naples and Lombardy). These units, however, varied widely in composition and strength – the largest was 3,500 strong, but the others were 2,000, 1,800 and 1,500. Similarly the number of companies varied – 10 was 'normal', but there were 15 and even 19.

That is why, once in Flanders, the Duque de Alba instituted the system that in The Netherlands Spanish tercios would have 12 companies of 250 men. In Spain and Italy, however, the tercios would continue to be of 10 companies each of 300 men. The pike companies of 250 men consisted of 11 *prima plana* (officers and staff), 111 *corseletes*, 108 *picas secas* and 20 musketeers. The arquebusier companies had 11 officers and assistants, 224 arquebusiers and 15 musketeers. The percentage of shot to pike, excluding the *prima plana*, in a tercio of 10 companies was 48.79 percent, while in a tercio of 12 companies it was 23.64 percent.

This theoretical model remained in place for several decades, but in practice was often different and companies generally had more firearms than the establishment called for. However, on campaign, if the enemy were considered to be strong in horse, the companies increased the number of pikes, to enable them to defend themselves better.

Nonetheless, the military literature and military instruction theoretically continued to emphasise the prevalence of pikes over firearms, but this was also due to budgetary factors – shot cost more than the pikemen. At the time horse and foot attacks could only be repelled effectively by forming a large square defended with pikes, so until the invention of the bayonet a unit had to have enough pikes to ensure its defence.

During the reign of Felipe II, the ratio of shot to pike would continued to grow in favour of firearms. In 1594, it was ordered that the new companies recruiting in Castile to serve in Italy should have 125 pikes, 100 arquebuses and 25 muskets. In 1598 a company of 250 men was to have 130 pikes, 100 arquebuses and 20 muskets; and in 1603 it was ordered that half of the companies in the tercios would be made up of pikes, and the other half with firearms. Again, in reality, the actual contemporary musters of the troops show that the proportion of firearms was higher than that prescribed in the Ordinances. For example, the musters of Spanish companies in Sicily in 1572 and 1574 show that between 70 percent and 80 percent of the foot had arquebuses and muskets, and in 1601 the Flanders army musters indicate that 62 percent of Spanish foot used muskets and arquebuses.

On 28 July 1632, King Felipe IV signed new Military Ordinances, which established the unification of the different types of horse and foot companies. These Ordinances sought to rationalise and standardise the organisation and composition of all tercios and companies across all of the armies of the Spanish Monarchy. Given that over the previous 100 years of their existence and with a continuous history of conflicts in such diverse and disparate theatres of operations (Flanders, Italy, North Africa, America, Asia), the armies raised had adapted to the political and military context of each area and extant organisations show a wide disparity.

This painting shows the interior of the Ridderzaal (Hall of Knights), one of the main rooms of the architectural complex of the Binnenhof in The Hague, during the Great Assembly of the States General in 1651; the painting is attributed to Bartholomeus van Bassen. The Binnenhof is a complex of buildings located in the city centre of The Hague, which housed the Seat of the States General of The Netherlands. In 1650, after the death of the Stadholder William II of Orange-Nassau (nephew of the great Maurice of Nassau), the States General held a special General Assembly to decide whether they wished to renew that political-military rank. In the assembly, the representatives of The Netherlands took the decision not to appoint a new Stadholder. The large number of standards and colours shown hanging from the ceiling and the walls of the Ridderzall taken in battle as trophies from the Armies and Navy of Spain is astonishing. A large number of these were captured by Maurice of Nassau in the battles of Turnhout (1597) and Nieuwpoort (1600). The colours with the Coat of Arms of Spain are 'Regimental Colours' of Tercios, while most of the colours with a white background are from companies of foot. In the background there are company colours with a blue background, and some standards of horse. At left is a colour displaying an arm in armour and a sword, possibly from a German regiment in the service of Spain, since this iconography is not common in the Spanish, Italian or Flemish Tercios. (Rijksmuseum, SK-C–1350)

The 1632 Ordinances differentiated the tercios garrisoned in Spain from the tercios located in the rest of the world. Thus, the strength of a tercio of Spanish foot for service in the Peninsula was set at twelve companies, each of 250 men. This total included the captain and his page, ensign and standard-bearer, sergeant, two drummers and a fifer, quartermaster, barber and chaplain, meaning there was a total of 239 NCOs and rank and file. The tercios serving outside the Peninsula were made up of fifteen companies, but of 200 men, with the same composition as the 'Peninsula' tercios although with only 189 NCOs and rank and file.

One of the obsessions of the minister Olivares was to try to get the nobility involved in the army. To this end, with the Ordinances of 1632 he encouraged their entry into the officer corps, giving priority to those of noble origin. In reality, this was counterproductive, as it only had the effect of encouraging favouritism to the detriment of veteran soldiers of humble origin, who saw their promotions limited to the benefit of young nobles without military experience, but who had an illustrious surname. Olivares believed that noble origins were synonymous with greatness and capacity for work, but on the battlefield, an illustrious surname conferred neither knowledge, nor courage, nor intelligence, which meant that their ability to command was often deficient.

Olivares' desire clashed with reality: the political expediency of placing nobles in the upper echelon of the army, in order to be effective, required that at least in the second level of command, there should be professional soldiers. This system worked for a while but it failed when the nobles, often younger sons in their early twenties, believed that they were capable of assuming these second level functions in order to reach the higher levels of command sooner. And all this was at the cost of postponing the promotion of the veteran officers, who previously had been content to remain at least in the second level.

The Ordinances of 1632 established the fixed composition of the garrison of the Army of Flanders: three Spanish tercios, one tercio of Neapolitans and one tercio of Lombards. It was also established that Walloon tercios and German regiments should be recruited, although the number would depend on the existing resources and the seriousness of the situation. However, on 20 March 1636, the Cardinal-Infante issued a regulation of his own, partially contravening the Ordinances of 1632, which regulated the composition of the units serving in the Army of Flanders and putting them into three groups: Spanish-Italians, Walloons and Germans.

On a practical level, with 15 companies per tercio, and 200 troops per company, the Spanish and Italian tercios (Milanese and Neapolitans), as well as the Burgundian and 'British' tercios (Irish, English and Scottish Catholics), were divided into companies of pikemen and companies of arquebusiers, in a ratio of three to two. The two types of companies had a staff of 200 men, with the same number of officers and non-commissioned officers (a captain with his page, an ensign with his standard-bearer, a sergeant, two drummers and a fifer, a quartermaster, a barber and a chaplain), so the number of troops was the same: 190 soldiers, eight of them corporals; the pike companies had 127 musketeers and 63 pikemen, and the arquebusier company had 30 musketeers and 160 arquebusiers. It is worth noting that the number of shot in a pike company was 63 percent, while the arquebusier companies consisted exclusively of shot; all this shows that the tercios had a high proportion of firepower, contradicting the traditional view that tercios were formations closer to ancient phalanxes or the early modern Swiss regiments.

The tercio had a *prima plana* company made up of the senior officers: the *Maestre de Campo* (Field Master, a rank roughly equivalent to a colonel), who was also the captain of the first company and had eight halberdiers, as a bodyguard, the *sargento mayor* (sergeant-major) and two assistants, a chaplain major and two ordinary chaplains, an auditor with two bailiffs, and a scribe, a field captain with four men, a quartermaster-major, a surgeon-major, a doctor and a drum-major (responsible for transmitting orders by the sound of his drum). Each nationality had a different drum beat, and the drum-major had to know them, in case he had to transmit orders to adjoining units.

The Reformed Officers

One of the peculiarities of the Spanish armies, although they were present in other countries but less frequently, were the reformed officers. These were from two different origins; sergeants and ensigns on the one hand, and captains on the other.

Ensigns and sergeants were appointed by their captain, although, their appointment had to be confirmed by the *Maestre de Campo* of the tercio, on verifying that they had fulfilled the requirements of seniority in the service. This requirement was four years of continuous service in war, or six years of service overall, but if they were noble this time was reduced to two years of continuous service. After three years they were to be dismissed, and their captain was required to appoint new individuals to those ranks; if there was a change of captain, the new one was to be dismissed to the lower ranks. The officers and NCOs who were dismissed could either take up a new post in another company, in the same tercio or another tercio, or they joined as private soldiers in another company. In both situations, their experience was put to good use on the battlefield, as a "reformed officer" brought experience, responsibility and all the knowledge gained from years of service, and this was very important in the front ranks during a battle. Reformed soldiers who served in the ranks were paid more, were given more consideration than the private soldier, and their status was classified as "reformed".

Captains were reformed when their company was reformed, i.e. disbanded, either because it was already understaffed, and merged into another unit in need of men, or because the Crown was short of resources and disbanded some units to save on pay. In either case, the reformed captains had the same options as in the previous case: to serve as reformed soldiers, or to be appointed as an officer or non-commissioned officer in another company.

In battle, the front rank of the pikes of a Spanish squadron consisted of reformed men, who had not only better equipment, but also hopefully the experience to defend their position with greater courage.

The senior officers of a tercio – *Maestre de Campo*, sergeant-major, et cetera – could also be reformed, but were often reinstated in another tercio or became part of the entourage of the Captain-General, as advisers on his staff.

An Army of Nations

The troops of the Spanish Monarchy were a faithful reflection of the conglomerate of states that made up King Felipe IV's dominions: Spanish, Italian, Walloon, German, Portuguese and Burgundian. In the Spanish Netherlands, the national contingents comprised, in order of importance, the Walloons, the Germans and Spanish, the Italians, the British (mostly Irish but including English and Scots) and the Burgundians.

Given the complexity of the extensive and distant possessions of the Spanish Habsburg Royal family, the territorial defence of the various

Spanish Pikeman, c1630-1640. Detail from a painting by Jan Martszen the Younger (c.1609-after 1647).
This well equipped pikeman – he has buff coat, back and breast with tassets, and a helmet – is in the drill position 'charge to horse' and his pike would be brought lower to come into line with the chest of his enemy's horse. Actually it is highly unlikely that he would be in this position, on his own, and in the middle of a melee but that is truly 'artistic licence'. Interestingly while most of the musketeers behind him have their sword worn from baldrics this man has opted for a waist belt, which would be hidden below the armour. (Collection of Michael Paradowski)

kingdoms was left in the hands of the natives of each country, complemented by the establishment of a nucleus of Spanish troops in each. Initially the Spanish units garrisoned the main cities and fortresses but the importance of the Italian territories in Charles V's European strategy had motivated these units to be enlarged and made of a permanent nature, giving rise in the period 1534–1536 to the permanent tercios of foot.

The tercios stationed in Italy were the most numerous, and in addition to providing protection against the Ottoman and French threats – these tercios could operate both on land and embark on the galleys and naval squadrons – they served as a training centre for conscript troops and as a base for supplying units to the theatre of operations in Flanders.

The defence of the various Spanish kingdoms was complemented by native troops from each territory, who not only ensured internal peace, but could also be sent to fight in Flanders, Spain or Germany. In addition, the Spanish armies also had mercenary units, mainly German, but sometimes Swiss.

Thus, the Spanish armies were made up of Spanish, Italians, Walloons, all subjects of the same King, but often with a different title, and Germans. These were not called "mercenaries" but "foreigners", with the size of each contingent varying according to the theatre of operations. Thus, in Flanders, the Walloons were the most numerous, followed by the Spanish; in Italy, it was the Italians (Lombards, Neapolitans and Sicilians, in that order), again followed by the Spanish.

As a general rule, the internal composition of the units was governed by the principle of not mixing individuals of different nationalities under the same flag. This was not due to any ethnic criteria or prejudice, but for more practical reasons: since the Spanish Army was so international, and a great many languages were spoken (Spanish, Basque, Catalan, Italian dialects, French, Dutch dialects, German dialects), it was absolutely necessary for all the men to understand the orders, so it was much more practical to put the men in units where they all spoke the same language, with the same customs, the same way of cooking, et cetera This was helped by the fact that the smaller units, the companies, were often made up of men from the same geographical environment.

The Portuguese were a specific case: they often formed separate units, also called tercios, who served as foot, but especially had also served in the various fleets against England – the Invincible Armada of 1588, Charles of Amésquita's raid on Cornwall in 1595, Martín de Padilla Manrique's expedition to Ireland in 1596 and to England in 1597. Portuguese troops could also serve in the Spanish foot companies, being considered as native "Spanish".

The people of The 'Spanish' Netherlands, divided between the French and Dutch language communities, were known collectively as "Walloons", corresponding to the inhabitants of the former Seventeen Provinces who had remained loyal to the King of Spain. During the long conflict of the Eighty Years' War, they initially served only in Flanders and in the invasion of France, but they later fought in Germany in the Palatinate War of 1620–21, in Catalonia and in Portugal. Distinct from the Walloons were the Burgundians, the inhabitants of Franche-Comté, formerly the Counties of Burgundy and of Artois. In gratitude for their contribution to the war effort, in 1602 they obtained the privilege of organising themselves into tercios, instead of regiments.

Both Walloons and Burgundians were considered to be good soldiers: they were acclimatised to the Flanders environment, knew the language and the territory, and were motivated to defend their country against aggression from the French and their former "brothers" in the northern provinces, now divided from them irreconcilably over religion.

The recruitment of Walloon troops was quicker and cheaper than for the units of the other nationalities. Moreover, their training was relatively fast, as there was a long tradition of citizen militia in the cities of the Low Countries, so that after a comparatively short period of military training, a shrewd marksman or civilian hunter could become a competent arquebusier or musketeer.

The Walloon tercios were composed of fifteen companies, without differentiation between pike and shot companies. The companies could be paid by the cities and in this case, the number of soldiers was around a hundred. Or they were paid by the States, either with their own money or money from Spain, and in this case, had a company strength in line with that of Spanish companies, of 200 men. The staff was similar to that of a Spanish tercio, and the same at company level (10 officers, NCOs and specialist NCOs), but with a different company structure of 144 musketeers and 46 pikemen, with eight corporals to command the squads.

As for the German mercenary units, the first difference was that their units were "regiments" and not "tercios". The Spanish classified the Germans according to their geographical origin, calling them "high" or "low": the former were from Imperial territories, while the latter were from Princely territories (e.g. the Bishopric of Liège or of Trier). "High" Germans were the more numerous group in the Spanish armies.

Since they were not subjects of the Spanish Crown, in order to solemnise the new dependence and obedience and not limiting it solely to the payment of a salary, when the regiment entered the service, a representative of the King of Spain gave the colonel his new colours through an act that represented the identification of the Royal person with the colours. Thus, in defending the colours on the battlefield, they defended their honour as a regiment, but also the figure of the King.

The composition of every German regiment was similar, although the number of troops and companies varied, depending on the resources available to the Spanish Crown in recruiting them. Thus, the *prima plana* of the regiment consisted of the colonel, who was the captain of the first company, with a small 'staff' composed of a secretary, six mounted men for his service, eight halberdiers, a drummer, a fifer and an interpreter. A lieutenant-colonel, who was the captain of the second company and was entitled to two halberdiers. A sergeant with a halberdier, plus a drummer and a fifer, an interpreter, a senior chaplain, a clerk with ten bailiffs, a sergeant-at-arms with a halberdier, a barrack-master with a halberdier, the commissary, the senior surgeon, a sergeant guide of the baggage; and a provost marshal, who had a team consisting of a lieutenant provost marshal, a chaplain, a clerk, six halberdiers, an executioner, eight servants and a jailer.

The organisation of the High German foot companies was fixed at 300 men. The company was commanded by a captain, with a lieutenant, an ensign, and a first sergeant – these four were each entitled to a page paid as a pikeman, a standard-bearer – a clerk, a quartermaster, a barber, two sergeants, two drummers, two fifers, two halberdiers for the captain's guard, an interpreter and a chaplain: a total of 22 individuals, almost double the number of posts in the units of the other nationalities. As for the troop types, there were 132 pikemen, including officers' pages, and 150 musketeers [NB this does indeed add up to 304].

For the "Low" Germans, it was similar: a captain with his page and two halberdiers, a lieutenant with his page, an ensign with his, a first sergeant with a page, two sergeants, a standard-bearer, a quartermaster, a clerk, a barber, two drummers, two fifers, an interpreter and a chaplain. The fundamental difference with the High German foot regiments was in the distribution of the troops, which was set at 150 pikemen, including officers' pages, 100 musketeers and 28 arquebusiers.

Finally, and to a lesser extent than in the French army, the Spanish also negotiated contracts to recruit Swiss – NB these were always from the Catholic Cantons. Generally the destination of the Swiss, called *esguízaros* in the Spanish accounts, were the fortresses of Lombardy, especially the garrison of Milan.

The differentiation between "subjects" and "foreigners" had an exception for the Irish units: for reasons of a religious nature 'in defence of Catholicism', they were always considered to have a special connection with the Spanish Monarchy. For example, the expedition of the Field Master Juan del Águila to Kinsale in 1601–1602, and the Irish troops came to be considered as subjects of the King of Spain, being granted the same privileges and advantages as the native Spanish. This distinction would later be extended to units from England and Scotland, always it was an essential requirement that these were formed only of Catholics.

Paradoxically, the multi-nationality characteristic of the Spanish armies is considered by French historians to be an element of weakness in the Spanish chain of command and tactics. According to the French historians, the disparity of territorial origin, the difficulties of language and the lack of a common link between soldiers of different origins were the seeds of discord and failure. By contrast, in the case of Rocroi, the presence of a Prince of Royal Blood at the head of the French army – d'Enghien's grandfather was first cousin of King Henri IV – brought his army together, and the other generals were also members of the higher nobility. On the Spanish side, most of the commanders were also members of the Spanish higher nobility. No doubt French historiography, imbued with the Nation-State concept, considered that the victory at Rocroi was ultimately due to the symbiosis of this idea and that, therefore, the French soldiers fought for the idea of Nation, while the Spanish did not. If this were so, at Honnecourt, only a year earlier, were the French soldiers not aware of their Nation?

As for the deployment on the battlefield of the armies of the Spanish Monarchy, the foot marched in three parts, which were then deployed specifically on the battlefield: vanguard (right flank on the battlefield), battle (centre) and rearguard (left flank). In turn, within each group, the units that marched first were those that would occupy the first line of deployment on the battlefield: in this way all companies knew where they were to be positioned and no time was wasted in forming up for battle.

The right flank of the deployment was by Royal order since the reign of Charles V always reserved for Spanish units. The right flank was considered to be the one of greatest risk and honour, and this extended to any deployment in combat – whenever native Spanish units were present, they should always be located in the place of greatest danger or closest to the enemy. For example, if the right flank was protected by a mountain or natural element, the Spanish would occupy the place of deployment that was considered the most dangerous, and in the case of a retreat, as the rear was the most dangerous place, it was the Spanish who formed the rearguard.

But greater risk also meant greater prestige and better booty, in case of victory. That is why the other nationalities objected to the privileges of their

French high ranking officer, c1630. 'Fight for Saint Martin on Île de Ré' Jacques Callot, 1629-1631. Another view similar to the illustration above of a General Officer by Callot. Note the baton of command and the elegant clothing. It is likely that in a field action he would have worn at least a buff coat over his coat and possibly a helmet although he may well have a secret either underneath his hat or on top of its crown. (Rijksmuseum, Amsterdam. Public Domain)

Spanish comrades-in-arms. The Neapolitans and Lombards were particularly belligerent in this respect, especially the former. Eventually, the Spanish Kings granted the Neapolitans the right to be second in the list of Nations, so they received the privilege of deploying alongside the Spanish, or to be located on the left flank, also considered a place of danger. Thus, the competition between nationalities to gain prestige and "emulate the Spanish" was conceived as a stimulus to combat.

However, this "healthy rivalry" had its risks, Gualdo Priorato recounts the unease of the Italian tercios during the 1643 campaign. At Rocroi, this manifested itself in, according to that author, their withdrawal from the field almost without fighting and while the battle was still undecided. Ostensibly because they were angry with Melo and Fontaine, who had relocated them and they were not at their 'correct post' on the left wing of the army's deployment, which they believed belonged to them by tradition, but they had been placed in the centre. Generally, the Walloons and Germans occupied the centre of the deployment on the battlefield.

The vanguard marched about a hundred paces ahead of the battle, and the battle marched two hundred paces ahead of the rearguard. Once on the battlefield, when each of the three parts deployed into several lines, the distance between each line varied between fifty and one hundred paces.

When a linear deployment was adopted, the units formed up in a checkerboard formation; that is, taking advantage of the space left by the units forming the preceding line, influenced by Roman military tradition. This formation was similar to that used by other contemporary armies, it made it easier for units in the rear lines to move forward to pass to the attack, or for the front line to withdraw.

When, in order to form am *escuadrón* (a foot squadron), it was necessary to use companies from different nationalities, the sergeant-major had only to know the number of troops and their nationality. The first bit of this information was used to establish the frontage and depth of the squadron; the second to establish the order and precedence within the squadron itself: the Spanish would always be on the right.

In the early decades of the seventeenth century foot no longer formed in large, phalanx-like units of several hundred or even thousands of soldiers armed with pikes. Since the emergence of the battalion-type unit concept, European armies gradually adopted smaller company formations, with a core of pikemen, and with a higher proportion of firearms. Interestingly, the strength of these "battalions" was similar across many armies: the Dutch battalion was of 550 men, the Spanish *escuadrón* was 600 men, the Swedish battalion was of 504 men and the Imperial and Bavarian formations were of 600 men.

Horse

The Spanish Horse

The 1632 Ordinance set out few rules for the horse. However, by tradition, the organisation of all horse companies (lancers, cuirassiers or mounted arquebusiers), regardless of the Nation, consisted of a captain, lieutenant, ensign, two trumpeters, farrier, chaplain, 3 corporals and 85 troopers.

The basic unit of the Spanish horse was the company, but, on the battlefield, horse companies were grouped into a "squadron". In the 1640s, the "regimental" horse unit in the Spanish armies was the *trozo* or *grueso*, which are synonymous terms, consisting of a varying number of companies, a fact that greatly hindered their operational capacity, since their actual strength varied in size. German horse served in regiments, raised like foot by virtue of Capitulations between the Colonel and the King of Spain. The commander of a troop was generally known as *Cabo de la Caballería* (corporal of the horse), and the most senior *Capitán de Caballos* (captain of horses). Occasionally there could be friction because one captain was considered to have greater experience than a more senior one; such disorder was corrected by the appointment of a *Comisario General de Caballería* (Commissary General of Horse) for each campaign.

In battle, the companies were grouped in *trozos*, of four to six hundred men each. Units of different types (lancers, mounted arquebusiers and *caballos-corazas*) were not mixed in the same troop. The *trozo* generally consisted only of *caballos-corazas* (cuirassiers), while the other units were formed in company-type detachments or in groups of several companies. In the attack, the lancers were placed in the vanguard, formed in a compact body, while the arquebusier companies were placed alongside the main bodies of the *caballos-corazas* with the intention that they should give them support with their fire.

The main reason why Spain eschewed the concept of a "regiment of horse" in favour of independent companies, which were grouped into *trozos* as required, was a chronic shortage of money. A regiment needed a large and costly *prima plana* structure to organise it and keep it operational, as well as a lot of money to house troops and horses, provide food and fodder, and so on. On the other hand, if the units were companies, they could be dispersed in different localities, guaranteeing their maintenance and avoiding conflicts with the civilian population. When a campaign was over, the Governor of Flanders could not risk discharging horse squadrons, since he always needed horse to be able to cope with an invasion, and, unlike foot, it was very expensive to re-assemble horse once they had been discharged. It was a long and expensive process recruiting and training horse and, if necessary, remounting them, et cetera. However, in the field, this system clearly showed its shortcomings, as the companies were not used to operating together, there was no relationship with a common higher command, et cetera.

Despite the defeat at Rocroi, and noting that the regimental horse model was proving successful in Sweden, Germany and France, the Spanish command did not choose to adopt it until the Regulation of 7 March 1649, by which the loose companies were grouped into 18 horse tercios. No doubt this decision had also been influenced by the dismal performance of the Spanish horse at the Battle of Lens on 24 August 1648.

As previously stated, Spanish horse was divided into three main groups: lancers, cuirassiers (*caballos-corazas*) and mounted arquebusiers, to which the figure of dragoons was later added, emulating the French, Swedish and Imperial armies. A separate category was the semi-regulars of Balkan origin, most commonly called "Croats" – similar to the Imperial and French armies – but whose ethnic origin was actually very broad (Albanians, Magyars, Cossacks).

The noble horse, which had dominated the European battlefields for several centuries, declined at the end of the fifteenth century, and it had a residual if minimal role throughout the following century. In the case of the various states of the Spanish Monarchy (e.g. Castile, Milan, Naples and Flanders), the nobility, as a symbol of their rank and thanks to their economic power, retained the right to have companies of armed horse, which were given different names in each Country. The most famous were the *Bandes d'Ordonnance*

Standard of horse captured by the Swedes in the early 1630s. Silk damask, with green floral decoration. On one side is the Virgin, on the other, a coat of arms in gold against black with a crowned lion and seven red roses. The text that is under the image of the Madonna is no longer legible, but traditionally the standard is said to have belonged to a Walloon Troop, so its origin could be from the Spanish Army on the Rhine or the Army of the Duque de Feria. (Armémuseum Stockholm, AM.081410)

ST 14:146

43

in The Netherlands, the companies of *Bandas d'Uomini d'Arme* (Men-at-arms) in Milan and Naples, and the *Guardias Viejas* (Old Guards) in Castile. Territoriality was their fundamental characteristic, both in their service and in their maintenance.

The reasons for the decline of the noble horse and, in general, of the medieval type of man-at-arms and lancer, were not only political – decentralisation of power of the monarchy – but also economic and military. A lance-armed soldier required a long and complicated period of training. Maintaining the rider and his horse was expensive – the horses needed to be of a far higher quality than that required for the rest of the mounted troops (they had to be strong, fast animals, given that their success depended on the impact of the charge, and this was only achieved with a strong and fast mount). Additionally firearm technology had improved the penetration capacity of bullets. Despite the reduction in their numbers, lancer companies still existed in many armies in the early 1630s, although their presence in the military was to decline in the years to come.

Spanish horse, by historical tradition and military utility, resisted the disappearance of the lancer companies. It must be said that warfare in medieval Spain had always been much more intense and rapid than in central Europe: the Arabs had fast horses and their tactics of mounted archery and enveloping manoeuvres made charges by heavy horse useless. Thus Spanish lancer companies were not as heavily armoured as their counterparts in the rest of Europe, and their use in the sixteenth and early seventeenth century was still accepted by Spanish military doctrine for warfare in Flanders. Lancers could engage their Dutch enemy on the battlefield, they could escort convoys and also charge disorganised or low morale foot.

The Italian Giorgio Basta, (Gjergj Basta, he was of Albanian origin), in *Il Governo Della Cavalleria Leggiera* (The Government of Light Horse, Venice 1612), stated that in order to have a first-class lancer it was necessary to have: a good mount, capable of reaching good speeds in the charge; to have hard and flat terrain, suitable for that charge; and to have a soldier well exercised in the handling of the lance. With regard to choosing officers of horse, Basta's experience led him to state that they should be candidates based on meritocracy and not according to noble titles, which did not guarantee experience, courage or intelligence.

Giorgio Basta theorised on the best type of deployment for light horse and considered that they should be used in small squadrons of 25 to 30 horse charging compactly, not in long lines. His reasoning was given that in battle only the first two lines would come into collision with the enemy; to maximise the power of the collision and not tire the mounts prematurely, the horses should go at a light trot, passing to a gallop, only within 60 paces of the enemy, when the maximum speed should be reached. However, from 1620–30 in the actions of the war in Germany the use of cuirassiers and dragoons was becoming more and more common and these changes influenced Spanish military thinking, which was already becoming largely in favour of cuirassiers, in Spain known as *caballo-coraza*.

Unlike lancer companies, cuirassier units were easier and quicker to train, cheaper to maintain, with more affordable mounts. Operationally, they were grouped in large compact formations that charged in ranks and

Fight between buff-coat wearing horse. Theodorus van Kessel, after 1640. Unusually both are using pistols as the primary weapon. Both combatants are wearing buff coats and have hats in place of helmets. The right-hand figure is probably wearing a back and breast over his buff coat, undoubtedly a great many horse of both armies would have done without this latter to lighten their equipment. (Rijksmuseum, Amsterdam. Public Domain)

could move across soft and uneven terrain. They used the trot to attack and to move across the battlefield to reach the place where they were needed, leaving the gallop for the pursuit only.

The companies of mounted arquebusiers were equipped with back and breast and a light morion or lobster-type pot. Their main weapon was the wheelock or flintlock arquebus, which they carried slung on the right side from a bandolier, in addition to their sword worn at their left from a second bandolier. The strength of a company of arquebusiers, be they Spanish, Italian or Walloon, was 100 men, made up of a captain and his page, a lieutenant and his page, 2 trumpeters, a farrier, chaplain and 91 troopers. The Spanish arquebusier companies did not usually have standards or guidons – since they fought in small, highly mobile units, there was a greater risk that in a skirmish the guidon would be lost.

The first documented reference to dragoon units in the Spanish armies dates from 1634, when the Cardinal-Infante, during his march from Italy to Germany, ordered 500 of his foot to take mounts and designated them as "dragoons", divided into five companies. Previously the term "dragoon" had been used only to refer to the aides-de-camp of the sergeant-major of a tercio, the only officers of a tercio who served on horse during a battle, charged with carrying orders across the battlefield.

Given the success of their performance at Nördlingen, and that seen in other European armies, the War Council in Madrid agreed to form detachments of dragoons that served in the Basque country, in the relief of Fuenterrabía and in Catalonia. Pedro de Santa Cecilia, who had commanded the Spanish dragoons at Nördlingen, was appointed Governor of Horse of Dragoons and ordered to recruit a thousand men and to appoint their Colonel.

Although they were initially different type units, in the Spanish armies, the terms "mounted arquebusiers" and "dragoons" referred to the same type of horseman: one who, armed with an arquebus, could fight mounted or on foot, moving around the battlefield on horseback according to the needs of the battle. Proof of this is that in Flanders and Milan there were units of "mounted arquebusiers", while in the Iberian Peninsula, in the mid–1640s, only the term "dragoons" is mentioned.

In fact, the peculiar situation of dragoons carried over into a confusion as to their position within the horse: they were regarded in the field as horse, although both mounted arquebusiers and cuirassiers regarded dragoons as foot. However for pay purposes, it was unclear where to assign them; eventually it was decided to assimilate the lieutenants of dragoon companies as if they were captains of mounted arquebusiers, for rank and pay, and captains of dragoons as the same as captains of cuirassiers.

The Captain-General of the Horse was the third in seniority in the Spanish armies, behind the Captain-General and the *Maestre de Campo General* (Field Master General). In the event of the latter two's absence, he took command of the army. The officer chosen for this rank had to be one of the oldest and longest-serving field masters, however there were exceptions, when nobles of high birth were chosen for the post.

The General was in direct command of the first squadron of the front line, which was placed on the right flank of the deployment. As a general rule, the horse was placed on the two flanks and in reserve, and its commanding General took the place of honour, the right flank. The Lieutenant-General of Horse, who was second in the structure of command of the horse, and considered of lower rank than a foot *Maestre de Campo*, took post on the left flank of the horse or on the left flank of the army.

The German Regiments of Horse

The colonel commanding a regiment of horse, as with the foot, was responsible for recruiting, arming, clothing and training the number of men provided for in his contract with the King. The regiment would only be admitted into the King's pay if it were considered that it had a sufficient strength. Like all regimental contracts of the time, it fell to the colonel to appoint the officers of his regiment, with the stipulation (usually) that they were required to have the number of years of service that made them capable of performing their duties.

The general trend in the German horse was for there to be a *prima plana*, consisting of 32 men, and for the companies to have 113 to 115 men. Thus, the detail of the senior ranks was as follows: colonel, lieutenant-colonel, sergeant-major with 2 aides, chaplain major, surgeon-major, quartermaster, field captain with 5 aides, 8 colonel's guard, a quartermaster, a wagon master, a secretary and an interpreter, 4 trumpeters and a 'timpanist'. The composition of a company was, a captain (and his page, pages were not counted as soldiers), a lieutenant (and his page), a cornet (and his page), a sergeant, two trumpets, a 'timpanist', two corporals, a farrier and a furrier, a clerk, a barber and 100 troopers.

Artillery

The Captain-General of the Artillery was responsible for the operational functioning of the artillery in battle. But his duties also included responsibilities outside of the campaign itself: supplying arms and supplies for the army, organising the artillery train, both the military and the civilian personnel, as well as the animals for the baggage and transport train (generally this last task was assigned to a civilian contractor, who provided the mule and oxen teams). Such was the importance of the Captain-General of the Artillery that his election was of the utmost importance and he was chosen from among the most senior field masters; it was a post normally reserved for natives of the Kingdom in which he served, unlike the General Field Master and the General of the Horse, who were customarily Spanish.

The Captain-General of the Army had to explain his plan of campaign to the Captain-General of the Artillery, so that the latter could make preparations for the stockpiling of provisions, organise the type and number of pieces of artillery needed for the campaign, both field and siege, arrange ammunition supply, carriages and draught animals, et cetera

The Captain-General of the Artillery was assisted by two Lieutenant-Generals, who usually came from amongst the captains of foot, but with experience in fortification. There was no standard artillery structure, but there were common ranks in all the Spanish armies, although the number of individual ranks depended on the resources available for that front:

Spanish cavalry, post 1625. Jacques Callot.
Carrying carbines these horse appear to be similar to the 'Mounted Arquebusiers' of an earlier period. Noteworthy is the positioning of the cornets in the second rank although the numbers of these are somewhat of an exaggeration – probably for effect in the engraving. In reality a body of horse of this size would be at most three troops and thus have three cornets. Similarly the formation is unlikely to have existed on a mid-seventeenth century battlefield and is again 'artistic licence'. (Rijksmuseum, Amsterdam. Public Domain)

accountants, miners, artillerymen, sappers, tentmakers, apothecaries, medics, et cetera.

As each master smelter applied his own tables in the creation of pieces, with similar materials, but in different proportions for their casting, there was a wide variety of pieces, names and calibres. Such was the chaos that in 1609 an order was published whereby in Flanders the number of calibres of guns was reduced to four: the cannon (firing 40 pound bullets), the demi-cannon (24 pound bullets), the quarter cannon (firing 6 pound bullets) and the fifth-cannon (a 3 pdr).

The larger pieces were used to batter fortifications, while the smaller ones were intended for use on the battlefield. Unlike the Swedes and a number of other states, the Spanish did not have guns assigned directly to the tercios. Instead all artillery was integrated into the artillery command. Since there were many fortresses in Flanders, the guns in the castles were often used for the campaign, and when the campaign was over, they were returned to the fortresses.

4

The Generals at Loggerheads

Louis of Bourbon

Louis de Bourbon (1621–1686), Duc d'Enghien. He became 4e Prince de Condé and Duc de Bourbon on the death of his father in 1646 and during his lifetime he also accumulated a number of further titles, Duc de Montmorency, Duc de Châteauroux, Duc de Bellegarde, Duc de Fronsac, Comte de Sancerre, Comte de Charolais. For his military successes and political power he was later nicknamed "The Great Condé".

d'Enghien, as he was known in 1643, was educated by the Jesuits in Bourges and then received military instruction at the Royal Military Academy in Paris. At the age of 16 he was appointed Governor of Burgundy. In 1639, he asked his father to allow him to take part in the Roussillon campaign, but the request was refused. At the age of 19, as a member of *Maréchal* La Meilleraye's staff, he took part in the conquest of Arras, alongside the Generals Gassion, Gesvres and La Ferté-Seneterre; and the following year, in the conquest of Aire-sur-la-Lys and Perpignan.

In addition to his Royal and noble birth, he was also related to Richelieu. In 1641 his father forced through a marriage between Louis and Claire-Clémence de Maillé-Brézé, which he was able to do because although Claire-Clémence was only 13 years old she was Cardinal Richelieu's niece. Both Louis XIII and Richelieu were pleased by the young Louis' courage and intelligence, and also by his personality, a mixture of energy, arrogance and charisma. This is why the dying Louis XIII recommended to his son, the future Louis XIV, to appoint Condé as General-in-chief of one of the armies that were to defend France against the almost certain Spanish invasion from Flanders.

When Condé was appointed commander of the Army of Picardy on 21 March 1643, over the head of the veteran *Maréchal* François de L'Hôpital, he aroused numerous misgivings and criticisms because of his youth, his inexperience in high command and the obvious favouritism shown him by Louis XIII.

After the Battle of Rocroi, and with the Kingdom saved from the Spanish invasion, Condé was sent to the Rhine to fight the Imperial Armies. In collaboration with Henri de la Tour d'Auvergne-Bouillon, Vicomte de Turenne, d'Enghien won victories at Fribourg (3, 5 and 9 August 1644) and Nördlingen (3 August 1645). In December 1646, after the death of his father

BOURBON-CONDÉ
(LOUIS II, LE GRAND)
1621–1686

Louis de Bourbon (1621–1686), Prince de Condé, Justus van Egmont (1601–1674), between 1654 and 1658. d'Enghien is shown here as an adult, portrayed during his stay in Flanders in the service of Spain. He took part in the victory at the Battle of Valenciennes (16 July 1656) fighting alongside his erstwhile enemies, and again was with the Spanish Army when it lost the Battle of the Dunes on 14 June 1658, another victory for Turenne. After the Peace of the Pyrenees (1659), he was pardoned by Louis XIV and again leading the French army fought against Spanish, Dutch and Imperial armies. (Wikimedia Commons)

Henri of Bourbon, he became 4e Prince de Condé. In the same year he took Dunkirk and, on 20 August 1648, won a victory at Lens against the Spanish Army of Erzherzog Leopold Wilhelm Habsburg.

During the Noble revolts of the Fronde, Condé adopted an ambiguous position: at first he defended the Court, but then he clashed with Cardinal Mazarin. His loyalty to Queen Anne of Austria led to the signing of the Peace of Rueil; but again his rivalry with Mazarin caused him to join the Fronde. On 18 January 1650, Condé, his brother Armand and his brother-in-law Longueville were arrested and imprisoned for thirteen months. On 7 February 1651, faced with an attack by the Fronde forces, Mazarin fled and the freed Prince de Condé took the lead of the "Fronde des Princes" and signed an agreement with Felipe IV of Spain and with the Republican Government in England.

With his army he headed for Paris. Louis XIV placed Turenne at the head of the Royal troops, who defeated Condé at Bléneau on 7 April 1652, Étampes, and then in the Saint-Antoine district. The Fronde army took cover in Paris, but in October they had to surrender to the King's troops. On 27 March 1653 Condé was condemned to death and his possessions confiscated, but he fled to Flanders, offering himself to the service of Spain. He took part in the Spanish victory at the Battle of Valenciennes on 16 July 1656, and in the Spanish defeat at the Battle of the Dunes on 14 June 1658, against a French army, and its English Allies, commanded by Turenne. After peace was signed between Spain and France by the Treaty of the Pyrenees (1659), Condé obtained a Royal pardon, granted in Aix-en-Provence shortly before Louis XIV married Maria Theresa of Austria, the daughter of King Felipe IV of Spain.

During the War of Devolution between France and Spain, Condé conquered Franche-Comté in three weeks (1668). He fought alongside Turenne again in the Dutch War, defeating William III of Orange at the Battle of Seneffe on 11 August 1674. After Turenne's death at the Battle of Salzbach on 27 July 1675, Condé marched to defend Alsace, fighting against the Imperial Commander, Raimondo Montecuccoli.

He retired from the army at the beginning of the 1680s, returning to live at his château at Chantilly, although he died at Fontainbleau in November 1686.

The French Chain of Command

The King of France was the supreme commander of the army, but unlike his father Henri IV, or his brother Gaston d'Orléans, Louis XIII took little effective part in any campaigns.

The second in command was the *Connétable de France* (Constable of France), the last being François de Bonne (1626); at the third level, the *Colonel Générals* who commanded the Foot, the Horse and the Swiss. In 1627, Richelieu abolished the rank of Constable, and it was the *Maréchals de France* (Marshals of France), formerly subordinate to the Constable, who became more prominent as independent commanders in the field.

The command echelon of the French army in the 1640s was: *Maréchal de France* (Marshal of France), *Maréchal de Camp* (Field Marshals), battle marshal, battle sergeant, *Mestre de Camp* and Colonel.

Sometimes an army could be commanded by one or more marshals, and there was usually a deep rivalry between them. The Bourbon dynasty granted the rank of *Maréchal* both to members of its family, the Princes of the Blood, and to veteran generals. After the abolition of the office of Constable, the *Maréchals de France* became the supreme commanders of the King's armies. The rank was not hereditary but did confer a great honour on the noble family whose members were rewarded with it (Montmorency, Noailles, Cossé-Brissac, Harcourt, Coligny).

The *Maréchal de Camp* was second in command to the commanding General, who was often a *Maréchal de France*. The functions of the *Maréchal de Camp* (literally, the General in charge of occupying the camp, i.e. organising the camp) initially centred on the accommodation and marshalling of troops in camp and on the march, going ahead on the road to reconnoitre possible places or towns where the troops could be accommodated. It was the function of the Quartermaster-General and the Major-General to put the *Maréchal de Camp's* orders into practice.

In an army on campaign a *Maréchal de France* usually had two or three *Maréchals de Camp*: one of them stayed with him, while the others could be the commanders of secondary detachments. In battle, the *Maréchals de Camp* were in charge of the reserve, or the main bodies of horse or foot.

By 1642 the figure of the battle marshal had been created, which was a specific post responsible for the execution of the commanding General's plans for battle, in the same way that the original functions of the field marshal were for billeting. The battle marshal was an operational 'Chief of Staff', in charge of marshalling the troops for marches and more especially for combat, and deploying them on the battlefield according to the General's instructions. He was also responsible for assigning or ratifying the senior officers in command of the units. The Chevalier de La Vallière was the first officer to hold the position.

The battle sergeants supported the above, prior to the creation of the position of battle marshal they had performed his functions. In case of absence or death in action of the senior officers, they assumed command of the army or the relevant wing or line. Their main function, however, was advisory, communication and execution of orders to the lower ranks and the inspections.

A French army of the early Thirty Years' War period was customarily commanded by a *Maréchal* as supreme commander with two field marshals, and two aides-de-camp. As armies grew, other General officers might be added, such as a battle sergeant, a Quartermaster-General, a Lieutenant of artillery, a Lieutenant-General of Horse and a General of army supplies.

Although the *Mestre de Camp* was originally an officer specifically appointed by the field marshal to take charge of encampment details of units, under Spanish influence, he became an operational commander, until he was eventually replaced by a regimental colonel-in-chief. The *Mestre de Camp* exercised disciplinary authority within his unit in the name of the King, and proposed to the King the names of the captains of companies.

According to the Ordonnance of 1629, the general staff of a permanent regiment was set out and fixed. The regiment was commanded by the *Mestre de Camp*, whose second in command was a *sergent-major* who took orders from the *Mestre de Camp* for the choice of position, battle array, alignment, and distances and intervals between the battalions, an *aide-major*, an *Provost de Justice* (responsible for policing), a conduct commissioner (responsible for intendancy), a quartermaster (who arranged the quartering of troops), a chaplain and a surgeon, five commissioners and five inspectors in charge of the musters.

At the general and officer level, Henri IV, inspired by the Italian academic tradition, promoted the creation of military schools, which proliferated in the following years, with the support of both the Crown and private initiatives. Military training also included a practical aspect, so that young officers, almost exclusively from the nobility, frequently rounded off their studies with a time in The Netherlands, serving under Frederick-Hendrick of Nassau and his generals, and then later in the Protestant German armies and those of Gustav II Adolph of Sweden.

François de L'Hôpital (Paris, 1583-Paris, 1660) was the youngest son of Louis de L'Hôpital and Françoise de Brichanteau. He was intended for an ecclesiastical life and at the age of 14 was appointed Bishop of Meaux, but in 1602 he decided to join the army. He was appointed *enseigne* (colour bearer and third in charge of the company) and then *sous-lieutenant* (second lieutenant) in the Gendarmes de la Garde (1615), obtaining command of a company in 1617. Two years later he was made a *Chevalier de l'Ordre de Saint-Michel*.

He was promoted to *Maréchal de Camp* in 1621, and the following year was Governor of the fortress-prison of the Bastille. During the following years he was successively at the sieges of Royan, Montpellier and La Rochelle, and then in Italy, Lorraine, Languedoc and Germany, where he was appointed *Lieutenant Général* (Lieutenant-General) in 1637. He was then transferred to the front of Lorraine, and appointed Governor of the newly annexed territory, directing the actions against the resistance (1639–1642), then was later appointed Governor of the province of Champagne. Mazarin made him second in command to be d'Enghien's military mentor, and indeed him to be the de facto commander of the Army of Picardy, but in reality d'Enghien acted on his own initiative and was influenced by Gassion. As a

François de L'Hôpital du Hallier (1583–1660), by Michel Lasne (c.1590–1667).
The exact date of this work is unknown, but from the appearance of L'Hôpital, it must be very close to the battle of Rocroi, when the General was 60 years old. L'Hôpital wears a cuirass, and displays the typical French custom of wearing his hair long, shoulder-length, with a moustache and goatee; all very different from the Spanish fashion. The veteran General, who began his military career at aged 19, rose to the highest rank of Maréchal de France. (National Gallery of Art, Washington, D.C.)

FRANCOIS DE L'HOS-PITAL DV HALLIER. Comte de Rofnay Chlier des ordres du Roy, Mar.ᵃˡ de Fran. Cap.ⁿᵉ lieut.ᵗ de la comp.ⁿᵉ des deux cens hommes darmes de fa Ma.ᵗˢ feul lieut. gnãl es Prou.ˡⁱᵉ de Champ.ⁿᵉ et Brie.

reward for his record of service, de L'Hôpital was appointed *Maréchal de France* on 20 April 1643.

In 1647 he resigned command of his company of *Gendarmes de la Garde* and in 1655 was discharged from the army to take up administrative duties as Governor of Champagne; he died in Paris, in 1677. During his long military career, he accumulated the titles of Sieur de Hallier and de Beynes and Compte de Rosnay.

Jean, Comte de Gassion (Pau, 1609-Arras, 1647). His family belonged to the Huguenot nobility of Béarn, but his father, Jacques de Gassion, was posted to various positions and the family followed him. Jacques wanted his son to enter a Catholic religious order, but Jean refused, maintaining his Protestant beliefs and faith. At the age of 18, he served the Duca di Savoia, Carlo Emanuele I, in his company of Guard Gendarme. Soon after, he returned to France to serve in the Protestant army of Duc Henri II de Rohan against the Army of Louis XIII. In 1629, Rohan submitted to Royal Authority and Gassion returned to the service of the Duca di Savoia; but when the French intervened in the War of the Mantuan Succession, Gassion enlisted in the French army of *Maréchal* de la Force, fighting against the Spanish.

In 1630 he entered the service of Gustav II Adolph[1] of Sweden, under the assumed name of Hontas. At the Battle of Breitenfeld on 17 September 1631, he received two sword wounds to the head and two musket wounds, but even though he was wounded, he managed to lead the capture of the Catholic artillery. His reputation for bravery grew and he returned to France,

---

1   Gustav II Adolph (1594–1632), King of Sweden 1611–1632, is more commonly, if incorrectly, called Gustavus Adolphus. This latter 'name' comes from a shortening of the way he was referred to after his death – Gustavus Adolphus Magnus (Gustav Adolph the Great), but it is not how he was usually known during his lifetime.

MONSIEVR DE GASSION MARESCHAL DE FRANCE.

B. Moncornet pcti

Jean, Comte de Gassion (1609–1647), by an unknown engraver c1650.
From an early age, Jean's destiny was to become a soldier. He trained in all the European theatres of war and had a well-deserved reputation for bravery and intelligence. He liked danger, living on the edge. The Gazette de France turned him into a hero for the general public, intertwining real stories with the thrilling adventures of journalists' inventions. On 28 September 1647, during an inspection at the siege of Lens, he was shot in the head with a musket ball, from which he died in Arras on 2 October. (Wikimedia Commons)

recruiting a company of 90 veteran horse, which became part of Gustav II Adolph's escort. He was subsequently rewarded with the command of three companies of horse and finally the command of a regiment of horse, with a strength of six companies. After the death of the King of Sweden, he continued in the service of the League of Heilbronn, under the command of Bernhard of Saxe-Weimar, with a regiment of horse of 12 companies and 1,200 men.

When he entered French service (1635), his brilliant record of service with Gustav II Adolph of Sweden led many generals to ask Richelieu to have Gassion serve with them. The Cardinal, recognising his worth, nicknamed him "Le Guerre". During his service in Germany with the Swedish army, Gassion assimilated perfectly to the shock tactics of the horse, and then transferred his experience to the French army. He obtained command of a sizeable body of horse, some 1,600 men, whom he trained in the Swedish manner. He also obtained the Royal grant of the privilege, usually reserved for foreign mercenary units, of appointing his own choice of officers and non-commissioned officers. Additionally his soldiers were answerable only to him, and he acted as their judge. Interestingly, as the head of his unit, Gassion was a colonel, while his counterparts in the French army were *Mestres de Camp*.

He served under Maréchal de la Force, excelling in command both in battle, Charmes and Neufchâteau, and in the sieges of Dole, Hesdin, Saint-Omer and Landrecies. At the battle of Raon in 1636, he destroyed Colloredo's regiment and succeeded in capturing the Catholic General, Colloredo. At the siege of Saint-Omer in 1637, he withstood the charge of Piccolomini's two cuirassier regiments (Alt-Piccolomini and Jung-Piccolomini) and forced their retreat. In 1639, Richelieu sent him to Normandy to suppress the peasant revolt of the *va-nu-pieds* (literally "barefooted ones") provoked by the imposition of a tax on salt in Cotentin. After his success there, he was appointed *Mestre de Camp Général de la Cavalerie*, a post he held from 1641 to 1646.

In character, Gassion was famous for putting service before comfort. He was reserved, active, capable of riding for hours on end and had a reputation for courage, intelligence but also a certain rapacious instinct for plunder.

History recognises his enormous role in command of the horse at the Battle of Rocroi, and as a reward for his service he was made Maréchal de France on 17 November 1643 at the age of thirty-four. During the following years, the French press, especially *La Gazette de France,* trumpeted his actions, mythologizing him. Gassion was the epitome of the virtues of medieval French chivalry updated to the seventeenth century. He was mortally wounded at the siege of Lens in 1647, and died on 2 October.

Henri de Saint-Nectaire, Marquis de La Ferté-Senneterre (1599-1681) was from the lower aristocracy of Auvergne. He rose through the ranks of the French administration: his grandfather was Maréchal Claude de La Châtre de La Maisonfort and his father, Henri de La Ferté-Senneterre, was both an ambassador and a minister.

From an early age he was destined for the army: as a young man, he marched to the Low Countries, serving under Maurice of Nassau, studying his tactics in depth. Back in France, his father recruited a regiment for the King's service for the siege of La Rochelle, and Henri served in it with the rank of captain.

During the siege of Privas in 1629, he took a shot from a musket that disfigured his face and henceforward he painted part of his face with plaster to conceal the wound. A jovial character, he gained considerable weight over the years and made jokes about his bulk.

He took part in the campaigns of the War of Mantuan Succession and the annexation of Lorraine in 1632. In 1638 he was appointed *Mestre de Camp de la Cavalerie,* and for his brilliant performance in the action of Hesdin on 29 June 1639, he was promoted Maréchal. In 1640, during the fighting at Chimay, he was wounded in the leg by a falconet bullet: in order to be able to walk, he tied his sword to his leg as a crutch.

His behaviour at the Battle of Rocroi was misguided, and he charged at the wrong time. However, he demonstrated great personal courage in battle, received multiple wounds, both pistol and sword, and was captured; but he was released after the surrender of the Spanish on the field.

In 1643, he was appointed Governor of the Duchy of Lorraine, and in 1648 was promoted *Lieutenant Général.* During the civil war of the Fronde, he remained loyal to the Crown and, under the command of Turenne, took several towns controlled by Condé. In 1652 he was made *Maréchal de France.* In October 1653, La Ferté launched the siege of Belfort, capturing the town in February 1654. He was taken prisoner at Valenciennes (1656) and ransomed by King Louis XIV, who, for all his services, raised the Marquisate of Ferté-Senneterre to the rank of Duc in 1665. He eventually retired to his possessions and died in 1681.

Roger de Bossòst, Seigneur d'Espenan (?–1646). Little is known about d'Espenan's youth, but in 1639–1640 he was the commander of the garrison of the fortress of Salses, after its capture and brief tenure by France.

He was one of the French representatives in negotiations with the Catalan deputies, who were plotting their rebellion against the King of Spain, Felipe IV. Espenan obtained the Catalans' commitment to accept King Louis XIII as the new sovereign of Catalonia, opening a war front in the interior of Spain, in exchange for French military aid.

In December 1640 he arrived in Barcelona with French troops and was appointed *Maréchal de Camp* of the French Army. He went on to defend Tarragona, against the Castilian Army of Pedro Fajardo de Zúñiga y Requesens, Marquis de los Velez. Faced with the superiority of the Velez's Castilian army, Espenan surrendered and managed to evacuate his army, although this caused deep unrest amongst his Catalan allies. Espenan was ordered to return to France as being very low on supplies, he sacked several Catalan towns on the way.

His role in the battle of Rocroi was somewhat sporadic, as he showed little initiative throughout the battle. The various accounts indicate that he played no role in the main course of the fighting, and that some of his foot units were disorganised by Isenburg's horse. When it was decided to attack the Spanish foot, he backed off and ordered a halt. Some of his units were partially disorganised and retreated following La Valière's orders, without his attempting to reorganise them.

Claude de Létouf, Barón de Sirot (Saône-et-Loire, 1600-Orléans, 1652). From a noble family of Italian origin (Létouf comes from the surname Tufo), at the age of 16 he applied for admission to Louis XIII's company of Royal Guards. After a number of years, he went to The United Provinces to learn the trade of arms in the army of Maurice of Nassau, and then after the conclusion of the Twelve Years' Truce (1609–1621), he joined the army of Carlo Emanuele I, Duca di Savoia. In 1625 he moved on to Hungary taking service with Army of The Empire and commanding a company of horse against the Transylvanian Bethlem Gabor. Afterwards he enlisted in the Imperial Army recruited by Albrecht Wallenstein. In 1627, while defending a post, he shot at King Christian IV of Denmark, killing his horse. In 1630 he had an opportunity for a shot at Gustav II Adolph of Sweden, and knocked off his hat. The Swedish King asked to meet him and offered him the command of a regiment of horse, which he accepted. When France went to war with Spain in 1635, he returned to serve his Country.

He was brave, jovial, hardened by many years of service, but with a certain reputation as a bully and somewhat overconfident about his own abilities, but his performance in command of the French reserve at Rocroi was decisive. In 1649 he was promoted to *Lieutenant Général* and then *Maréchal de Camp*. During the following campaigns he took the towns of Thionville, Courtray, Armentières and a number of others. He died in 1652 at the assault on Le Pont de Gergeau, during the civil war of the Fronde.

Francisco de Braganza and Melo

Francisco Melo de Portugal y Castro (1597–1651), a member of a collateral branch of the Royal House of Braganza, he was an example of the Portuguese higher aristocracy in the service of Spain. Melo was a diplomat and politician and accumulated the titles of 1st Marqués de Vellisca, 1st Marqués de Tordelaguna, 1st Conde de Asumar and Vizconde de Caseda, many of these titles specifically created to honour his services to the Spanish Habsburgs.

Don Francisco was the first-born son of Constantino de Braganza y Melo, state councillor to Felipe III, and nephew of the archbishop of Évora, José de Braganza.

Sent at a very young age to the Court in Madrid, Melo decided to join the entourage of the Royal valide, Gaspar de Guzmán, Conde-Duque de Olivares. Both men came from outlying regions of Castile and from cadet branches of illustrious noble families (the House of Braganza and the House of Medina Sidonia, respectively) and sought social and political advancement to level up with the senior branches of their families. Thus, with the approval of Olivares, Melo became a part of the entourage of Isabelle de Bourbon, daughter of the French King, Henri IV, and then wife of Felipe IV. In 1631 he was appointed *Mayordomo* to the Queen (the rank is literally 'butler', but represents so much more in Spanish Court hierarchy).

During the following years he showed his support for Olivares, being rewarded with the position of *Gentilhombre de Cámara* (Gentleman of the King's Chamber). Melo received his first diplomatic post in 1632 when he was sent as ambassador to the Duca di Savoia and then, from 1632 to 1636, he was Spanish ambassador to Genoa, and then ambassador to Rome, being subsequently replaced by the Marqués de Castel-Rodrigo. No doubt at the behest of Olivares, on his return to Spain his very effective ambassadorship in Italy was rewarded with several rewards from the Crown. He received the title of Conde de Asumar and was raised to the dignity of becoming a member of the Council of State of the Crown of Portugal.

In March 1637, he was sent to the Court of the new Emperor, Ferdinand III, and in 1638 returned to Madrid to explain his embassy. He was posted to Italy as Viceroy of Sicily between 1638 and 1639 and in 1640 he was again appointed Ambassador to the Imperial Court in Vienna, this time to attend the Diet of Ratisbon. When the Portuguese revolt led by his relative João de Braganza broke out, Francisco de Melo remained a firm supporter

Francisco de Melo (1597–1651), by Anthonie van der Does (1609–1680).
Melo was the Governor of the Spanish Netherlands and Captain-General of the Army of Flanders. He is shown with a simple collar "a la valona" (Walloon collar), the red scarf as a symbol of the Spanish Monarchy, a General's baton and a rapier with a concentric rings style guard. As fencing evolved more and more towards the use of the point, greater protection for the hand was required, so that metal plates (shells) were often added between the rings of the guard; in some later examples the rings are entirely covered with metal plates, a style which eventually evolved into the cup hilts of later rapiers. (Rijksmuseum, RP-P-OB-50.137)

EXCEL.^{SIMO} D^{NO.} D. FRANCISCO DEMELLO COMITI DE AZUMAR. &C. EQUITI ORDINIS CHRISTI: ET QVINQVE COMMENDARUM IN LVSITANIA COMMENDATORI: OECONOMO SUPREMO REGINÆ CATHOLICÆ PHILIPPO IIII. HISPANIARUM REGI A CUBI- CULIS; ET A CONSILIIS STATUS AC BELLI. AD PRINC^M OMNES ITALIÆ. CÆSAREM. ET PONTIF.^M MAX. LEGATO EXTRAORDIN.^O IN DITIONE MEDIOLAN.^{SI} ALSATIA. ET BELGIO. EXERC^{TUM} IMP.^{RI} NUPER REGNI SICILIÆ PRO-REGI. ET AULÆ PRINC. CARD!^{HI} HISP. INF. PRÆFECTO MAX.^{MO} NUNC AVTEM PRO PACE SANCIENDA PLENI-POTENT.^{RIO} ET BELGII AC BURGUNDIÆ GUBERNATORI; ANT. VANDER DOES. L.M.D.O.

of King Felipe IV. Upon the instructions of the Olivares, he requested and obtained the arrest of the Infante Duarte de Braganza, the brother of João de Braganza, who was serving in the Imperial Army. Duarte had left Portugal in 1634 with the avowed purpose of achieving military fame in the service of The Empire in its ongoing struggle against the Protestant powers.

Melo was posted to The Netherlands, in the entourage of the Cardinal-Infante, in 1641. Faced with the power vacuum caused by the death of the Cardinal-Infante, Felipe IV established the joint government of Flanders between Melo, Jacques Boonen, Archbishop of Mechelen, and Pieter Roose, President of the Privy Council. To avoid disagreements that would hinder the work of government, the King decided that Melo should assume sole command, and he was made acting Governor of the Low Countries on 4 December 1641. On 7 December of that year his troops succeeded in recapturing the town of Aire-sur-Lys.

In the spring-summer of 1642 he launched a campaign against the French, winning the important victory of Honnecourt and as a reward, the King elevated him to the rank of Grandee of Spain and granted him the title of Marqués de Tordelaguna. Despite his lack of military experience, all these victories raised hopes in Madrid, even after the fall of his protector Olivares in January 1643.

After the defeat at Rocroi, he swiftly reorganised the surviving forces, but lost the fortress of Thionville on 8 August 1643 in the French summer offensive. He returned to Brussels to face popular fury: his house was sacked by the angry mob who blamed him for the defeat and the pro-French riots that followed. There were also disturbances in Ghent and Bruges.

Worse still was the renewal of the Dutch alliance with France in January 1644. In the next five years the French conquered more places in southern Flanders than the Dutch had conquered in twenty years of campaigning. Melo's prestige declined further and the Marqués de Castel-Rodrigo arrived in Brussels to succeed him in June 1644; Melo returned to Spain in November. There were rumours at Court that he would be tried for four crimes (failure to follow the advice of his staff, failure to wait for Beck's troops to arrive, failure to entrench to besiege Rocroi, failure to secure the baggage with army money). However as Fontaine's death in the line of duty redeemed him for his dismal performance at Rocroi, in the end there was no trial.

Despite the fall from grace of the Valide Conde-Duque de Olivares, de Melo's political protector, he managed to survive his friendship and military disasters. He was appointed to the Council of War and the Council of State in 1644, where he frequently advocated peace with The Netherlands, France and the Catalan rebels as a means of seriously undertaking the reconquest of Portugal. He was appointed Viceroy of Catalonia in 1645, and of Aragon in 1648. In 1648, after being rewarded for his services with the title of Marqués de Vellisca, he was sent as Spanish Plenipotentiary to the Congress of Westphalia. However, he was never again to occupy positions of prominence.

Despite his precarious political circumstances, Melo lived out his last years quite comfortably off. He died in Madrid of an unknown illness on 18 September 1651.

The Spanish Chain of Command

The General officers who made up the Spanish high command in Flanders were, in order of importance: the Captain-General (who was also the Governor-General), the Field Master General, the Captain-General of the Horse and the Captain-General of the Artillery. At a secondary level were: the Lieutenant-General field masters, usually one for each of the three main nationalities, the Lieutenant-General of the Horse, the Commissary General of the Horse and the Lieutenant-General of the Artillery.

The Captain-General, in agreement with the Council of State and the King, defined the military strategy for the campaign. It basically came down to two alternatives: either to stay on the defensive or to attack. As enemies existed both to the east and the west, the Captain-General had to decide on which front to make the most resources available for the campaign. The need to divide his forces into two armies and the growing French military effort forced him to react defensively most of the time, thus largely losing his ability to act as he wished.

With the outbreak of war against France, the Army of Flanders had to face two simultaneous threats, and the Governor-General had to divide the army into two, called the "army against France" and the "army against The Netherlands". The experience of the war against the French showed that they used to divide their army into several contingents, in order to threaten more territories in Flanders, so they had to be imitated. The tercios were distributed throughout the border provinces, but there was no coordinated or overall command, with the field masters of each tercio deciding for their unit, creating a hierarchical imbroglio.

To alleviate the responsibilities of the Captain-General when it was decided to create the two armies, the position of *Gobernador de Armas* (Governor of Arms) was created to command the secondary army.

The second in command of the main army was the *Maestre de Campo General* (Field Master General), who was in charge of implementing the campaign strategy devised by the Captain-General (e.g. to present a field battle or to besiege a town). The Field Master General chose the route, the terrain to deploy the army, the deployment on the battlefield, and thus had command over all the units of the army. However, after the death of the Cardinal-Infante, the Captain-General of the Horse began to claim for himself absolute independent command of the horse, below the Governor-General. Previously the Captain-General of the Horse had been second to the Field Master General and followed his orders.

The Captain-General of the Artillery was the third in the hierarchy and commanded the army if the two senior officers were not present. As commander of the Artillery, he organised the logistics of the guns, their transport, ammunition, et cetera

The second 'level' of general officers acted as "chief of staff", advising their respective Captain-Generals and transmitting their orders to the third level of command – the field masters and horse corporals.

The Flanders theatre of war had traditionally been where the largest army in the Spanish Monarchy was concentrated, and where the great generals such as the Duque de Alba, Johann de Austria, Alexander Farnese, Ambroggio Spinola, and the best senior commanders – Julian Romero, Sancho Dávila, Conde de Bucquoy, Tilly – stood out.

After Spinola's death in 1630, and until the arrival of Cardinal-Infante in Flanders in 1643, there was a succession of Captain-Generals of Flanders who, despite being very competent, did not arouse the unanimity that previous officers had enjoyed. Something similar happened after the appointment of Melo as successor to the Cardinal-Infante. In addition, the increase in the size of the Army of Flanders, which had to simultaneously fight both the Dutch and the French, and its greater collaboration with the Imperial Armies, created the need for a General Officer who could assume part of the responsibilities of the Captain-General and also have sufficient prestige to rival the higher ranks of the Imperial Army. The rank of "Sergeant General of Battle" was suggested, but the Council of State refused the idea.

After the defeat at Rocroi, Melo again insisted on the creation of this rank, and also proposed the appointment of Esteban de Gamarra as Sergeant General of Battle for the Spanish Tercios, Count de Grobbendonck for the Walloons and Ottavio Guasco for the Italians and Germans – his suggestion was rejected. Finally, however, this rank actually was created on 13 April 1646, establishing the specific rank for each of the four main Nationalities of the Army of Flanders.

For the campaign of 1643, Melo appointed Count Paul-Bernhard de Fontaine as General Field Master of the Army of Flanders, the Duque de Alburquerque as General of Horse and his brother Álvaro de Melo as General of the Artillery.

Paul-Bernhard de Fontaine (Lorraine, 1576-Rocroi, 19 May 1643), was the son of François de Fontaine, Sieur de Cierges, a nobleman of Basque descent, Governor of Stenay and Steward to the Duc de Lorraine. Both de Fontaine's father and mother, Suzanne d'Urre, died before he was a year old, so it was his maternal grandfather, Jean d'Urre, Sieur de Tesières, who looked after him. Tesières resigned his guardianship in 1584 because of his advanced age, he was 87, and died two years later. After that Charles d'Urre, de Fontaine's uncle, took care of him.

At the age of 20, in 1596, de Fontaine entered the service of the King of Spain as a volunteer. In 1597, he was captain in the Walloon Regiment of Foot of Colonel Claude de la Bourlotte. In 1604 he was Captain of Horse and by 1610 he took command of the regiment previously commanded by Colonel Nicolas de Catris. As Colonel of Regiment of Foot, Fontaine took part in the War of the Cleves-Jülich Succession and in 1610,was seriously wounded. He took part in several important battles against the Dutch, including Hulst, Kallo and Antwerp. From 1616 to 1638 he commanded the unit known as the "Tercio de Fontaine". During the Twelve Years' Truce, 1612–1621, he had a series of fortifications built from Knokke to Lapscheure, a series later known as the Fontaine Line. In 1631, as commander of the Spanish troops, he broke the siege of Bruges against Prince Frederik Hendrik of Orange-Nassau. In 1627 the Emperor Ferdinand II conferred on him the title and rank of Zählen (Count).

In 1637 he was appointed *Bailli* (Constable) of Bruges, and the following year became second in command of the army against France and was also appointed General of the Flanders artillery. In 1638 he was made the Master of Artillery General, for operations against the Dutch. He defeated the Dutch at Hulst and, at the end of remarkably fast march through the

Count Paul-Bernhard de Fontaine (1566–1643), by Pieter de Jode (1628–1670).
De Fontaine is wearing three-quarter armour with reinforcements at the shoulders. In his right hand he holds a baton and in his left hand rests on a close helmet, an evolution from the visored sallet. This type of helmet was used by the heavy, pistol-armed, cuirassiers into the mid–seventeenth century. In this case, it gives a knightly and chivalric aspect to the figure of Fontaine, perhaps by way of artistic licence.
(Rijksmuseum, RP-P–1906-706)

flooded lands of Campine and Limburg, forced Frederik Hendrik, Prince of Orange, to abandon his campaign against Geldern. By this time, however, he was chronically ill and, in truth, unfit for military service. He participated in the Rocroi campaign from a transport saddle, as he was unable to ride.

Why did Melo choose Fontaine as his second in command, if he had more experience on the Dutch front than on the French? The explanation must surely be found in Melo's lack of military experience and the 1632 Ordinances' heavily favouring of the nobility.

On the one hand, Melo was a diplomat and politician, but he had little battlefield experience. The victory of Honnecourt had primarily been achieved by the actions of Jean de Beck, and Melo wanted an experienced military man like Fontaine at his side. Secondly, since the Spanish Military Ordinances of 1632 had introduced the possibility of relatively rapid promotion through the military ranks for the nobility. Young noblemen, such as the Duque de Alburquerque, the Conde de Garcíez and the Conde de Villaba, could occupy posts as field masters with only a few years of service. Thus, Francisco Fernández de la Cueva, Duque de Alburquerque, was 21 years old when he was appointed Field Master, and only 24 when he was promoted to Captain-General of the Flanders Horse over the veteran Andrea Cantelmo, who was 45 years old, with more than 25 years of service. Therefore, to compensate for Albuquerque's lack of military experience (in only five years he had gone from soldier to General) Melo called for Fontaine's presence as Field Master General, to advise both Alburquerque and himself. This favouring of the nobility was not unique to Spain – the Duc d'Enghien was 21 when he became General, ahead of the veteran Maréchal François de L'Hôpital.

In Spanish sources, Fontaine is known as "Conde de Fontana" or "Conde de Fuentes", a literal Spanish translation of his surname. Throughout his career, Fontaine showed himself to be more of an efficient administrator than a military strategist and he was chief bailiff of Bruges and of the Franconate of Bruges, Governor of Damme and superintendent of the gendarmerie in the County of Flanders.

Francisco Fernández de la Cueva (Barcelona, 1619-Madrid, 1676) was an example of the high nobility that Olivares wanted to involve in the military. He was 8th Duque de Alburquerque, 6th Marqués de Cuéllar and Conde de Ledesma and Huelma. Through his father la Cueva belonged to a reputable line of high-ranking officials who had held the rank of Viceroy in various Spanish territories – in Aragon, Navarre, Naples, New Spain, Sicily, et cetera

He began his military career at the age of 19 as a simple soldier at the siege of Fuenterrabía (1638), but later rose through the ranks because of his noble birth. Felipe IV sent him to Flanders in 1640, and appointed him Field Master of the Tercio de Saavedra at the age of 20. He fought in the campaigns of 1641 and 1642, and was prominent at the Battle of Le Châtelet, for which action he received a letter from King Felipe IV thanking him for his bravery.

His appointment as head of the Flanders Horse was not without controversy. Although Alburquerque was known for his courage and intelligence, it was also true that he was still very young, and that his meteoric career rise was due to his noble origins. Alburquerque commanded his own Tercio, and on 15 April 1643, Melo appointed him General of the Horse of the States of Flanders, removing the Conde de Bucquoy the previous holder of the post. This latter offended the Walloon units as a whole, who felt it was an affront to them that a native noble of such prestige should be put out by a young Spanish noble. It was said that Alburquerque was courting Melo's daughter. Melo had not only upset the Walloons, but also the Spanish: the veteran Andrea Cantelmo refused to

Francisco Fernández de la Cueva, 8th Duque de Alburquerque (1619–1676), by an unidentified painter, in 1693.
The Duque was prominent in the government of the Viceroyalty of New Spain, which included present-day Mexico, Louisiana and Florida, southern United States, Guatemala, Cuba, Puerto Rico and Santo Domingo. He was the 22nd Viceroy and also the youngest at 34. Faced with the danger of English troops landing in Mexico, one of his first actions was to reinforce the defences of Veracruz and San Juan de Ulúa, he sent arms and ammunition to Jamaica and Havana and reinforced the naval forces. In his founding and settlement work, he sent a hundred families to New Mexico, and the town of Albuquerque, among other places, was founded in his honour. The City is known today by the abbreviation ABQ and is the most populous in the State of New Mexico in the United States. (Museo Nacional de Historia de México, Q6940502)

serve under Alburquerque, since Alburquerque had been Cantelmo's subordinate in previous campaigns, and the Italian considered it an insult to serve under such a young and inexperienced officer.

The veteran Commissioner General of the Flanders horse, Pedro de Villamor, was also upset by the distribution of posts among the nobility and forced subordination of himself and other veterans in favour of the nobles. For this reason he asked Melo for permission to return to Spain. The Governor found himself in the middle of the political balancing act between the nobility and the professional military. He denied Villamor's leave, but promoted him to Lieutenant-General of the Horse of the Army against France, a post in which he served until 1647, but in return, he had to serve as Alburquerque's assistant.

After the battle of Rocroi, Alburquerque wrote a long letter to the King in which he offered his exculpatory view of the battle, exaggerating his youth, listing the mistakes made by Melo and Fontaine and arguing that he had offered advice on how to correct them, but that it had been rejected.

The stain on his service record for his actions at Rocroi was erased by his subsequent brilliant military services a few years later. He was again elevated to high command because of his noble origins, he was promoted to Captain-General of the Galleys of Spain. He excelled in the defence of Tortosa and, especially in the siege of Barcelona in 1650, intercepting four French ships carrying five hundred foot. In 1653 he was rewarded for his military service with the post of Viceroy of New Spain (Mexico), returning to Spain in 1661. On 9 July 1663 he was appointed Captain-General of the Navy of the Ocean Sea, and held this post until his appointment as Lieutenant-General of the Navy the following year. From 1668 to 1670, he was Viceroy of Sicily. He died while serving in the Royal Palace, after Carlos II had appointed him "gentleman of his chamber", chief steward and member of Councils of State and War.

Although in the nineteenth century, Henri d'Orléans, Duc d'Aumale, questioned Alburquerque's courage at the Battle of Rocroi the Spanish historians Cesáreo Fernández Duro and Antonio Rodríguez Villa refuted the claims, providing information from witnesses to the battle, such as Melo himself, and official documents from the Court of Felipe IV.

The General of the Artillery was Álvaro de Melo. Initially it was planned that it would be the veteran Andrea Cantelmo, but when Alburquerque was appointed General of the Horse, ahead of Cantelmo, to avoid rivalry between the young man and the veteran, it was decided to compensate Cantelmo with the position of General Field Master of the second army, that operating against The Netherlands. It was then that Melo decided to appoint his brother Álvaro as the General of the Artillery. This appointment was criticised, but the Melo defended his decision by pointing out that Álvaro was the most senior Field Master of Foot and had a great deal of experience on the battlefield. In fact, the performance of the Spanish artillery at the Battle of Rocroi was far superior to that of the French; Álvaro de Melo deployed his guns well, and had ensured that they had sufficient ammunition. Little, however, is known of Don Álvaro's life.

Ernst von Isenburg (Isenburg, 1584-Brussels, 1664). He was Graf von Isenburg-Grenzau, in the Holy Roman Empire. His father, Salentin, 9th Count of Isenburg-Grenzau, was initially Archbishop and Elector of

Spanish Senior Officers and Foot in column of march. Jan van de Velde (II), 1632. (Rijksmuseum, Amsterdam. Public Domain)

Cologne (1567–1577) and Bishop of Padeborn (1574–1577), but, in 1577, he left the clergy and married Antonia Wilhelmina of Arenberg. In 1574, Salentin recruited a regiment of 2,000 horse for the service of the King of Spain in his fight against the Dutch Protestant rebels, initiating a relationship of loyalty and service to Spain, which his sons continued. The heir to the title, Salentin 10th, died in Bohemia in 1619 while serving as a captain in Albert Waldstein's Cuirassier regiment. At his death, Ernst inherited the family titles.

Ernst began his military career at the age of 16 as Colonel of a mixed regiment of horse – five companies of cuirassiers and five of arquebusiers. This was paid for by his father, to serve in the Palatine War (1620–1622) under the prestigious General Ambroggio Spinola. In 1622 he recruited a German regiment of foot of ten companies, which he commanded at the Battle of Fleurus on 29 August 1622, and in the sieges of Berg-Op-Zoom in October 1622, and of Breda, from 1624 to 1625, appearing in the painting by Velázquez that celebrates the surrender of the City.

In 1626 he led an auxiliary corps of 6,000 men and six guns into the Palatinate to the aid of the Imperial Army, contributing to the Danish defeat at Lütter-am-Bamberg on 25 August 1626, and their final expulsion from Germany. For this, Felipe IV made him a Knight of the Order of the Golden Fleece, 24 January 1628.

In 1633, when 3rd Duque de Feria, Gómez Suárez de Figueroa y Córdoba, organised the Army of Alsace to secure 'the Spanish Road' so that the Cardinal-Infante could reach Brussels, Isenburg was appointed Field Master General, a rank he sometimes held simultaneously with that of Governor of Arms, i.e. second in command. In 1643 he was appointed Commander of the Army of Alsace, sent to reinforce Governor Melo's spring campaign.

After the death of the Count de Fontaine, he was appointed Field Master General of the Army of Flanders, a post he held until his appointment as Chief Financial Officer of the Spanish Netherlands in 1645.

Given his prestige throughout the Army of Flanders, he continued to hold the colonelcy of his German regiment, although he left operational command in 1628. He held a number of civilian posts for several years until his death in 1664.

Beck Capelle, Jean George (Pfaffenthal, 1588-Arras, 1648). Of humble origins – his father was a messenger and Jean himself was a shepherd and messenger – he entered the Imperial Army in 1618, at the age of 30. By 1627 he was a lieutenant-colonel and in 1629 a colonel. Wallenstein noticed him for his military qualities and in 1632 appointed him Major-General and Commander of the Prague garrison in 1633. He remained loyal to Emperor Ferdinand II and contributed to the downfall of Waldstein, being rewarded with a noble patent of The Empire on 25 February 1634, the vacant colonelcy of the ex-Regiment of Aldringen on the same day, and the barony of Widim in Bohemia on 18 April 1637. From 1636, he cooperated with the Spanish Army of Alsace and he participated in the invasion of France with Piccolomini's army. He took part in the Siege of Saint-Omer in 1638 and of Thionville in 1639, in which he stood out for his flanking manoeuvre against Maréchal Pfeuquières' army.

Beck felt that he was outclassed by Piccolomini, who, as General-in-chief took all the credit, so he asked the Emperor to serve him in Spain, whilst retaining the colonelcy of his German foot regiment. Felipe IV quickly promoted him, appointing him Field Master General of the Army of Alsace in April 1640, to operate alongside the Duke of Lorraine. For his achievements on campaign, on 18 January 1642, Felipe IV made him Governor and Captain-General of the Duchy of Luxembourg and of the County of Chiny. In reward for his services, Emperor Ferdinand III made him Barón Beck.

Beck participated brilliantly in the Battle of Honnecourt (26 May 1642) and was considered the architect of the victory. After the battle, while Melo operated in the province of Boulonnais, Beck was left in command of a detachment to defend the provinces of Artois and Hainaut against a second French army, under the command of the Count of Harcourt, before which he took the castle of Dolhem on 7 August. At the end of the campaign, the troops under his command marched to winter in Luxembourg.

In April 1643 he received orders from Melo to join the spring campaign and led his army to Rocroi, but was unable to

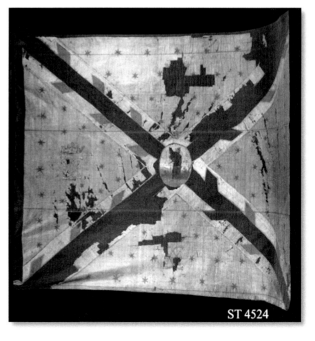

Catholic company colour, with the Cross of Burgundy at its centre.
On the colour is a monogram believed to belong to Erzherzogs Alberto and Isabel Clara Eugenia, who ruled as regents of Flanders from 1599 to 1621, the date of Alberto's death. Isabel remained in power, as Governor until her death in 1633. Thus, it could be the colour of a Walloon or Burgundian unit in service in the Army of Flanders or of the Duque de Feria. (Armémuseum, AM.084274)

ST 4524

arrive in time for the battle. He nonetheless, managed to reorganise the survivors to prepare for the defence of Flanders. When the French army besieged Thionville on 17 June 1643, Beck, who had arrived only the day before, organised the defence with the troops he was able to bring out of Luxembourg. On this occasion, however, there was no relief and he had to capitulate on 8 August. He saved the garrison, with which he was able to march to Luxembourg, but his resistance at Thionville had disorganised the French army, which was unable to take any further action that year.

In 1644, the Duc d'Enghien attacked Luxembourg, but Barón Beck resolutely opposed the attack and forced the French to abandon the campaign.

King Felipe IV appointed him Governor and Captain of the Duchy of Luxembourg, and also granted him the *hábito de Santiago* (the habit of St. James) on 9 April 1644 – an honorary title which allowed him to be honoured as a knight and entitled him to receive an allowance.

During the campaign of 1645, Beck commanded the second army operating against The Netherlands, resisting the Dutch offensive. He was seriously wounded in early October and Frederik Hendrik of Nassau took advantage of his absence to lay siege to Hulst, which surrendered on 4 November after a 28-day siege.

The King made him Field Master General of the Spanish Netherlands on 12 November 1645, the second most important military post. Shortly afterwards his Governorship of Luxembourg was given to Felipe Francis de Croy, Count of Solre. Beck took advantage of his convalescence to acquire the castle and manor of Beaufort, which he had rebuilt in the Renaissance style.

In the campaign of 1646 he was given command of the Army of Alsace, cooperating with his former General Piccolomini. Although he was second in the chain of command, his initiative enabled the surprise action on Maréchal Rantzau's quarters at Kuurne on 23 June. He was subsequently responsible for the defence of the Scheldt posts between Termonde and Ghent. He then returned to Brussels to arrange for the cantonment of the troops.

On 20 August 1648 he faced the Duc d'Enghien for the third time at the Battle of Lens. Erzherzog Leopold Wilhelm was now Governor of Flanders. Beck placed himself at the head of the Alsatian squadrons of horse, practically the same ones that at Rocroi under Isenburg's command, had overwhelmed the French horse in front of them. They succeeded again, even dispersing Châtillon's heavy horse, which had come to support. But, as at Rocroi, the Croats began to plunder the baggage and Beck's horse did the same, while d'Enghien took advantage of this to reorganise his troops and counter-attack. Beck, exasperated by this failure, went on the attack almost alone against the French horse and was shot and seriously wounded. He was identified on the battlefield and d'Enghien offered his carriage as an ambulance to take him to Arras. There, overwhelmed by his failure, he refused medical assistance and died three days later.

5

The Road to Rocroi

In France, the death of Richelieu on 4 December 1642 and news of the agony of the tubercular Louis XIII augured a climate of political instability during the youth of the Louis XIV, who was only four years old. There was the growing threat of a noble revolt in France, motivated by the nobility's rejection of the influence of the Queen Regent, Anne of Austria, and of the new Prime Minister, Cardinal Mazarin.

Meanwhile, in Flanders, Francisco de Melo began preparations for a new campaign in the spring. The Governor of Flanders was determined to be the first to attack: his strategy was to invade France to capitalise on the impact of the previous year's successful campaign, with the victory of Honnecourt, which had been partially ruined by his excessive caution. Following instructions from the Court in Madrid, Melo sought to attract France's war efforts towards Flanders in order to take pressure off the situation in Catalonia.

The Portuguese General was aware that his economic and logistical resources for this campaign were considerably less than in previous years, although they had never been optimal. The average income from Spain for the years 1635 to 1641 had reached 4 million *escudos*, in 1642 it had been 3.3 million, but in 1643 it was only 1.5 million *escudos*.

To try to make up for the lack of resources from Spain, Melo turned to the provincial authorities in Flanders. He managed to get a subsidy, but it proved insufficient; the bankers in Antwerp did not want to lend him money, nor did some of the Portuguese bankers, still undecided between loyalty to King Felipe IV or to the new King João IV. But others did, and he managed to raise 300,000 *escudos*, although at the cost of putting up his own fortune as collateral.

Thus, with the financing partially resolved, Melo began to prepare his plan of campaign. The existing documentation does not allow us to know at what point he decided what his campaign objective would be, but it does allow us to reconstruct the sequence of events.

At the beginning of April, Melo ordered his widely dispersed army to concentrate at various points. In the military terminology of the time, these places were known as *plazas de armas* ('place of arms', the location for parades and for mustering). Most of the foot (the tercios of Albuquerque, Ávila, Velandia, Villalba, Garcíez and Castellví) under the Duque de Albuquerque, at Béthune and Douai. The Italian tercios, Visconti, Strozzi and Ponti, and the Walloon tercios of Ligne, Ribacourt and Grange, concentrated around Festubert, under Melo's command. Another body of four

German foot regiments, 70 companies of horse, and his own horse regiment of 12 companies, at Quiévrain, Mons and Valenciennes under the command of Albert de Longueval, Conde de Bucquoy. The Army of Alsace, so-called because it had fought on German soil, and consisting of five German regiments of foot, six German regiments of horse and a Croat regiment of horse, was concentrated around Namur commanded by the Count of Isenburg. The Flanders companies of horse, mainly the *Bandes d'Ordonnance*, under Claude Lamoral, Prince of Ligne, assembled in the area of Lens. And in Luxembourg, around Paliseul, the troops of Jean de Beck were assembled, initially intended to protect this Duchy and Franche-Comté this force consisted of about 1,000 horse and 3,000 foot, although some sources put the number of men at nearer 6,000.

To disguise his intentions, Melo toured the coast of Flanders to inspect the coastal towns (Bruges, Ostend, Nieuwpoort and Dunkirk) to give the impression that he was preparing a coastal defence in anticipation of a Dutch invasion, and as if he was planning to act solely on the defensive in 1643.

On 15 April, Melo left Brussels to join Count de Fontaine in Lille. At a meeting of his General Staff, he debated whether the main war effort should be against France or The Netherlands. With news of Louis XIII's illness and a climate of rebellion among the French nobility, the Marqués de Velada suggested preparing the army for a campaign against France, but to wait on events. If there was some kind of noble uprising, it could be used as an opportunity to make a surprise attack on a border town and force negotiations with a supposedly weakened French monarchy. Furthermore, the army's food supplies could be supplied at the expense of the inhabitants of the conquered region, which, as well as being a relief for the inhabitants of Flanders and an embarrassment for the French, would save money for the Crown.

Melo did not specify what the objective of the campaign of 1643 would be, but he did say that it would be against France. He was convinced that the campaign would be not only a political and military success, but also a personal victory. His political career had been so closely linked to Olivares that he needed to stand out for his own military merits to avoid being dismissed. To this end, he conceived a more ambitious plan than a mere delaying action: a determined action on the French border. His thinking was probably that, in the best-case scenario it would even allow him to march on Paris, thus preventing the invasion of the Franche-Comté and provoke the French withdrawal from Catalonia. The overall situation in 1643 was bad for the Spanish: Marshal La Meilleraye was intending to conquer Burgundy, and it was known that an army of 10,000 French was preparing to enter Catalonia. To follow Madrid's 'guidelines', Melo has two possible actions.

Firstly, he could move into enemy territory, locate one of the French field armies and attempt to beat it while it was separated from support, as he had done successfully at Honnecourt the previous year.

The second alternative was that of manoeuvre and to seize a specific target of strategic and propaganda importance that would force the French to modify their campaign plans in an attempt to recapture it.

Melo opted for the second alternative, as it entailed fewer risks and a higher return. He opted for the capture of Rocroi, located just three kilometres

Reinforcing breastplate (c1625–30), Italian, probably Milanese.
Made of steel and silvered, it was intended to be worn on top of a Cuirassier's primary cuirass. Designed to be bulletproof, these pieces were extremely heavy, so they were removed from the main breastplate when not engaged in combat. On this cuirass you can see a dent, made by a bullet or a strong blow from a mace, and known as a 'proof mark'. As for its decoration, it has a pentagram, the letter 'F' and a crown that surrounds a pair of crossed palm branches: this is the personal emblem of the Duque de Feria, Gómez Suárez de Figueroa and Córdova. It is conjectured that while he was Governor of Milan (1618–1625 and 1631–1633) he ordered the manufacture of an armour, now preserved in the Royal Armoury of Turin, this reinforcing breastplate and a pistol (both preserved in the Metropolitan Museum of Art, New York). This piece was in the Royal Armoury of Madrid until 1836. Its dimensions are: height 40.6cm; width 41.9cm; weight 6.662 Kg. (Metropolitan Museum of Art, 14.25.867)

from the northern French border. According to his spies Rocroi did not have particularly impressive defences and the garrison, according to those spies, was only of 400 musketeers. Moreover, given the proximity of the Meuse, it could be more easily supplied once captured. But for fear of French spies, Melo explained nothing of his plans to his generals.

From 19 April, the various army detachments were on the move. Henao's troops went to Valenciennes and the Artois detachments concentrated at Carvin, 15km from Lille, where Melo's headquarters were located.

Thus, Melo concentrated his army in the region between Valenciennes and Le Quesnoy, to make the French believe that he was preparing to besiege Landrecies. He called for reinforcement troops from Luxembourg and ordered the Isenburg and his horse to move from Namur in a south-westerly direction, following the course of the Sambre on its north bank, so that, before reaching Maubeuge, they would cross the river at Thuin. While the whole Spanish Army moved westwards by various routes, Melo remained in Brussels, giving no indication to French or Dutch spies of his real intentions. When the concentration of his forces was complete, he moved to Lille and ordered the army to move nearer the French border, without giving any indication of where he would cross.

The French meanwhile had deployed three armies on the border with Flanders: one in Picardy, one in Champagne and a third in Burgundy, to threaten Alsace and Franche-Comté. The commander of the Picardy army, concentrated in the valleys of the Somme and Authie, was Louis de Bourbon, Duc d'Enghien, aged just 21. The Army of Champagne, commanded by the Compte d'Espenan, was concentrated between Chauny and Guise. The Army of Burgundy was garrisoned around Langres, commanded by Maréchal La Meilleraye.

The Duc d'Enghien arrived in Amiens, headquarters of the Army of Picardy, on 20 April, was informed of the state of his army. It consisted of 20 regiments of foot concentrated between Abbeville and Montdidier, and 21 regiments of horse around Amiens and Doullens: 12,000 to 14,000 foot and 7,000 horse. He found that not only was the army poorly paid, poorly equipped and scattered, but especially worrying was that they were demoralised and lacking discipline. The defeat of Honnecourt, the lack of pay, the absence of a unified command and the indiscipline of many officers – given the proximity of Paris, many had abandoned their units to live in the capital – had led to the disappearance of their operational ability and poor morale and desertions were more common than in other French armies. d'Enghien set out to reverse the disastrous situation and concentrated on restoring discipline, increasing the level of training and improving the army's combat capabilities.

Under d'Enghien's command was *Lieutenant Général Maréchal* de L'Hôpital, and three field marshals (Jean de Gassion, *Mestre de Camp General* of the light horse, the Marquis de La Ferté-Senneterre, and the Barón de Sirot). On his appointment, the instructions that d'Enghien had received from Mazarin and Le Tellier were somewhat vague, focusing on staying on the defensive, preventing a siege and avoiding engaging the Spanish in the open as much as possible.

The Duc's intention was, in truth, to take action as soon as possible, and to accomplish a major feat of arms. If the Spanish remained on the defensive, he would attack an important town, Thionville in Luxembourg for example, or if the opportunity arose, force a field battle.

The general situation of the Army of Picardy was quite pitiful but the good news was that d'Enghien learned that the Army of Burgundy, under Maréchal La Meilleraye, would be divided into three bodies, one of which would be attached to the Army of Picardy.

On 25 April, spies reported to d'Enghien that the Spanish Army consisted of some 15,000–16,000 foot and 6,000–7,000 horse and that it appeared to be heading towards Arras. From Arras, General Guiche sent word to d'Enghien that the Spanish were preparing for some important action.

Melo's spies informed him of the location, and of the morale, of the Army of Picardy. Melo therefore decided to move his army in a way as to make the French believe that they were going to attack between Guise and Vervins. The reports from French scouts indicated this, and the Duc d'Enghien wrote to his father, "The enemy will enter France on the Vervins side". The Spanish commanders also thought that this would be their objective, since Melo kept it a secret that the final destination was actually Rocroi. Francisco Fernández de la Cueva, Duque de Alburquerque, in his account of the 1643 campaign, wrote that the Spanish Army crossed the border without the soldiers or their commanders knowing what their objective was.

By early May, all the Spanish detachments had been concentrated around Carvin. On the French side, d'Enghien informed the King that his army was leaving winter quarters and concentrating at Doullens.

On 9 May, Melo ordered Jean de Beck to take the castle of Château-Regnault, on the Meuse River, to ensure a safe location to move supplies from one side of the river to the other. On the same day he sent orders to Isenburg, concentrated at Namur, to move south, with the intention of taking Rocroi. To conceal his actual plans, he ordered the rest of his army to make several marches: one detachment to Valenciennes and another corps to Cambrai.

Spanish artillery train on the March. Engraving by Jan van de Velde (II), 1632. Note the large number of wagons needed to support the guns. Contemporary lists show that the guns themselves represented only a tiny proportion of the actual train. (Rijksmuseum, Amsterdam. Public Domain)

Spanish artillery train on the March. Engraving by Jan van de Velde (II), 1632. (Rijksmuseum, Amsterdam. Public Domain)

That same day, 9 May, d'Enghien called in all his horse in the area of the Oise River and his foot from the area of the River Authie. He put the garrisons of the Towns of Picardy on alert, also fearing the invasion in the area of Cambrai. d'Enghien and his staff headed for Péronne and Saint-Quentin. The Marquis d'Heudicourt, Michel Sublet, remained cantoned with his detachment at Landrecies. Quincé remained at Guise with the Regiment of Rambures, and several Swiss companies. At La Capelle was the Marquis de

Roquépine with the Régiment de Biscaras, two companies of the Regiment de Piémont and two Swiss companies.

However, the Spanish were not going to attack from the area of Cambrai. Isenburg's horse left Namur for Labuissiere, halfway between Maubeuge and Thuin, and threatening to march towards Landrecies. Melo's army meanwhile was at Carvin and began the march towards Douai, and the day after towards Valenciennes.

On 12 May the Duc d'Enghien was told that the Spanish appeared to be marching towards Landrecies, so he moved his army eastwards past Albert, and by dusk they had reached the vicinity of Péronne. d'Enghien and his staff billeted at the village of Moislains, seven kilometres north of Péronne. Shortly before nightfall Maréchal La Ferté-Senneterre also arrived at Moislains with his foot, and Gassion, at the head of 2,000 horse, also arrived at Moislains. In this central position, controlling the roads of the Saint Quintin-Cambrai-Arras line, d'Enghien's army could block the Spanish Army direct route to Paris.

In the absence of reliable news about where the Spanish were heading to, d'Enghien sent detachments of horse to scout the territory and sent orders to d'Espenan to reinforce the garrisons at Guise and La Capelle. A letter from d'Enghien's father alerted him to Louis XIII's terminal condition, and also warned him that Cardinal Mazarin planned to relieve him of his command and give it to the veteran L'Hôpital. d'Enghien desperately needed to locate the Spanish and beat them as soon as possible.

The French scouts initially positioned Melo's army at Hirson, and d'Enghien suspected that they would enter France to attack Vervins. Some in his personal circle advised him to return to Court to be present when King Louis XIII died, but d'Enghien refused, saying that it was his duty to remain at the head of the army.

Meanwhile, Isenburg's horse, which had been extremely active at the sight of the French scouts in the Landrecies area, had made a change of march southward during the night of 11 May, riding swiftly for a whole day, to appear in front of Rocroi on the morning of 13 May. The veteran Isenburg surrounded the town with such speed that the peasants who had risen early to work in the fields, on seeing the enemy horse, did not have time to warn their fellow-citizens, and took refuge in the hamlet of Sévigny-la-Forêt. Rocroi was cut off so swiftly that the Governor, *Monsieur* Geoffreville, was unable to send messengers to alert the Duc d'Enghien.

Isenburg sent messengers to Melo that he had surrounded the town and that, according to the captured peasants, the garrison numbered only 400 musketeers. The main Spanish Army then marched towards Rocroi, spending the night at Dompierresur-Helpe. That night Melo assembled his staff and finally told them that their objective was to besiege Rocroi.

The commanders outlined the negative points of the plan, that there was a lack of siege artillery and a lack of supplies for an army that had to camp and fortify itself to besiege a fortress. Melo argued that this was all part of his intention to mislead the enemy. They had entered France with only field artillery in order to give the French the impression that they were looking for a pitched battle, thus they would be concentrating their army to protect the countryside towards Paris, not imagining that what the Spanish were really intending was to take French towns. Melo explained that he had sent messengers to bring a convoy of artillery and supplies from Flanders, as soon as the town had been encircled by Isenburg's men.

The Generals complaints were fully justified – the Spanish Army numbered around 20,000 and there were only 50 wagons with supplies. Melo insisted that he had ordered supplies to be assembled in Namur, and that the train was waiting for his order to bring the supplies to whatever place he ordered. Since they had already isolated Rocroi, he had sent word that the convoys could now leave. Melo's caution was later confirmed. When the messenger arrived in Namur and explained that the destination was Rocroi, the first convoy set out but it was intercepted by a French detachment. According to Spanish sources, a French spy had infiltrated the convoy's contractor and had informed d'Enghien of the destination of the convoy.

At dawn on 14 May, Melo broke camp towards Chimay and from there, without giving his troops a rest, continued on and reached Rocroi on 15 May. In the meantime, Isenburg's troops had started to emplace and to dig trenches.

During the march to Rocroi, Melo's army passed through Avesnes-sur-Helpe, entered France at La Capelle and turned towards Hirson. The Croat irregulars plundered the region, forcing the peasants to take refuge in the fortified towns, but the Croats created such a wave of horror at their outrages that as many as 4,000 volunteers enlisted to fight them. Melo banned looting and arson on pain of death.

When Melo surveyed the environs of Rocroi, he felt that the town would not hold out for long and he dispensed with the construction of lines of circumvallation and contravallation lines. Indeed, hardly any shoes or shovels had been carried in the baggage train because reports had indicated that the town's defences were weak.

The City was fortified with five bastions and protected by demi-lunes. It was protected on the west by the river Oise and by the lush forest of La Thiérache, which reached almost to the foot of the ramparts. To the east the river Meuse ran close and the forests of the Ardennes made approaches difficult. On the south-west of the town lay a wide plain, bordered by woods and marshes and divided in two by a gentle depression in the ground, which was reached from the south-west by a narrow path.

On 13 May, d'Enghien received a worrying letter from his father announcing the imminent death of King Louis XIII. The Prince de Condé asked his son to come to Paris, as he felt that he needed his presence to support the regency. d'Enghien replied that it was his duty to remain at the head of his army.

Louis XIII died on 14 May when d'Enghien was at the Abbey of Fervaques, at the source of the Somme, and as his army reached the Saint-Quentin area.

On 15 May, the French army reached the valley of the river Oise, bound for Guise and Vervins. d'Enghien sent messages to Gesvres, who was at Origny-Sainte-Benoîte, and d'Espenan, who was at Brunehamel, asking for their cooperation. Meanwhile, Gassion, at the head of a force of 1,500 men, advanced in a screen of protection and reconnaissance, from Vervins to Maubert-Fontaine.

To complete the encirclement of Rocroi, Melo dispersed his army throughout the countryside into five camps surrounding the City. The main camp was located opposite the Climey area, and a short distance away was the artillery cantonment. Another camp was set up on the Mézieres road.

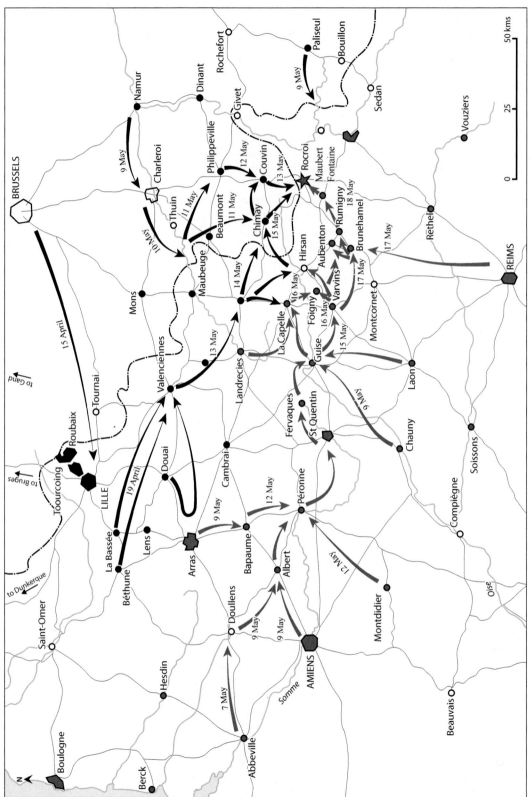

Route of the contending armies, and showing the marches and countermarches carried out by the Spanish to try to disguise their intention of attacking France via Rocroi. The French army tried to cover the whole length of an extensive border but once the Spanish invasion route was known, it concentrated in Rumigny.

Alburquerque's horse was positioned on the Rocroi plain, and, closing the encirclement, was the encampment of Isenburg's horse.

However, this location was not optimal. The Duque de Alburquerque warned Melo that there was a gap of about 3km between his post and the Spanish foot positions, where the French could enter to relieve the garrison. Melo visited the area, realised the mistake and assigned a strong detachment to cover this erstwhile gap in the Spanish line.

Because of the small garrison and the weakness of its walls Melo was convinced that the town would soon fall; he believed that the City could be taken in three or four days. Thus no fortification work was done of circumvallation and contravallation. Melo's information on the situation in France also allowed him to be optimistic and the various French armies were scattered and so far from Rocroi that it would take several days to unite them (d'Enghien was in Amiens, La Meilleraye in Langres, and the Marquis de Gesvres was near Paris).

The four nationalities in the Spanish army began to dig the approach trenches, with each of them being assigned a bastion as a 'target', except for the Germans, who had two. The Spanish would attack the bastion of the "Chain" (on the south-east); the Italians the bastion of the "Lost Fort"; the Walloons the bastion of the "Little Fort"; and the Germans the bastions of the "Dauphin" and the "Citadel".

On the first day, the Spanish trench was occupied by the Alburquerque's tercio, the Italian by Ponti's tercio, the Walloon by the Count of Meghem's troops, and the German by the Count of Rittberg's regiment.

On 16 May, d'Enghien's army left Guise for Vervins, where it halted to await the arrival of the garrison detachments from Landrecies, Guise and La Capelle, as well as d'Espenan's force of some 6,000 troops. d'Enghien settled in the village of Foigny, 8km north of Vervins, and there received two pieces of bad news. A messenger from the Court brought a letter from the Queen informing him of the death of King Louis XIII, and another messenger arrived informing him that the Spanish had surrounded Rocroi. According to this messenger, it was not the whole of the Spanish army, but a strong advance detachment, although other troops were rapidly approaching to reinforce the besiegers.

In a letter written to Mazarin, d'Enghien reiterated his commitment to expel the invaders and stated that he would arrive at Rocroi on 18 May and do all he could to relieve the town. To gain time, he sent Gassion with a corps of 1,500 horse – the Duque de Albuquerque said that there were 1,800 but Vincart says there were only 500 – to try to get reinforcements into the town, telling him that they were to meet the next day in Rumigny. d'Enghien ordered the army to make a forced march to Rocroi, they had to arrive before the town fell, because if that happened the Spanish would be holding it with a strong garrison, which would have to be expelled, while their field army could ravage more of the French countryside.

At Rocroi, the Spanish intensified the artillery bombardment and continued with the siegeworks, rotating new units in the trenches: the Spanish tercio de Castellví, the Italian tercio of Visconti, the Walloon tercio of the Count of La Grange, and the German regiment of Frangipani. Such was the commitment of the soldiers of each nation that in just two days the trenches reached the counterscarp and ramparts.

Melo ordered the outer defences of the City to be taken, and since they did not have sufficient artillery, there was no option than a direct assault. Three artillery pieces were placed in the Italian camp, and the order was passed to the four active units that, when three cannon shots were heard, the attacks were to be launched simultaneously. Although the assault was bloody, the defenders fired their grapeshot causing a great many casualties, in the end the assault troops managed to take the outer defences of the City. Despite this initial success, the conquered positions were a trap for the attackers: the defenders, positioned on the Rocroi walls, were higher than the attackers in the bastions and continued to fire on them, causing further heavy casualties, especially among the Italian tercios.

Although the outer defences had been captured, the experienced Spanish generals told Melo that the City could not be taken as quickly as initially thought. And since they knew that the French armies would sooner or later come to the town's rescue, they advised Melo to begin fortification works, to prevent an attack on their rear and a sortie by the defenders. Melo still claimed that Rocroi would soon fall, but his generals insisted that the next few hours should be devoted to fortifying their positions, to prevent a surprise attack. Melo refused, believing that the courage and experience of his men could make up for the lack of fortifications, and he reminded them of the successful sieges of Lens and La Bassée in the campaign of 1642.

The same afternoon, Melo received a letter from Alonso Pérez de Vivero y Menchaca, Count of Fuensaldaña, who was General Field Master of the army of the Dutch frontier. The letter informed Melo that spies in the Court at Paris had reported the death of Louis XIII, and that an army of over 10,000 men, horse and foot, was on its way to the relief of Rocroi. Melo seems to have been comforted by this news: the French field army was inferior to his own, and was commanded by the *Duc d'Enghien*, an inexperienced General.

In the face of Dutch inactivity, Fuensaldaña showed his initiative and sent Melo an additional 4,000 men. Melo became even more confident and convinced in his decision of not fortifying his lines. He was certain that he would shortly receive reinforcements of Beck's 5,000 men, when he had completed the conquest of Château-Regnault, and the 4,000 sent by Fuensaldaña. Confident that he could beat the French in battle and in the siege.

As Melo had kept the intention of taking Rocroi a secret, no adequate supply of bread had been contracted for, so that for three days the Spanish troops had had hardly anything to eat.

Meanwhile, Gassion's 1,500 men passed through Maubert-Fontaine and, crossing the forest of Pothées, reached the vicinity of the besieged town on the night of 15–16 May. Gassion personally led forward a detachment of 500 horse, and taking advantage of the cover provided by the neighbouring woods, came close to Rocroi. He was discovered by the Croat scouts; however, the French force was stronger, and they drove the Croats back. However, the noise of the fighting alerted the company of horse of Commissary General Antonio de Ulloa, which was on guard duty. They attacked the French advance guard, who, in the face of the onslaught, retreated. The veteran Gassion countered this setback and ordered Captain Saint-Martin to dismount his company of the *Fusiliers à Cheval de Son Eminence*, between

Broadsheet describing and illustrating the Battle of Rocroi, 1643 (Amsterdam, van Hilton 1643). The engraving is by Salomon Savery. (Rijksmuseum, Amsterdam. Public Domain)

100 and 150 men, and together with 25 to 30 men of d'Enghien's Guards, to take advantage of the confusion to infiltrate the enemy. Using the advantage of the darkness and the trees, the French musketeers managed to pass through unseen, to attack the Italians who were guarding the demi-lune at the Porte de Maubert (Maubert's gate), and to enter Rocroi. Having thus succeeded in his task, Gassion returned to report to d'Enghien.

At Rocroi, the arrival of reinforcements boosted morale and there was now a regular garrison of about 600 musketeers, plus the citizen militia of about a further 100 men. The Governor of Rocroi was Monsieur de Geoffreville, but his delicate state of health made him unfit to command the defence, which fell to Major Pierre Noël.

According to French accounts, before dawn on 17 May, Noël led a sortie at the head of all available men, including the reinforcements that had entered during the night, from the Porte de Maubert against the Spanish trenches, and in particular against the demi-lune defended by the Italians of Visconti's tercio. The French were so quiet that they managed to cut the throats of the sentries and enter the redoubt without being detected. They then engaged the rest of the defenders, while other French troops demolished the parapets, and whatever else they could – they also noted that the Italians had no cannon in their position. The fighting alerted the rest of the Italians in the camp, and led by Visconti, they rushed to join the fight. Noël ordered a cautious retreat, withdrawing in an orderly fashion towards the moat of the ramparts, protected by the fire of his guns firing grapeshot at the Italians. The French attack caused between 60 and 150 Italian casualties, depending on which source you read, and the French claim to have suffered very few casualties.

The few large artillery pieces that the Spanish had at their disposal needed a flat surface on which to deploy, so Álvaro de Melo, commanding General of the artillery, urged his men to work harder to have the esplanades completed as soon as possible. He also ordered them to prepare fascines so that, the following night, they could throw them against the ditches so that the foot could cross and scale the walls. In the trenches, the soldiers of the four nationalities were busy constructing fascines, cuttings, gabions, bales, and everything necessary to cross the moat. Isenburg's men had made great haste to be the first, and had already filled the moat with their fascines.

That day, 17 May, the French army had left Vervins at first light, and without stopping, passed through Aubenton, arriving at Bossus-lès-Rumigny, where, at nightfall, it was rejoined by Gassion's force. They were also joined by the last reinforcement detachments of the Army of Champagne. That night, d'Enghien sent scouts north towards the forest of Pothées, the entrance to Rocroi.

At noon, Melo received the news that the Duc d'Enghien's Army was rapidly approaching. Shortly afterwards, the Croats further informed him that detachments of French horse had been seen beyond the forest.

That evening, at Bossus, the Duc d'Enghien held a council of war with his general staff; according to the latest reports, the Spanish Army consisted of 18,000 foot and 9,000 horse. Gassion reported, after his reconnaissance the night before, that the besieged town could not hold out for more than a further 36 hours. He also explained the details of the terrain they would have to traverse to reach the city: the woods, the gorge, the plain that opened before Rocroi. d'Enghien told to his generals that the King had died, but proposed that they should keep quiet about the news so as not to demoralise the troops.

d'Enghien was still determined to attack, so asked the opinion of each of those present of the two alternatives. To either relieve the City with the whole army, even at the risk of a battle, or to reinforce the garrison with a detachment carrying food and ammunition to try to prolong the siege and thus gain time to wear down the Spanish. Maréchal L'Hôpital, supported by other senior officers such as d'Espenan, La Ferté-Senneterre, La Vallière and La Barre, opted for the second alternative. For the veteran L'Hôpital, to risk losing the battle would mean not only the destruction of the armies of Picardy and Champagne, but also the subsequent fall of Rocroi. This would leave the whole frontier unprotected, with the high possibility that the Spanish would attack other important towns, such as Arras, Saint-Quentin, and Cambrai. Moreover, the new King's prestige would falter badly if his reign began with a defeat.

But d'Enghien was determined to engage in a battle. He told L'Hôpital that his task was to save the Kingdom from invasion, and to do so, before saving Rocroi, it was necessary to fight a battle. His speech was seconded by Gassion, de Sirot and de Persan. For the Duc, attempting to reinforce the garrison could mean losing that detachment before it could even cross the Spanish lines, and that would lead to the loss of the town as well as the detachment and the supplies it would be carrying. In that situation, the Spanish would also remain the masters of the initiative, and could then engage in battle against the dwindling French army.

Since Gassion had observed that the Spanish had not built any defences to protect themselves from a relief army, d'Enghien insisted on the opportunity to attack them from the rear. Moreover, the terrain available to them for deployment was ample, with wide opportunities for manoeuvring by the horse. And if they ultimately lost the battle (something any General had to be aware might happen), the surviving troops could regroup and could be supported by Maréchal La Meilleraye's 15,000-strong army covering the Champagne and Bassigny frontiers. If fortune smiled on them and they won the battle, not only would they liberate Rocroi and inflict heavy casualties on the enemy, but the Spanish would be cut off from their bases in Flanders, demoralised, and easily prey to further operations before they could reach Flanders.

L'Hôpital believed that the Duc was too influenced by the aggressive ardour of the Gassion. 'It was not for nothing that Louis XIII had appointed L'Hôpital as Lieutenant-General to the Duc d'Enghien, he had hoped his prudence would moderate the ardour of the Duc's youth', wrote Robert de Harlay, Barón de Monglat. The veteran General tried to use his reputation and prestige to persuade d'Enghien, but the latter was convinced from the start to pursue a pitched battle. Reluctantly, L'Hôpital conceded and placed himself at d'Enghien's disposal, as did the other generals.

d'Enghien then began to plan the battle and assigned each of his generals to their place in the deployment. The right wing would be commanded by Maréchal Gassion and the left by La Ferté-Senneterre, while d'Enghien himself, accompanied by L'Hospital, d'Espenan and La Vallière, would be in the centre. The Barón de Sirot would command the reserve of 2,000 foot and 1,000 horse.

6

The Battle is Coming

At dawn on 18 May, between 5 and 6 o'clock, the French army began its march towards Rocroi. Gassion's horse formed the vanguard, followed by the horse of d'Enghien, the bulk of the foot, the horse of La Ferté and finally the reserve corps under Sirot's command. It was decided to leave the baggage in the villages of Aubenton and Aubigny-les-Pothées, in order to be able advance as quickly as possible. The main body of the French army arrived at Maubert-Fontaine a few hours before noon, deploying on the plain, with its front in the lush forest of Pothées.

At that point, the main road split in two, to cross the forest. The historian Paulin Lebas identified these two roads as the Echevé and the Anières roads. The northern, the Anières path, was narrow and passed through the thickest part of the forest and then led to the Hardy-Pré swamp and a large plain. The southern road, the Echevé road, was even narrower and steeper and went to Savigny-la-Foret, and from there, continued on to Rocroi. d'Enghien sent a party of 50 Croats to reconnoitre these routes, fearful of encountering the Spanish on the far side, or that the army might be ambushed in the forest.

The scouts returned and reported that they had found no obstacles, no fortifications and no trace of the Spanish in the forest, and that the road was safe all the way to the plain in front of Rocroi. d'Enghien decided to seize the opportunity and secure access to the plain, and sent a strong force under Gassion, consisting of the Croat detachments of Schack and Raaband and a part of the Régiment Royaux, to get a foothold on the plain. Gassion encountered a party of 50 Croats in Spanish service scouting the ground, and drove them off, clearing the route.

At about one o'clock Gassion's detachment emerged from the forest and advanced across the plain, where it was seen by the Spanish sentries, who promptly raised the alarm. Gassion nonetheless had time to see that a hill overlooking the Spanish camp had not been fortified, nor even occupied by the Spanish. He sent word of this to d'Enghien, urging him to get through the forest as soon as possible, before the Spanish could deploy their army. d'Enghien sent Gassion reinforcements to secure his position: the *Fusiliers a Cheval de Son Eminence*, and the Régiments Gassion, Lenoncourt, Coislin and Sully. He also put companies of foot in the most vulnerable places to protect the pass through the forest.

When Melo and his staff were alerted, there was some astonishment, as they did not believe the French army was so close. Melo was clear about his battle plan, but did not want to share it for fear of spies. Thus when the Spanish scouts reported that the French were approaching, he failed to call a council of war, provoking the anger of officers such as the Duque de Alburquerque, the Count of Garcíez and the Count of Villaba. Melo claimed that everything was proceeding as he thought it would, and that when Beck's detachment of 3,000 foot and 1,000 horse arrived, French sources put Beck's force at 5,000 to 6,000, everything would be perfect.

Melo was overconfident: he had won at Honnecourt and now felt doubly confident. He was confident of taking Rocroi before d'Enghien's army could approach; and confident that, if d'Enghien did reach the vicinity, the Spanish Army would defeat him, as in the previous year. Moreover, Spanish intelligence reports had failed to report that d'Enghien's army had been reinforced with fresh troops. The French army was not the 12,000 or 13,000 men Melo originally expected, but actually numbered between 15,000 and 16,000 foot and between 7,000 and 8,000 horse. Perhaps this is why Melo was so confident that the situation was under control, because he believed that his army could easily beat an outnumbered army?

Melo was blindly confident in the numerical and qualitative superiority of his army, belittling his adversary. According to the Duque de Alburquerque, Melo told them that 'the French General was a Prince of only 18'. His generals took the opportunity to insist on giving battle: if the enemy was weak and commanded by an inexperienced General, so much the better for them, as they could crush them without difficulty. If, on the other hand, he thought it better to let them advance and give battle the next day, it was better to be prepared and fortify themselves as much as possible. They cited the example of the redoubts erected during the night on Albuch Hill, which decided the Catholic success of the Battle of Nördlingen (5–6 September 1634).

Alburquerque wrote that he offered to lead a charge with 1,500 horse to drive the French beyond the forest, but Fontaine refused. However, just in case, Melo sent messages to Beck urging him to bring his army to Rocroi

French Horse at Rocroi. Detail from Illustration 26. (Rijksmuseum, Amsterdam. Public Domain)

as soon as possible. He also ordered the army to suspend the siege actions against Rocroi and to stay on alert.

On the French side, in his memoirs Barón de Sirot wrote that if the Spanish had attacked with 5,000 to 6,000 men, the French would have been defeated. In fact, it was clear that there was a great danger for the French passing through that area. L'Hôpital probably warned d'Enghien of this, but d'Enghien was determined to press on towards the plain to engage in battle. He may have misled the Maréchal, reassuring him that they were only probing the enemy, since La Moussaye wrote that the Duc 'persuaded L'Hôpital that he was advancing towards Rocroi only to provide assistance in the form of men and ammunition, through the surrounding woods'.

It is impossible to know what Melo was thinking, we only know what he did, and did not do. He did not attack the French vanguard and did not defend the approaches to the Rocroi plain. Why? Historians have ventured various explanations. Perhaps he did not want to defeat the French vanguard for fear that the rest of the enemy army would flee intact and attack him later when he displayed some weakness? Perhaps he was afraid that a sortie would be made from Rocroi against his rear while he was fighting the French field army? Or perhaps he was convinced of the strength of his own forces and that Beck's contingent would arrive in time to fight a great pitched battle that would completely defeat the army of the Duc d'Enghien. Melo considered that he had defeated the French at Honnecourt, and in Flanders the Spanish armies had always been victorious in their attacks against the French – so perhaps, overconfidence or an underestimation of the enemy?

Between one-thirty and two o'clock, when Melo realised that the entire French army was deploying in battle order on the plain, and that this was not just an attempt to reinforce the garrison, he ordered his army to begin deploying as well, including the guns that had been firing on the town. Since the Rocroi garrison was still believed to be weakened, the troops garrisoning the trenches abandoned their positions and similarly formed up for battle, leaving only a company of foot and Colonel Suárez's (German) regiment of horse to watch the City and its garrison.

While the bulk of the French army was still inside the forest, the Spanish high command reconnoitred the terrain to ascertain the most advantageous positions at which to await the enemy. The terrain features of the plain were a marsh on the right hand side, a shallow stream that split the plain in two, and a forest on the left.

Near the swamp was a very steep slope, virtually impossible to ascend or to skirt, so Alburquerque and other officers proposed that the flank of the army should rest on that area. Melo rejected this proposal, observing that if the army remained behind the swamp, it would not have enough space to deploy all of its battalions and companies of foot and squadrons of horse. In rejecting the proposal, he pompously stated that his rank as a General of the King of Spain did not permit him to show signs of fear by positioning himself behind a swamp. With this decision, Melo ordered Fontaine, as General Fieldmaster, to deploy on the other side of the stream, and gave him the freedom to deploy the whole army there as he saw fit. In his letter, Alburquerque states that by advancing the position, the army would be at the foot of another hill, much gentler than the previous one, and that if the French occupied that hill, they could do a lot of harm. This was the hill that Gassion had seen was unoccupied on his first reconnaissance. Fontaine ignored Alburquerque's observations, and continued to order the army's deployment according to Melo's instructions.

Both armies began their movements and deployment for the battle ahead; but while the information on the French army's deployment is abundant and illuminating, the Spanish deployment is more confusing and unclear.

The Order of Battle of the Spanish Army

The man responsible for the Spanish deployment was the field master, General Conde de Fontaine, whom Belgian historians consider a hero, but Spanish historians consider the main cause of the defeat at Rocroi. Spanish accounts state that Fontaine had the army formed as if "on a parade ground" rather than as if "in battle", i.e. it was deployed as if it were a parade with the various units stretched out and with large gaps between them. Perhaps it was deployed in this way to give the appearance that the army was larger and to buy time for Beck's troops to join the battle? According to the sources, the Spanish Army on the field numbered between 15,000 and 18,000 foot and 8,000 to 9,000 horse.

Again according to Spanish sources, there had previously been a dispute between the Duque de Alburquerque and the Conde de Bucquoy, and Melo settled it in favour of the former. According to the accounts, as a Portuguese, Melo was biased in favour of the Spanish over the Walloons, and ordered Bucquoy to march to the City of Mons; his regiment of German horse was placed under the command of his lieutenant-colonel and second in command.

While the French were still arriving on the Rocroi plain and deploying, Fontaine ordered the deployment of the Spanish line facing south, resting its western flank on a pond and its eastern flank on a copse at the foot of a hill. The two wings of horse of 28- to 30 squadrons between them, the one on the right under Graf von Isenburg, and the one on the left under the Duque de Alburquerque, assisted by his two Lieutenant-Generals, Pedro de Villamor and Juan Pérez de Vivero. In the centre were the Spanish and the foot of the other nationalities, Italian, Walloon, et cetera. However, it seems that Fontaine miscalculated the space between the pond and the forest and the Spanish foot had to position themselves in the centre, boxed in by the other units, without forming up properly.

To this day, we do not know exactly what the deployment ordered by Fontaine looked like. The sources available do not give us a clear picture, and only very fragmentary information. Historians have therefore come up with their own theories in an attempt to make the information from the sources match. Throughout this book, the reader will find the various hypotheses put forward by the authors whose works have been consulted in the writing of it. All of them are acceptable, all of them present reasoned and coherent theories, but it is easy to see how very different they are from each other. It is for all these reasons that, in the following paragraphs, I will attempt to set out my own conclusions on the deployment of the Spanish Army.

As for the horse, there is usually agreement about the deployment on the flanks, and that the two wings deployed in two lines. On the left flank, under the command of the Duque de Alburquerque was the "Horse of Flanders", and the 12 squadrons deployed in two lines. In the first line, under the command of Pérez de Vivero, were the companies of Gaspar Bonifacio, Juan de Borja y Aragón, Césare Toralto, Antonio de Butrón y Mújica, Antonio López de Ulloa and Virgilio Orsini. In the second line, under the command of Villamor, were the companies of Ottavio Moron, Juan Antonio Barraquina, Rodrigo de Rojas, Ernesto Bentivoglio, João Mascarenhas and the Barón de Gramont. Spanish sources suggest that there was a reserve of horse, under the command of Barón d'André, Felipe Charles Hypolyte Spinola.

On the right flank, resting against the Houppe marsh, was the "Horse of Alsace", commanded by Ernst, Graf von Isenburg, composed of several *trozos*, and which was also formed into two lines. The first, under Isenburg himself, composed the companies and *trozos* of Conde de Bucquoy, Conde de Linares, Pierre de Broucq, Carlos de Padilla and Doneckel, some sources add the company of the Barón de Bicht (or Vichet). In the second line, under the command of Jacinto de Vera, the squadrons of Vera himself, Warlusel, Henin and Savary; also forming with this horse were about two hundred Croat horse, under Captain Ystvan, who served as scouts. The horse of Alsace, veterans of a number of campaigns, had at its disposal a full complement of troops, and with their squadrons having long experience of fighting together.

As for the foot, most sources agree that the total number of units in the Spanish Army was 21 tercios and regiments. The researches by José Palau and José Luís de Mirecki identify the following nineteen (two may have deployed as more than one body):

> five Spanish tercios – Bernhardino de Ayala, Conde de Villalba; Antonio de Velandia y Arellano; Duque de Alburquerque (as Alburquerque was serving as a General of Horse, his tercio was commanded by his sergeant-major Juan Pérez de Peralta), Hernando de Quesada Mendoza, Conde de Garcíez; and Jorge de Castellví (formed mainly of Sardinians).
>
> five Walloon – Adrien de Bryas, Lord of Granges; Ambroise de Hornes, Conde de Bassigny; Albert François de Croy, Conde de Meghen; Claude Lamoral, Prince of Ligny and Jean Conrad d'Aubermont, Barón de Ribacourt
>
> three Italians – Alonso Strozzi; Giovanni delli Ponti and Luigi Visconti
>
> one Burgundian – Jacques Nicholas de La Baume, Conde de Saint-Amour
>
> five German regiments – Johan Ferdinand, Count of Rittberg/Riberghe; Ottavio Guasco, Guilio Antonio Frangipani; Charles de Gavre, Barón d'Hembise; Jacques Renier, Barón de Rouveroy).

As already mentioned, it is clear from the various Spanish sources that there was a reserve of horse of four squadrons, commanded by Felipepe Charles Hypolyte Spinola, Barón of André, and consisting mainly of companies of the *Bandes d'Ordonnance* of Flanders. From existing documentation,

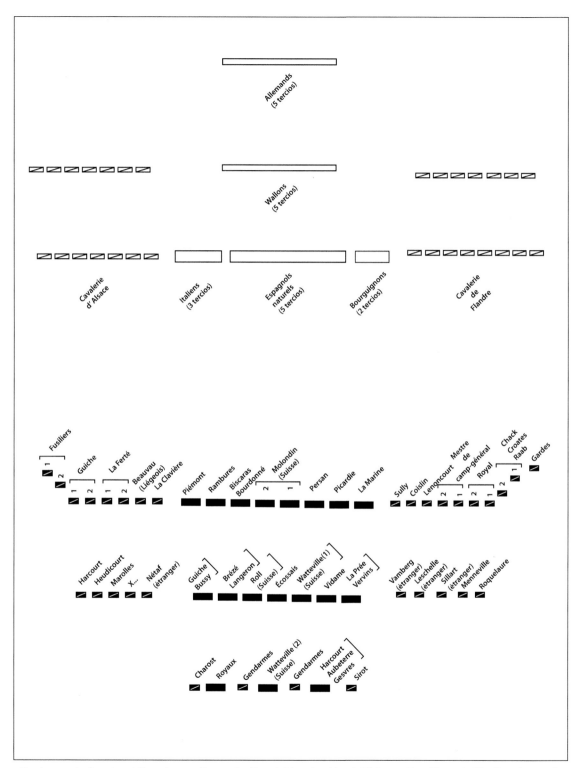

Deployment of armies at Rocroi according to the French historian, Henri d'Orleans, Duc d'Aumale. The French army is clearly and accurately shown in some detail; however, the deployment of the Spanish army is considerably less so. The map shows the Spanish tercios in the centre of the deployment, although their customary position was on the right of the infantry lines, which was considered the decisive position from which to carry out any encircling manoeuvre.

it is likely that Albert François, Prince de Croy, commanded part of this Walloon contingent. The following captains of horse have been identified, these officers probably commanded the reserve companies: Antonio Vicentino, Carlo Colombo, Conde d'Umego, Prince of Croy and the Barón d'André himself.

The only unanimity of opinion is that all the versions agree that the tercios deployed on a much wider front than usual, and it was only as the battle progressed that they became more compact, as was their custom. The tercios formed a squadron called *frente prolongado* ("extended front") or *gran frente* ("large front"), as this deployment gave them a wider frontage and therefore more firepower facing the enemy. This open, linear formation was not to the liking of some Spanish officers, who preferred a greater depth to face the shock of the charge of an enemy regiment of horse. This is why the Duque de Alburquerque, in his letter, constantly repeats his assertion that Fontaine's deployment was more appropriate for a military parade than for a battle.

The starting point for the Spanish deployment is the text of Juan Antonio Vincart, who was the secretary of the secret war notices of Governor-General Melo. In his account of the battle, he describes the following deployment:

> With this, the Field Master General, Count de Fontana, arranged the battle in five battalions of Spanish in the vanguard with two pieces of artillery between each battalion, another three battalions, one of Italians and one of Burgundians, to the battle, five of Walloons to the rear and five of Germans for the reserve, and the horse on the right and left of the said battalions of infantry, disposing a very large front, as all believed that the enemy's intent was only to try to relieve the town and not to venture a battle in the conjuncture that France was in by the death of his King.

This innocent and descriptive paragraph conceals two major problems. Firstly, it refers to the Spanish units as "battalions", and not tercios or squadrons – which suggests that in the aforementioned deployment, they did not form full tercios, but squadrons created *ad hoc* for the battle. Vincart therefore used the new term "battalion" because of the strong influence of the Dutch and Swedish tradition from the 1630s onwards.

From a literal reading of the above text, it can be deduced that Fontaine ordered his army to deploy in four lines. This deployment does not correspond to the traditional Spanish battle order, which was usually two lines or, at most, three. In the Spanish military terminology of the time, the vanguard of the battle was equivalent to the vanguard of the deployment and of the march, i.e., the units that went first on the march (remember that as a rule they were native Spanish troops) occupied the vanguard of the battle, the right flank. Thus, the battle formed the centre, and the rearguard occupied the left flank. Interpreting the deployment in this way, the Italians occupied the centre of the deployment – not an honourable position, and according to Gualdo Priorato, they were offended by this post. The Walloons occupied the left flank, a privilege granted to them by Fontaine, who felt more attached to them because of their origin, language and traditions.

1. Spanish Army of Flanders cavalry trooper
(Illustration by Sergey Shamenkov © Helion & Company 2022)
See Colour Plate Commentaries for further information

2. Spanish Army of Flanders veteran pikeman
(Illustration by Sergey Shamenkov © Helion & Company 2022)
See Colour Plate Commentaries for further information

3. Spanish Army of Italy veteran musketeer
(Illustration by Sergey Shamenkov © Helion & Company 2022)
See Colour Plate Commentaries for further information

4. Croat Cavalry Trooper
(Illustration by Sergey Shamenkov © Helion & Company 2022)
See Colour Plate Commentaries for further information

5. French King's Guard cavalry trooper
(Illustration by Sergey Shamenkov © Helion & Company 2022)
See Colour Plate Commentaries for further information

6. Swiss Pikeman
(Illustration by Sergey Shamenkov © Helion & Company 2022)
See Colour Plate Commentaries for further information

7. French Pikeman
(Illustration by Sergey Shamenkov © Helion & Company 2022)
See Colour Plate Commentaries for further information

8. French Musketeer
(Illustration by Sergey Shamenkov © Helion & Company 2022)
See Colour Plate Commentaries for further information

Additionally maybe he wanted to compensate the Walloon units in some way for the slight caused by the punishment of Bucquoy.

Indeed, this interpretation of the Spanish deployment is consistent with Vincart's own description of the French deployment:

> They placed four infantry battalions and five horse squadrons in the vanguard, in battle, seven infantry battalions and nine horse squadrons, and in the rear four infantry battalions and five horse squadrons with a reserve of 6,000 men (infantry and horse).

We know that the French deployed detachments of foot mixed in with their horse on both flanks – Vincart describes them as vanguard and rearguard. He says that the foot formed in the centre with seven battalions although in reality, there were twice that many, but it seems likely that Vincart, from a distance, could not distinguish the troops in the second line.

Secondly, Vincart's expression 'five battalions of Spanish in the vanguard with two pieces of artillery between each battalion. Three other battalions, one of Italians and one of Burgundians, in the battle' would indicate that in the "battle" line there were five other battalions: three of Spanish, one of Italians and one of Walloons. However, that would suggest that the five Spanish tercios deployed in eight battle squadrons, of which three were with the Italians and Walloons. Remember, there were three Italian tercios, and a single Burgundian regiment. It seems strange that the three Italian units formed only a single battalion therefore some Spanish historians have considered this to be an error by Vincart, who they believe may have intended to write 'three other battalions of Italians and one of Burgundians'.

Each tercio deployed in extended formation, that is, with a frontage three times its depth. This contradicts the traditional Anglo-Saxon view that tercios were monolithic units, with a great depth and little frontage. Fieldmaster Francisco Dávila Orejón, who fought at Rocroi as a captain of foot in Jorge de Castellví's tercio, wrote in *Política y Mecánica para Sargento Mayor de Tercio*[1] (Policy and Mechanics for the Tercio's Sergeant-Major) that he had never seen any Spanish tercio squadron in more than nine ranks deep. Thus, at Rocroi the Spanish units deployed at most in eight or possibly nine ranks deep.

If all of these units of foot had deployed in a single line, the Spanish battle line would have been immense. It has to be concluded, therefore, that they were deployed in two lines, in a chequer-board formation.

In this hypothetical first line, the Spanish would form on the right flank, the Italians and Burgundians in the centre, and the Walloons on the left. Therefore, in the second line, in the space between the Spanish and Italians, and between the Italians and the Walloons, the German regiments would have been positioned. However, according to this deployment, the Spanish front would have been too wide and would not have fitted in the confined space of the battlefield.

---

1   *Política y Mecánica para Sargento Mayor de Tercio*: Sargento Mayor Detercio [Francisco Dávila Orejón]. Madrid, Julian de Paredes 1669.

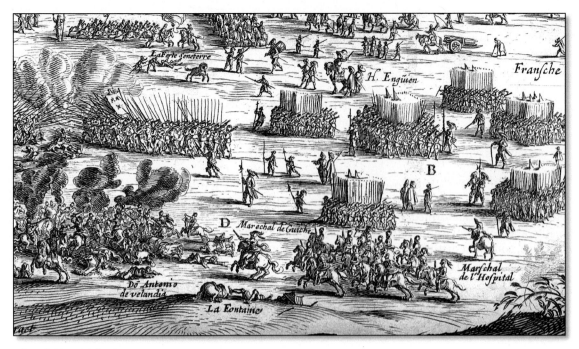

The image text labels include: *La Forte Seneterre*, *H. Enguien*, *Fransche*, *B*, *D Marechal de Guiche*, *Marschal de l'Hospital*, *Do Antonio de velandia*, *La Fontaine*

French Horse defeating and routing their Spanish counterparts. Detail from Illustration 26. (Rijksmuseum, Amsterdam. Public Domain)

Some historical sources describe the Spanish deployment in a different way in line with Vincart's text. In the first line, the five Spanish tercios – from right to left, Villalba, Velandia, Alburquerque, Garcíez and Castellví, although some sources change the order, from right to left: Garcíez, Alburquerque, Villalba, Velandia and Castellví. In the second line would be the three Italian tercios of Strozzi, Ponti and Visconti, and the Burgundian of Saint-Amour. In a third line the Walloon units would have been deployed – from left to right: La Grange, Bassigny, Meghen, Ligny and Ribacourt; again some sources indicate a slightly different order: Ribacourt, La Grange, Meghem, Bassigny and Ligne. The German units are then further back and forming the reserve – from left to right: Rittberg, Guasco, Frangipani, d'Hembise and Rouveroy; or another source gives: d'Hembise, Rouveroy, Frangipani, Rittberg and Guasco.

The historian and politician Antonio Cánovas, aware of the often erroneous interpretation of Vincart, reinterpreted what was written and argued that the Spanish were in the vanguard, on the right of the line, that the Italians and Burgundians formed on their left in the battle. The rearguard, which always followed the battle was, according to his version, not on the left flank of the first line but in the second, putting the Germans in the third line as a reserve:

> This was not, and could not be, the formation of a Spanish line, which was deployed, according to the proper order of march, taking the vanguard, the right; the battle, the centre; and the left, the rear.

The Duque de Alburquerque described the formation of the army thus:

> There were 21 tercios of infantry, five of them facing the enemy and the rest were facing the enemy to the bias from the sides, and all the King's horse on the left wing and on the right another wing of some of the King's horse and the rest of the German regiments and horse.

The key element is to discern what Alburquerque meant by the expression "faced the bias from the sides" (*hacían frente al sesgo por los costados*). No similar expressions are preserved in modern Castilian. The simplest interpretation is that five tercios, Alburquerque does not specify whether they were Spanish or from the other nationalities, coincided with the front of the enemy foot, while the others occupied the flanks, beyond the enemy foot. However, as we know that the French front was longer than the Spanish, this assumption is questionable. We can consider that, keeping the five tercios in front of the enemy, the others formed obliquely, covering the flank of the front line tercios and forming diagonally to the front; but this solution is perhaps too novel.

The most plausible solution would be to interpret "bias" as referring to the space or gap left by the front line units, i.e. that the units were in a staggered or chequer-board formation, as was usual at the time. However, Alburquerque only specifically mentions the first line, without saying whether the other 16 units occupied a second and subsequent lines. It is conceivable that, because of the limitation of the Rocroi plain, there had to be at least a second and third line, to accommodate the other units – for example 5 + 6 + 5 + 5.

In my opinion, taking into account all the sources and the Spanish military tradition, Fontaine arranged a deployment in two main lines, but with the various squadrons forming a checkerboard pattern, in order to facilitate their movement depending on the how the battle developed, and with the Germans in a third line, as a reserve.

Alburquerque's criticism was that Fontaine had deployed the army more for show than in battle formation, because there was hardly any reserve. And the fact that the reserve was the German regiments and a small contingent of horse would indicate exactly that the Spanish Army *could not* deploy in four lines of battle, as the literal meaning of Vincart's words would indicate.

Thus, according to my beliefs, the Spanish Army would be deployed as follows. Given that the Spanish tercios were on the right flank, as the most exposed place, they must have been positioned according to the number of men, but also according to tradition and as a matter of their precedence. A brief history is given below.

The tercios of Garcíez and Villalba, 1,400 men and 1,200 men respectively, trace their origins to the tercios of Lombardy and Naples that entered Flanders under the Duque de Alba in 1567. The former corresponded to the County of Flanders and the latter to the County of Brabant; both had been commanded by Fontaine and had very similar military and combat records. The tercio of Alburquerque, 1,400 strong, originated in the campaign to conquer Portugal in 1580, and was assigned to the defence of The Netherlands but had also served under Fontaine. The Velandia tercio, 900 men, had been created in Spain in 1639 and served in Flanders thereafter. The tercio de Castellví, 500 men, was also created in 1639, and was paid for by the Kingdom of Sardinia – which belonged to the former Crown of Aragon – with the requirement that its Field Master, sergeant-major and principal officers were to be native Sardinians.

I would suggest the following deployment, after taking into account the contemporary documentation and the various hypotheses on the location and deployment of the Spanish tercios. In the first line, from left to right of the line, the tercios of Villaba, Garcíez and Alburquerque, as they were the oldest and most numerous. In the second line, from left to the right, the tercios of Velandia and Castellví, since they were more junior and numerically weaker. Thus, having the tercios with more troops in the front line, Fontaine had more 'shot' at his disposal to harass the enemy from a distance, maintaining Melo's order to delay the fighting until Beck's arrival. The Spanish musketeers and arquebusiers had heavier weapons than their French enemy, which, although more cumbersome to carry and reload, had a longer effective range.

For the deployment of the units of the Nationalities of the Spanish Army, I have opted, in the absence of information from the period, to use a similar criterion. The most veteran units would be closer to the left flank and in the most exposed place, or else because they were the units with the most troops. Thus, at the extreme right of this deployment, closest to the Spanish, must have been Strozzi's Italian tercio, 600 men, which had been raised in 1634, to form part of the army that escorted the Cardinal-Infante, participating in the battle of Nördlingen. In Flanders this tercio distinguished itself in the siege of Diste in 1635 and La Bassé in 1642, where it suffered heavy losses. Next to it, forming the side of the Walloon tercios and closer to the left flank because of its prestige and seniority, the Lombard tercio of delli Ponti, 600 men. This tercio had its origin in a tercio recruited in Milan in 1597. At the battle of Avein, 20 May 1635, it was at the side of Ladron's Spanish tercio, also suffering heavy casualties. Finally, in its second line, right to left, the Italian tercio of Visctoni, 600 men, which was formed for the Palatinate campaign (1621) from independent Italian companies, and the Burgundian tercio of Saint-Amour, 400 men, whose origin goes back to a German tercio of 1579. This tercio, mainly composed of Burgundians during the following years, in 1602 obtained the privilege of being renamed "tercio", since the majority of its soldiers were subjects of the King of Spain.

Regarding the left flank of the foot deployment, corresponding to the Walloon tercios. At its most exposed flank must have been for the Meghem tercio, 600 men, created in 1596. Its first field master was the mythical Charles Bonaventure de Longueval, Conde de Bucquoy. The other units do not stand out one from another for their origin or service record and so it is difficult to follow this criterion for their deployment on the battlefield.

Finally the German regiments; they were raised in the 1630s to fight in Germany and Flanders. By the seniority of their field masters, Guasco and Frangipani who had fought at Nördlingen, the two flanks would have been occupied by their regiments, while the other three, d'Hembise, Rittberg and Rouveroy, would have occupied the centre.

Finally, with regard to the deployment of the horse. The references to their deployment are indirect – throughout the various documents they are named and one can get an idea of their place, whether in the first or second line, but little else. Thus their exact location on the plan is arbitrary and is based on the information of other historians, who have also provided their personal assessment, rather than any actual documentary evidence.

The Ordinances of 1632 established that the right flank, in general, the place of greatest danger, should always be occupied by Spanish. That is why the second most dangerous place, the left flank, was coveted by the other nationalities. Traditionally, the Italians had succeeded in having that place assigned to them. However, on this occasion Fontaine wanted to reward the

Walloons with a place on the left flank. Perhaps this was to compensate for the conflict between Alburquerque and Bucquoy, or simply because, as a native of Lorraine, he felt closer to the Walloons. What is certain is that, for the Italians, the location in the centre of the battle was not to their liking. So, in the centre of the formation were the Italian tercios of Strozzi and Ponti, and behind them the units of Visconti and the Burgundian Saint-Amour. On the left flank, the units of La Grange and Bassigny, with the tercios of Meghem, Ribacourt and Ligne behind them. Finally, in reserve, were the regiments of von Rittberg, Guasco, Frangipani, Hembise and Rouveroy.

Where Alburquerque's horse were deployed there was a large open space to the left of his line of battle. This was an open area running down to a wood, such that a horse detachment could slip in and attack the Spanish from the rear. Alburquerque asked Melo to reconnoitre it. Melo then asked Pedro de Villamor if he dared to guard that post, the officer replied that he did not. Alburquerque said that it could be protected by digging a ditch to prevent passage, to which Melo replied that they had no picks and shovels. Alburquerque took the opportunity in his letter to lambast Melo for his lack of foresight, writing,

> really have to be either very bold or very careless to pretend take a city and start a siege without the most necessary tools, such as picks and shovels.

Alburquerque then asked whether the area could not be protected by sending a detachment of 1,000 horse. Melo replied that it could, but that he and Fontaine did not think it appropriate, as such horse would have to come from Isenburg's units and they did not want to weaken that formation. He agreed, however, to the creation of a detachment of 1,000 musketeers, to be drawn from across the tercios, and commanded by the lieutenant Field Master General Baltasar Mercader. This body was tasked with defending the forest and, if the occasion arose, to hinder any movement of the enemy in that sector.

While the Spanish Army began the movement from its rallying point opposite Rocroi to take up the deployment indicated by Fontaine, the French continued to form up across the plain, as more and more troops emerged from the forest.

At around 2 o'clock, half of the French army had passed through the gorge and was deployed on the plain. d'Enghien ordered the hill on the Spanish right flank, which was still unprotected, to be taken and occupied. French and Spanish sources disagree on the sequence of events. The former state that the French occupied the position, the Spanish sources indicate that Fontaine finally ordered the position to be occupied, and that the French aborted their movement when they saw that the Spanish were advancing to the hill. Then, observing that the French detachment was turning back, Alburquerque shouted to the rest of the commanders that they should charge, but Fontaine forbade the attack. Angry, Alburquerque asked Melo for an audience and explained the situation. To this Melo replied that he was waiting for Beck's contingent that was still some 15km away, and that he 'did not want to go out in search of the enemy when he could wait and await the reinforcement of Barón Beck, and that by waiting he had lost very few victories'.

Melo had arranged for the artillery that had been firing at Rocroi, it was all field artillery, to be now distributed in pairs between the gaps between the tercios of the front line. The Spanish baggage was placed in the centre of the plain between the Spanish line of battle and the trenches. It was perhaps the only place available since the route Beck had to take to join the battle had to be kept clear. However the way the wagons were arranged hindered the movement of fresh troops and support troops from one flank to the other. As the Spanish Army deployed, Melo again sent messengers to Beck to come as quickly as possible.

At around 4 the Spanish artillery was deployed in front of the tercios and began the bombardment of the French. Their fire caused a considerable number of casualties – about 300 men according to French sources, including François de Vaudetar, Marquis de Persan, who was seriously wounded and had to be taken from the field. By comparison, La Moussaye's account and Sirot's memoirs both claim that there were close to a thousand casualties. The French artillery responded, but their skill was inferior to that of the Spanish and moreover, they had not been able to deploy their pieces properly – clearing and flattening the ground – so they were unable to effectively carry out proper counter-battery fire.

Sirot wrote that the Spanish artillery was better placed, was also much better served, and its gunners were more experienced and more skilled than the French.

The Order of Battle of the French Army

By six o'clock in the evening, the French army deployment was nearly complete and d'Enghien took up position next to the Régiment de Picardie, which, as the oldest regiment present, was at the right of the line. L'Hôpital was positioned next to Piémont, the next oldest Regiment, on the far left of the French line.

French sources are much more complete than those of the Spanish in describing the deployment of their army. The French army consisted of around 16,000 foot, 7,000 horse and 12 cannon. The foot comprised 21 regiments, including three of the *Vieux Corps* (Picardie, Piémont, La Marine) totalling 30 companies, two of the *Petits Vieux* (Rambures and Persan) of 30 companies, three Swiss regiments (Molondin with 10 companies, Watteville with 10 companies, and Roll with 12 companies), the Gardes Écossaises of 12 companies), 12 wartime regiments of 20 companies each (Bourdonné, Biscaras, Vervins, La Prée, Vidame d'Amiens, Langeron, Brézé, Bussy, Guiche, Harcourt, Aubeterre, Gesvres), and 12 Royal Companies.

The horse was divided into 24 regiments and 7 companies forming 32 squadrons. 6 companies of gendarmes, a company of d'Enghien's Guards, a regiment of dragoons (*Fusiliers à Cheval de Son Éminence*), 16 *chevau-léger* regiments (Cardinal-Duc, Mestre de Camp General, Lenoncourt, Coislin, Sully, Roquelaure, Menneville, La Clavière, La Ferté, Guiche, Marolles, Heudicourt, Gesvres, Aubeterre, Harcourt, Chârost); one Liégeois regiment (Beauveau), three German regiments (Zillard, Leschelle and von Bergh), two Regiments of Croats (Raab and Schack) and one Hungarian regiment (Sirot).

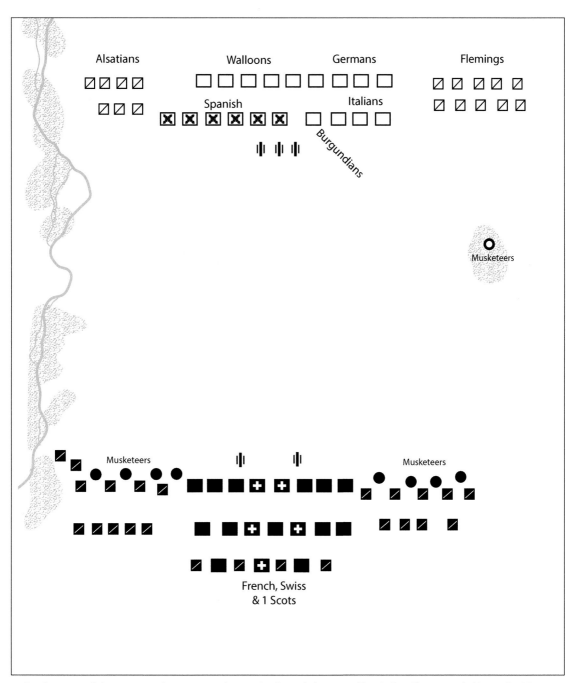

Deployment of the armies at Rocroi, according to the Spanish historian, Tomás San Clemente de Mingo. De Mingo shows the Spanish army deployed in two lines, with the Spanish tercios on the right flank, all in line and extended to occupy part of the centre of the infantry line. No units are shown in reserve; although historical sources indicate that the German regiments were positioned towards the rear, even though de Mingo shows them in the second line.

d'Enghien ordered the deployment approximately 900 metres away from the Spanish, on the side of the smooth valley.

On the left wing, the 13 squadrons of horse under La Ferté-Senneterre and L'Hôpital, deployed in two lines. The first was made up of two squadrons from the *Fusiliers a Cheval de Son Eminence*, two from the Régiment de Guiche, two from the La Ferté, one from the Liégeois Régiment de Beauvau, and one from the Régiment de La Clavière. In the second line there was one squadron from the Régiment d'Harcourt, one from the Régiment d'Hendicourt, one from the Régiment de Marolles, and two from the Régiment de Netaf. In addition, in the first horse line there were five detachments of commanded musketeers.

At the centre of the line was the foot, in 15 battalions, and also deployed in two lines, commanded by d'Espenan and La Vallière. The first line consisted of eight battalions (Piémont, Rambures, Bourdonné-Biscaras, the Swiss Molandin in two battalions, Persan, La Marine and Picardie); the second line consisted of seven battalions (Bussy-Guiche, Langeron-Brézé, de Roll Suisse, Gardes Écossaises, de Watteville Suisse, Vidame and Vervins-La Prée), it was positioned about 250 metres behind the front line.

The first line of the foot comprised the veteran regiments, while the second line was made up mainly of wartime regiments, some of them newly recruited. Since up to 11 detachments of musketeers had been formed to support the two wings of horse, the battalions of foot were not at their usual strength of 800 to 900 men, and probably only 500 to 600 men, half pikes and half muskets. They each probably only occupied a frontage of 60 paces, and additionally there was another 60 paces between each battalion. Guthrie says the battalions had a maximum front of 85 men and were 10 ranks deep, although the smaller battalions would have had to reduce their depth to keep their front line at 85 men. Guthrie himself however, admits that at the time, given the disparity in strength of the French regiments with 30, 20 or even fewer companies – the foot could have deployed in the traditional 10 deep, or the Swedish 6 deep formation, or an intermediate system of 8 ranks.

The right flank, resting against the Bois de Rouge-Fontaine (tradition has it that this wood gets its name because, after the battle, everything was stained with blood) was under Gassion, and comprised a total of 15 horse squadrons, in two lines. 10 squadrons in the first line, with the two squadrons of the Régiment de Raab-Chack, Gardes du Duc, the Régiment Royal in two squadrons, Mestre de Camp Général in two squadrons, and one squadron of each of the Régiments Lenoncourt, Coiselin and Sully. In the second line were the squadrons of the Régiments de Roquelaume, Menneville, Sillart, L'Eschelle and Vamberg. In addition, in the first line there were six detachments of commanded musketeers.

Vincart's account reports that between each squadron of horse there was a detachment of foot so perfectly aligned that, "the heads of the horses did not pass the line of the footmen". Each of these detachments of musketeers must have been quite numerous, with a minimum of about 250 men, as was the Swedish practice, or perhaps even 300 or more, since the Spanish accounts indicate that they were "battalions", that is they were sufficiently strong to give that impression. As squadrons of horse and detachments of musketeer were both deployed in the front line, the total space was constricted. It can therefore be conjectured that the French squadrons on both flanks, about

Spanish (left) and French (right) foot in combat. Detail from Illustration 26 The cross of Burgundy on the Spanish colours and the Fleurs de Lis on the French have become simple 'shorthand' to identify the troops of the two nations. (Rijksmuseum, Amsterdam. Public Domain)

200 men per squadron, could not have deployed in their usual 3 or 4 ranks, but more probably in five to eight ranks.

The reserve was commanded by Barón de Sirot, and was deployed 350 metres behind the foot in the centre. It composed four squadrons of horse (Hungarian Régiment Sirot, Gendarmes Condé-Guiche, Gendarmes Angoulême-Vaubecourt and Régiment de Chârost) and three battalions of foot (Royaux, Watteville Suisse, and a mixed battalion of Harcourt), intermingled. In total, some sources including Sirot, indicate that there were 1,000 horse and 2,000 foot. The battalion Royaux was made up of 8 companies from the elite *Milice Royale* raised by various nobles, and the battalion of Harcourt was a composite from the 3 regiments of Harcourt, Aubeterre and Gesvres.

The artillery was commanded by Henri de Chivré, *monsieur* Le Barre, Lieutenant-General of the French artillery, and consisted of 12 pieces, 4 and 8 pdrs, placed in front of the front line of foot.

After 6:30, with the French deployment having only just been completed, the impatient La Ferté-Senneterre launched his horse, without orders, in an apparent attempt to get reinforcements into Rocroi. There is speculation as to whether he was encouraged to attack by L'Hôpital, who wanted to avoid battle and the veteran therefore incited La Ferté's attack by the example of Gassion's success the night before. It seems that L'Hôpital may have wanted to get the Régiments de Piémont and de Rambures into Rocroi, using La Ferté's horse as cover or distraction.

La Moussaye writes that La Ferté-Senneterre was envious of Gassion's successes, and since he had managed to get reinforcements into the besieged Rocroi, La Ferté wanted to achieve a similar triumph.

The French horse, followed by five battalions of foot, crossed the stream separating the two armies, exposing the rest of the left flank, which had not yet fully deployed. This advance was slowed by the marshy terrain, however, the French reached the Rocroi countryside, where the German horse under Colonel Suárez moved to try to prevent them from entering Rocroi. The Duc d'Enghien, as soon as he was told of La Ferté's movement, clearly saw that it exposed his left flank. d'Enghien ordered the army to halt any movement and to go onto the defensive, galloped to the area and sent messengers to stop the advance of his first line of horse, but they were unable to stop the charge.

The French passed through the marsh and arrived near Rocroi, only to be stopped by Suárez's regiment, which was guarding the area. The Graf von Isenburg, seeing Suárez repulsed, sent the rest of his regiments of horse, under the command of the battle sergeant-major Jacinto de Vera, to Suárez's aid. The French horse were forced to retreat and as they passed through the swamp, they were fired upon by Spanish musketeers and arquebusiers who had been moved to support their horse.

d'Enghien, seeing that all the entire Spanish right flank were going to fall on La Ferté-Senneterre's horse, ordered the second line of horse to charge in support. Isenburg, noted the French movement, but having no orders to start the battle, gave the order to halt, thus allowing the French horse of the first line to return to their starting point, although after having taken heavy casualties.

If Fontaine and Melo had given the order to attack, the outcome may have been different, but this was not to be the case. For La Moussaye, "this incident only succeeded in delaying the battle and caused no other inconvenience than to allow the Spanish to better prepare their position", as they advanced their line a few metres in front of the French left wing. Once his men were safely withdrawn, La Ferté-Senneterre apologised to d'Enghien for his mistake.

After 7:00, the last detachments of Sirot's reserve deployed onto the plain and the deployment of the French army was complete.

Alburquerque wrote that, after dark, he proposed to Fontaine to alter the deployment that the French had already seen. He proposed that the "parade" formation be changed to a "battle" formation; and because he had observed that the French horse had detachments of commanded shot, he asked Fontaine to send him some *mangas* of arquebusiers and musketeers to support his own horse. Fontaine did not agree to the proposals: he believed that his deployment was adequate to "frighten" the enemy and that, seeing the size of the Spanish Army, the French would not put up a fight and would withdraw. This would allow the Spanish army to refocus on its objective of capturing Rocroi. Alburquerque contacted Melo, but he would not listen to Alburquerque either, and replied that he had already sent a force of 500 musketeers into the forest and was not going to send any more. In response to this, Alburquerque states in his letter that he warned his officers of the dire fate that awaited them, 'We shall soon see the enemy attack us and cut us off, gaining us the rear and victory'.

Dusk brought the cessation of hostilities; the soldiers of both armies remained on the battlefield, lying in the open while sentries watched for any enemy movement, warming themselves by their campfires. In Sirot's words:

> Our soldiers had slept in battle order with their weapons, they just had to get up, blow their match, aim their cannon and fire on the enemy. And the enemy, since their intentions were the same as ours, their troops found themselves in the same position.

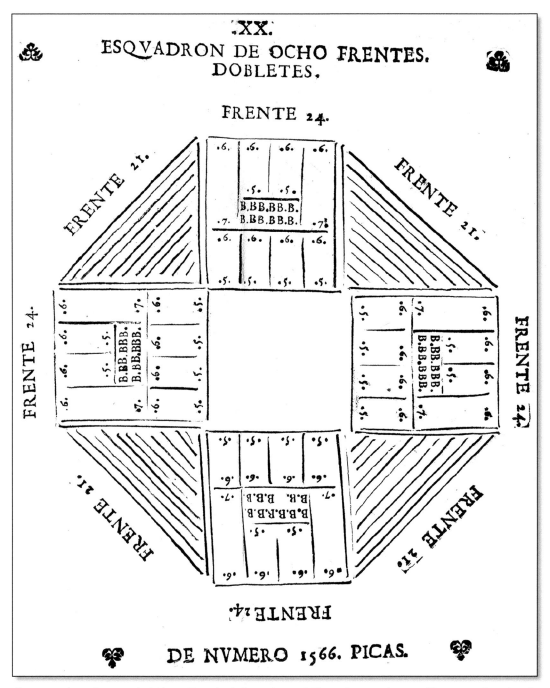

Illustration from Compendio Militar y Tratado de Escuadrones (Military Compendium and Treatise on Squadrons), Saragossa 1644, Sargento Mayor Miguel Lorente Bravo.

Throughout the seventeenth century, numerous books written by former officers were published in Spain, in which the battle tactics, organisation of units and the logistics of armies were explained. Almost all of them also taught how to "escuadronear", that is, form ad hoc units based on the available troops, the terrain and the enemy. Using complex mathematical formulas, it was the task of the Sergento-Major of the tercio to be able to assign the companies in this type of unit. This illustration shows, as complex as it is implausible, a total of 1,566 pikemen are available and an all-round defence is required: 4 rectangular squadrons are formed, with a frontage of 24 men and a depth of 11 men, as well as 4 triangular squadrons that are inserted into the formation, of a 21 man frontage and 11 man depth.

Melo went round his army several times to give encouragement. He observed that the French were in the same positions and did not seem to want to make any further attempt to succour Rocroi, so Melo ordered Isenburg to return Jacinto Vera's detachments to the main frontline. Despite this "meticulous" activity of their commanding General, the Spanish generals muttered. Although the French had been outnumbered and in dire straits on several occasions – when Gassion's contingent was alone on the plain, then at the crossing of the forest and the gorge, and when Gassion had tried to occupy the hill, and finally during La Ferté-Senneterre charge – at no time had the order for a general attack been given. And now, in the early hours of the morning, with no news from Beck, Melo held no council of war to prepare the strategy for the next day.

At around 9 o'clock, the Duc d'Enghien assembled his staff to deliberate whether, taking advantage of the darkness, it would be feasible and advantageous to send help to Rocroi, or whether it was better to attack the Spanish in a pitched battle. Opinions were divided: L'Hôpital, La Ferté-Senneterre, d'Espenan and La Valière supported sending reinforcements to Rocroi, while Gassion, Persan and Sirot wished to give battle, an option favoured by d'Enghien. The various French sources conclude with the same argument, although they differ in the vehemence of the discussions, with some saying it was certainly heated, especially the arguments of L'Hôpital and Gassion defending their opposing views. It was also discussed whether they should attack at night or wait until the morning – it was agreed to wait until dawn.

7

The Battle

According to the sources, the Spanish Army consisted of between 15,000 and 18,000 foot and 8,000 to 9,000 horse and the French army had between 15,000 and 16,000 foot and 7,000 to 8,000 horse. All sources agree that the two armies were fairly evenly matched.

On 19 May, d'Enghien was awakened at three in the morning: his scouts had captured a Spanish deserter, some sources suggest that he was a French spy, who reported that Melo was expecting the arrival of Beck's 4,000 men, and that they could reach the Spanish camp by about 7:00 am. With this reinforcement, it was Melo's intention to attack. The deserter/spy also informed d'Enghien that there was a detachment of 1,000 musketeers hidden in the grove and that some of Isenburg's horse had withdrawn from the front to return to their original camp, because Melo was afraid that either a sortie would be attempted from the town or that the French would try to send in reinforcements.

Aware of the gravity of the situation, d'Enghien decided to anticipate enemy movements and ordered his troops to muster in silence. He meanwhile armed himself in a beautifully decorated cuirass, bulletproof armour, and a distinctive hat with long white feathers – worn by the French "Princes of The Blood" since the Battle of lvry, 14 March 1590. At 4:00 am, d'Enghien joined his army on the field. French sources are fairly reliable and abundant, allowing us to reconstruct their deployment relatively accurately.

An illustrative example of the complexity of the study of the battle is the question – admittedly, a somewhat minor question – of the initial position of the Duc d'Enghien, since there are several versions. It has to be said that the account of the Battle of Rocroi from the French point of view generally praises the generalship of d'Enghien, portraying him as an intelligent, courageous leader who was present at all the main events of the day. While no one doubts his ability to command, it is doubtful that he could have been in so many places during the battle, because of the impossibility of moving from one side to the other, and he would have become too focused on one part of the battle to the detriment of other trouble spots. According to La Moussaye's version, d'Enghien was with Gassion on the right wing, the place where the victory was forged. This is, in fact, the most widespread and the most plausible option. However, authors such as Gualdo Priorato, Ormesson and Montglat claim that he was with La Ferté-Seneterre on the left, the French wing that was defeated by the Spanish horse. Yet others, place him in a position between Gassion's horse and the centre of the foot. Finally, General Sirot, in his memoirs, puts the Duc in the centre with the foot.

The battlefield was bounded on one side by the La Houppe marsh and on the other by the forest of the Potées. The terrain where the French army deployed was higher than that of the surroundings and extended imperceptibly into the plain. On the left, the large swamp of La Houppe and the woods, not thick in this area, did not prevent squadrons from forming up. Opposite the hill occupied by the French there was another, almost identical ridge where the Spanish were deployed and with the same frontage as the French, more or less, Between the two armies was the dip of a valley. According to historian Paulin Lebas, this plain was called *Champ des Pretres* (Field of the Priests) by the locals.

According to the Duque de Aumale's calculations, the Spanish Army occupied a front of about 2km, while the French front was 2.8km. Fontaine had deployed his foot squadrons with an extended front, but if he had done it in the more traditional way – with almost equal frontage and depth – the French could have overrun the Spanish line and outflanked it easily. The distance between the two armies was about 900 metres.

According to Guthrie's calculation, the plain at its longest was about 2.5km, while its width varied according to where you measure, as it was hedged in by the forests, marshes and hills. The foot of the armies occupied about 1,000 metres in the centre of the deployments, while the wings of horse occupied between 600 metres, for the Spanish, and 750 metres, for the French, each side of the lines of foot.

Before the battle began, d'Enghien went through the ranks of his army to encourage his men. The General harangued his army,

> Frenchmen, this says it all. Before you, you see our old enemy. These proud Spanish have long since disputed your glory and your Empire. Their furious General shudders to see a seemingly secure conquest wrested from him, and has to abandon the siege of a town whose capture would have brought him our fairest provinces to the gates of Paris. The enemy comes to take vengeance with all the pride of his nation; let us oppose them with all the pride and valour of our own. I left the Court to lead you and promised to return only if I came back victorious. Do not disappoint my hopes. Let us all remember the battle of Cerisoles. Follow in the footsteps of your ancestors who triumphed there, and I will follow in the footsteps of my ancestor who led them into battle. May the name d'Enghien, borne by this your Prince of Bourbon blood, be a good omen for you and for me, and may the enemy we defeated on the fields of Cerisoles honour our triumph again today with his defeat on the plains of Rocroi.

He then ordered the two contingents of horse to be ready for battle. Melo also harangued his troops, encouraging them to fight with the memory of the victories they had achieved and to show their courage in the name of their King.

At around 4 o'clock, the French guns began firing, and the Spanish guns responded; given the darkness of early morning, the fire was not very effective.

Between 4 and 4.30, Gassion's horse on the right wing advanced, skirting the grove containing Baltasar Mercader's detachment of musketeers on the right. According to Albuquerque these musketeers numbered 500 men, according to Montbas they numbered 800, and 1,000 according to La Moussaye. Gassion had positioned his men, by passing this position, to charge directly into the flank of Albuquerque's horse.

The second line of French horse under d'Enghien, supported by the musketeers of the *enfants perdus* under the command of the sergeant-major of the Régiment de Piémont, attacked the grove head-on, and fierce fighting ensued. Although French sources claim that the defenders of the grove were wiped out, Spanish sources state that Mercader's men put up stiff resistance and held off the first wave of French horse. It is hard to believe that an experienced force of shot, well equipped and entrenched in a forest, could be annihilated by horse without the support of foot in the half-darkness of the early morning. It is therefore more plausible to think that the Spanish troops did indeed hold off the attack by the horse, but could not also resist the musketeers accompanying the horse, whom d'Enghien had ordered to cooperate the previous evening. But while the Spanish foot defended themselves in the forest, at no point did they receive any help from the horse of the Duque de Alburquerque, who, annoyed by the rebuffs he felt Melo and Fontaine had shown him, devoted himself to holding the line without trying to help the men on his flank.

In both versions the ending is the same: the Spanish in the forest were either killed, or had to retreat or be taken prisoner, like Mercader himself. Gassion and the first line of horse moved around the copse from the east, hidden from the view of the Spanish by the forest, to fall by surprise on the flank of Alburquerque's horse. At the same time Alburquerque was charged head-on by the second line of French horse under d'Enghien's direct command. The twin attacks broke Alburquerque's horse and forced its flight. French sources point out that Gassion's manoeuvre caught Alburquerque unawares, and that he had not foreseen that he might be attacked on his flank. This was probably because he was confident that the musketeers in the forest would repel any enemy attack. It should not be forgotten that in the front line of the French horse on the right flank were two of the best regiments, *Royale* and *Mestre de Camp Général*.

Given that, according to the various Spanish sources, the French horse were supported by foot – and not just by the initial detachments of commanded musketeers – it may be implied that several of the French regiments on the right flank of the front line of foot took part in the attack. These would have been the Régiment de Picardie and the two regiments that the Spanish identified as "Swiss" – Molondin's or Watteville's battalions. It is also likely that the other two regiments of foot deployed in this sector, La Marine and Persan, took part or were close by in support.

This version does not, however, agree with Vincart and Cánovas. For the former, the French attack on the grove had initially failed, and seeing that the French horse was badly mauled, Alburquerque launched the attack. Thus the General led his first line of horse, accompanied by his two Lieutenant-Generals, Juan de Vivero and Pedro de Villamor, and exhorted his men to combat, "Now is the time to make like who we are".

He then attacked and defeated Gassion's horse: Captain Gaspar Bonifacio's company defeated two companies of French horse and César Toralto's company annihilated a squadron of horse of more than 300 men. Vincart says that Alburquerque's horse not only defeated part of the French horse, but also a regiment of French foot and another of Swiss. Then, passing through the gaps in the broken French line, they reached the artillery and captured some pieces of artillery, according to the administrative report on the granting of a pension to the captain of lancers Cristóbal Berrio de Barrionuevo, of Alburquerque's troop of horse. As Juan Luís Sánchez says,

> Barrionuevo charged a detachment of French horse fighting a company of Spanish horse, forcing them to retreat and in the pursuit captured some enemy cannon; he subsequently regrouped and with other remnants of Spanish horse, charged a battalion of French foot and routed it.

Captain Juan de Borja, with two squadrons of horse, also annihilated a French battalion of foot. However, it is likely that the defeated French foot were not the regiments of the front line, but the detachments of musketeers who were present on both flanks and who were there to support the horse. If the Spanish sources describe them as battalions, perhaps some 300 to 500 strong, it is because their numbers were probably larger than the usual between 100 and 200 shot at most. Thus the Spanish accounts believed that they were a full battalion. But it was not all victory and Spanish sources indicate that a squadron of French horse defeated Virgilio Ursini's company.

Wilson also believes that Alburquerque's horse broke the first line of French horse and their supporting foot. But that, at the moment of defeat, the French horse was able to prevail over the Spanish horse thanks to its better organisation, because the officers were able to reorganise it quickly and while the Spanish horse were still scattered. For Vincart as well, the success of the French horse is explained by the fact that it was better organised, in regiments, than the Spanish horse and had twice the number of officers per company.

However, this version raises some problems. Even assuming that Alburquerque's horse could defeat the first line of French horse and foot, there was still the second, commanded by d'Enghien; and it is hard to believe that Alburquerque could break the two lines of horse, and both the *enfants perdus* and the regiments of foot located on the right centre of the deployment. It was one of Alburquerque's criticisms that he did not have foot in support and the enemy did. Secondly, the accounts indicate that the French artillery was deployed in front of the foot, so it is likely that it was more centrally located, rather than being positioned on a wing. And even supposing that there were some guns located further to the edge, these were probably only a couple of pieces, and not the whole artillery park that Alburquerque suggests in his account.

For Aumale, Gassion's squadrons were in the front line and it was they who attacked Alburquerque's first line head-on, while the French second line, commanded by d'Enghien, and hidden from Alburquerque's view by the copse, carried out the flanking manoeuvre, charging the Spanish on their flank.

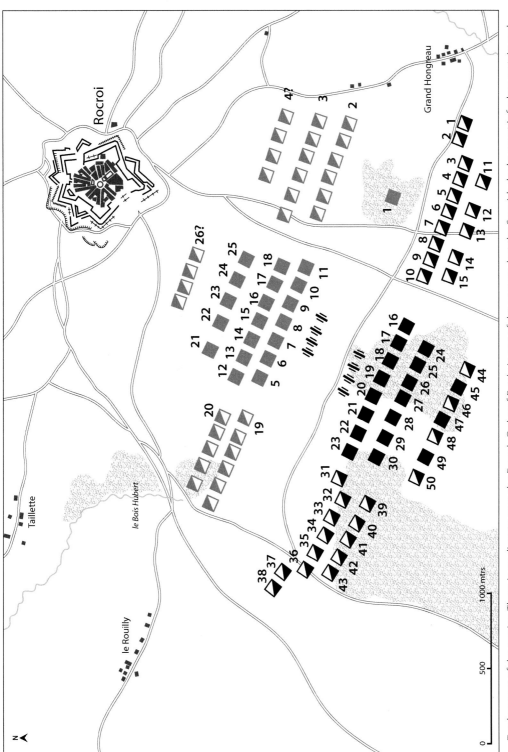

THE BATTLE

Deployment of the armies. There is no dispute as to the French Order of Battle in any of the sources, but the Spanish deployment is far less certain and still a point of argument. In this hypothesis, the Spanish tercios, formed in two lines, occupy the right flank. The Italian tercios are located in the centre, conforming to the hypothesis that they were unhappy that they had not been posted on the left flank, the second post of importance, because Fontaine wanted to reward the Walloon and Burgundian units (see main text for the discussion of this). See appendices I and II for the orders of battle of both armies, which include numbered keys to formations shown. Formations in light grey are Spanish, those depicted in black are French.

103

According to Spanish sources, more in agreement with the French sources, the performance of Alburquerque's horse was not so brilliant. When it was noticed that the French horse was overrunning the forest, Alburquerque alerted his wing, but it seems that they were distracted by d'Enghien's horse, who were attacking them head-on. When he received Melo's authorisation, Alburquerque charged with his horse, but was attacked from the left by Gassion's first line of horse. This double attack, effectively forming a pincer against the Spanish, succeeded in disrupting it and throwing it into chaos. The various *trozos* of horse were almost surrounded, and some units began to flee through the gap that still remained even while the fighting continued in the front.

According to Aumale, Alburquerque and his officers Vivero and Villamor rallied their second line of horse behind the left of the foot and launched an attack on some foot. These are believed to be the Régiment de Picardie, which was emerging from the copse and was vulnerable as it was reforming, but it hastily formed an 'hedgehog' and resisted the attack of the retreating

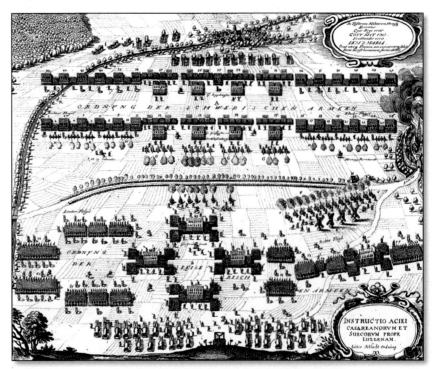

Battle of Lützen, 16 November 1632.
In this decisive battle between Swedish and Imperial forces, Sweden prevailed but at the cost of heavy losses. Gustav II Adolph lost his life, but his fame and success remain. In this engraving, the Imperial troops appear deployed in a "Tercio" type formation, although this was not actually the case, but rather they deployed in a mixed model, in smaller units. However, we can see what the theoretical appearance of a "Tercio" was like: the centre was made up of pikemen, around them was a guarnicion (literally 'garrison') of musketeers, and in the corners, the mangas ('sleeves') of arquebusiers. In contrast to the Imperials the deployment of the Protestants is more reliable, since they formed in the style of a "Swedish brigade", although it seems that the customary depth of their ranks was reduced. (Theatrum Europaeum, period 1629–1633, Edition 1646)

Spanish horse. This successful resistance by the Régiment de Picardie allowed that sector to hold firm for the rest of the battle. French reports indicate that there were no casualties among the officers of the regiments in the second line behind Picardie. Alburquerque's Spanish horse thus did not break the French first line of foot, thanks to the resistance of Picardie, nor the second, and the Spanish success in that sector was limited to taking the artillery deployed in front.

It is in this context, that part of the French horse and musketeers were defeated, that a rumour spread in French Court circles that d'Enghien had fled when he saw his men defeated, and that it was thanks to Gassion's initiative and courage that the affair was saved. Gassion rallied the fugitives and sent them into combat, and then sent a message to d'Enghien to return to the battle. Lefevre d'Ormesson, who wrote a few days after the battle, described this story and repeated the rumour. d'Enghien had many enemies – at least the Spanish were fighting him head-on; palace intrigues could do a lot of damage.

Seeing the danger to his left flank, where Alburquerque's horse was in the throes of defeat, Melo rode there with his escort guard and tried to rally the horse. Bonifaz, Borja, Toralto and Orsini's squadrons all rallied and charged the enemy horse and foot. One Spanish account extols their performance and states that they managed to partially disrupt the French attack. Gassion, however, managed to reorganise his horse and, after heavy fighting, finally scattered all of Alburquerque's horse.

In general terms, both French and Spanish sources end up agreeing that the French broke the two lines of Alburquerque's horse. The fugitives were followed by Gassion's horse, by the Croats according to Aumale, who pursued them to the entrance of the nearby woods and prevented them from rallying and rejoining the battle. d'Enghien had instructed the horse to concentrate on breaking the resistance of their Spanish counterparts and not to engage in any pursuit that would draw the French horse away from their immediate objective of destroying the Spanish army.

The Duque de Alburquerque himself acknowledges that his horse was defeated, but lays the blame on Melo and Fontaine. According to Alburquerque, his horse had to face the French horse and foot alone, and Fontaine did not send any foot to him. Fontaine also did not order an advance of the foot to press the French centre and divert their attention away from Alburquerque's wing.

Melo and Fontaine should perhaps have placed companies of foot with Alburquerque's horse, but in any case, Alburquerque should have positioned his horse to be able to better resist the French onslaught. In addition, when attacked by the French horse, Alburquerque should have organised his defence better, and regrouped his men under the protective fire of the tercios, but he did not do so.

Perhaps the Spanish horse fled into the woods rather than the centre of the deployment because that was where the baggage wagons were located and would make movement difficult. Maybe, but Alburquerque should have foreseen the need for a rallying point. The man who was always ready to give advice on the deployment of units he was not in charge of, was unable to deploy his own men correctly.

The Duque de Aumale claims that the Alburquerque himself was one of the first to flee and that he did not stop until he reached Philippeville, more than 30km from Rocroi, leaving his Lieutenant-Generals in charge of the horse and trying to rally them. A few years later, the Spanish historians Cánovas del Castillo and Fernández Duro made a fiery defence of Alburquerque's role in two books based on the study of contemporary testimonies and official documents in the Spanish archives. They pointed out his errors but they also lauded his courage and honour,

It seems that routing of Alburquerque's horse was not as sudden as French sources tell us, but that heavy fighting ensued between loose Spanish detachments and the French horse. Melo tried to rally his horse until the last moment, and in the chaos of combat and pursuit, rode towards a unit of horse marching from the battlefield, shouting at them to return to the fight. However, his escort told him that they were mistakenly following a French unit, so they quickly turned back before the French realised and attacked them – the lack of any identifying uniform in the armies at the time could lead to such mistakes....

While this was happening on the French right wing, fighting was also taking place on their left wing. According to some sources, La Ferté-Senneterre had received express orders from d'Enghien not to advance until he received a direct order. However, the General attacked on his own without orders upon detecting the movement of forces on the Spanish right wing. It was part of Isenburg's horse, which was hastily joining the line of battle, as they had been busy during the night before in watching Rocroi and in preventing the garrison of the town from attacking the Spanish rear. In fact, the French spy who had alerted d'Enghien to the Spanish plans had also told him that the Alsatian horse was tasked with the prevention of any sortie from the Rocroi garrison. It seems that La Ferté, noting that the enemy horse were not deployed in that sector, and thus seeing the opening in front of him, ordered the attack.

Perhaps the main issue is not that La Ferté launched his attack before receiving d'Enghien's order, maybe he did receive such an order, but that, in the haste to reach the line of Alsatian horse before it was reinforced by the remainder of the troops arriving from Rocroi, La Ferté's charge was launched from too great a distance. It would have been wiser to start the movement at a walk and then a trot. It was the same area La Ferté had encountered the previous evening and perhaps, because of this and in order to reach the 'combat zone' before the Spanish horse, La Ferté ordered the charge at full speed. These circumstances meant that the French arrived in disorder to face the opposing horse.

In any case, the French horse arrived tired and disordered. Isenburg was ready however and, at the head of Bucquoy's regiment of horse charged the French, who were easily contained and he managed to encircle and annihilate them. This caused chaos and a disorderly retreat of the French, leaving behind many dead and wounded men, including La Ferté with a bullet wound and two sword wounds. His horse was killed and La Ferté fell to the ground and was taken prisoner by the Spanish horse.

Remembering that Bucquoy had been dismissed from army command for his argument with Alburquerque Isenburg knew that this unit was disgruntled. So, he set out to ensure the regiment's reliability and placed it at the head of the charge, ensuring that the fighting itself would clear up any lingering doubts and the pent-up anger could be channelled against the French rather than into sedition.

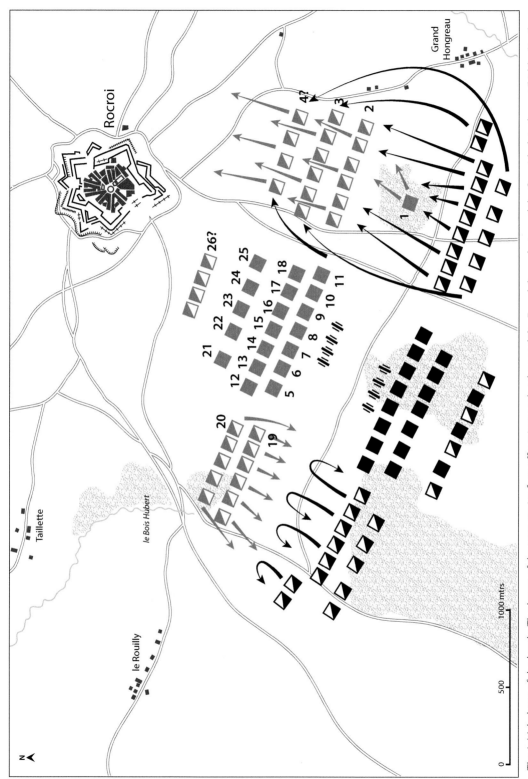

The initial phase of the battle. The horse of the two armies face off against each other, and the French have destroyed the Spanish detachment 'hidden' in the forest. The Conde of Alburquerque's cavalry has been defeated and is dispersed across the field. Issemburg's horse have defeated the French left-wing horse and subsequently occupied their positions.

The French second line, commanded by L'Hôpital, then went into combat; but the second line of Spanish horse charged as well and, supported by the first Spanish line, broke L'Hôpital's men. L'Hôpital was wounded by a shot in the arm, and had to retreat protected by his escort, while his men were broken and surrounded in small groups, defeated by Isenburg's men. The Alsatians also destroyed the musketeers who accompanied L'Hôpital horse, and seized the French cannons on that wing. Having annihilated La Ferté, the Spanish horse halted and rallied.

The French account by Jean de Serres[1], narrates this event in a totally different way:

> At the first charge we reached their cannons that fired incessantly at us; but the enemy troops that opposed our left flank, receiving at the same time the rescue of all the horse of their left flank that had folded, made such a great effort that they regained their posts and pushed part of our squadrons and battalions back to our battery.

It is the only account that indicates that the French reached the Spanish artillery and came into contact with the foot. Moreover, it states that the Alsatian horse came to the aid of the foot, although we know from other sources that the fighting between La Ferté's and L'Hôpital's horse against Isenburg's Alsatians was a direct combat and was not caused by the French seizing the Spanish guns or fought in support of the Spanish foot.

It was 5 o'clock in the morning. The French foot and the two wings of horse had begun the advance, but as they advanced, they were met with fire from the musketeers and arquebusiers of the front line tercios. The French advance became slower as they drew nearer to the Spanish lines. D'Espenan looked to his flanks. d'Enghien's horse seemed to dominate the field, but they were still fighting Alburquerque's horse. On his left flank, L'Hôpital's horse has been swept aside. It was not a good time to advance unprotected and d'Espenan ordered a halt, and awaited developments.

Isenburg's horse, after the action against the French horse, wheeled inwards and charged the flank of the foot of the French centre. On that flank the regiments of Biscarras, Rambures and Piémont were deployed, and they had to partially alter their front to be able to fire a volley of musketry at Isenburg. This was ineffective and they were unable to stop Isenburg's horse, which broke into Biscarras' formation and forced the other regiments to retreat. Isenburg then fell on the French artillery, which they took from behind. La Barre was killed defending his guns, as were a great many of the gunners and of the foot.

The remnants of the French horse on the left then counter-attacked and recovered the artillery. A fresh charge by the Spanish horse, supported by the musketry fire of the tercios still in position, repulsed the French horse and seized the guns again. These were then served by some Spanish troops and turned against the French. The Spanish were now able to use 30 artillery pieces against the French centre and the French had no artillery with which

---

1   Jean de Serres, *Le Véritable Inventaire de l'Histoire de France…* Paris, Arnold Cotinet, Jean Roger, François Prevveray, 1648.

German Three-Quarter Armour, early seventeenth century. Weight 25.75kg; weight of helmet approx. 2.25kg.
This armour came from the private collection of Graf Zierotin, at Castle Blauda in Bohemia. This type of armour generally served as equipment for cuirassiers. Because they were mass produced, such armour is also called "Munition armour", to be stored in large armouries, to equip both foot and horse. Munition armour was of a standard pattern with interchangeable pieces. It was often made of iron or sometimes an alloy of iron containing a small amount of phosphorus, which gave a marginal increase in hardness. (Metropolitan Museum of Art, 29.152.4a–m)

to respond. The French official reports admit to high casualties in the Regiments of Rambures, Biscaras-Bourdoné and Brezé-Langeron, particularly when compared to the other regiments of foot in the battle. The accounts that the Alsatian horse forced the retreat of the French foot is thus quite plausible.

As they watched Isenburg's German horse take the guns, the Spanish foot still in line of battle had not yet been ordered to advance. They threw their hats in the air and shouted "victory", anticipating that, with the French right flank and centre broken, they would be given the order to advance and reinforce the front line.

Guthrie, following French sources, states that Isenburg's attack was supported by Visconti's and Velandia's tercios, and together, they not only captured the French guns, but had also driven back the French foot[2]. It should be stressed that no Spanish source states that the tercios moved forward to fight, so Guthrie's assertion is strange. Moreover, it is also implausible that these two tercios, one Spanish and one Italian, went forward on their own, exposing this flank. Perhaps, in an attempt to lend credibility to the French claim that the tercios attacked, it could be said that it was not the entire tercios, but rather the usual *mangas* of shot that went forward to support the horse and consolidate the capture of the artillery?

This hypothesis would tie in with the claims of some French sources that indicate that in the fighting between the French regiments and the tercios (sic), the French had to retreat. Again, it should be said here that it was not the entire tercios that moved forward, but rather their detachments of musketeers and arquebusiers that advanced to harass the French with their fire. It is worth remembering that the composition of a Spanish tercio of this period had a very high ratio of firearms to pikes – an official ratio of almost

---

2   William P Guthrie, *The Later Thirty Years' War: From the Battle of Wittstock to the Treaty of Westphalia.* Wesport USA, Greenwood Press, 2003.

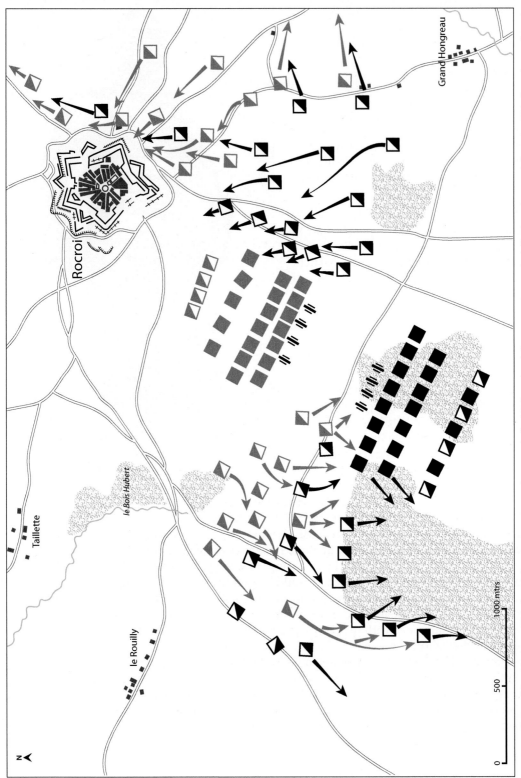

Middle phase of the Battle, 1. d'Enghien's horse is positioned to attack the Walloon and German units on their flank and rear, while part of his force is employed mopping-up dispersed bodies of the Spanish left-wing horse that are still resisting. Issemburg's horse have captured the French artillery and caused the withdrawal of some French regiments of foot. At this point, it appears that victory is within the grasp of the Spanish army.

Grand Hongreau

Rocroi

le Bois Hubert

Taillette

le Rouilly

0   500   1000 mtrs

3 : 1. Thus it is likely that Fontaine ordered the field masters of the front line to order their shot to deploy and advance to consolidate the capture of the artillery, but without committing the main line, keeping it back and waiting for Beck, as was originally planned.

If the order to advance had been given at that time, it is likely that the French centre would have collapsed, and only the horse on the right flank of d'Enghien and Gassion would have remained operational, so that the tactical situation up to that point would have been very different. Why was the order not given to attack? Here it can only be guessed at. Perhaps Melo did not give the order because he was out of his command position, either on the left flank, rallying Alburquerque's horse, or on the right flank, with Isenburg's horse. Maybe his second in command, Field Master General Conde de Fontaine, did not give the order because his instructions were to defend and not to attack, or to "put the army for show and not for battle", as the Duque de Alburquerque accused him.

La Moussaye's account states that the bulk of d'Espenan's foot stayed in line, as the French General, noting the different results of the fighting of the horse on both flanks, decided to wait upon events, limiting himself to skirmishing, and as he saw, 'the Spanish foot waiting with great pride and in good order'.

Other sources indicate that, at this point, to avoid the total defeat of the French centre, *monsieur* de La Vallière ordered the withdrawal of the remaining regiments of foot. Aumale describes how La Vallière went from regiment to regiment to assess their morale and state. Apparently, nobody knew where d'Enghien was, but they had seen that the French left wing horse had been defeated and the Alsatian horse had taken the artillery. At this point, assuming that d'Enghien was fighting with the horse on the right wing, the French army was deprived of its commander-in-chief. It is in this context that La Vallière took command of the centre and ordered the tactical withdrawal, to protect the foot from the onslaught of enemy horse and their cannon fire. At the time, the battle seemed lost for the French, and if Melo had ordered an aggressive advance of the Spanish foot, the French front would probably have collapsed.

Between 5 and 6 a.m., the French had been driven into the abyss: their horse on the left had been defeated, they had lost their cannons and their foot were beginning to retreat. But Melo had made the same mistake as d'Enghien and, emboldened by the fighting, had joined first Alburquerque's horse and then Isenburg's, so that the Spanish centre was also without a commander-in-chief. None of the field masters present (Villalba, Garcíez and Velandia) took command or made the decision to attack at that crucial moment in the battle.

Turning now to the flanks of the battle. At about 6.30, d'Enghien organised his second line of horse, while Gassion kept up the pressure against the remnants of Albuquerque's horse who were still offering resistance. Then, according to the traditional French version, d'Enghien had the brilliant idea of moving his horse to the enemy rear and charged with his men against the formations of foot. However, the Marquis de Monglat attributes the idea of attacking the enemy horse to Gassion,

> He [Gassion] saw the disorder of the men of the other flank and
> the victorious Spanish … pillaged the luggage as though they had

nothing left to fear. So he turned back to the right and marched on to take them from behind.

It makes perfect sense that d'Enghien, after reforming his squadrons, would make a flank or rear movement to attack the Walloon and German units from behind, these the ones closest to where he was. If d'Enghien attacked the foot from behind, and the foot was formed up with the Germans behind, he had to attack the Germans first to catch the foot off guard. However, if he attacked the Walloons first; then the Germans were already warned. Nonetheless the French probably attacked the Walloons on their left flank, and not from the rear.

According to Montbas's account, Gassion told him that there were two enemy battalions at a distance of 20 paces. One appeared to be Spanish and the other, in his words, a mixed unit of Italians and Walloons, each of more than 3,000 men. We know that there were no mixed units at the start of the battle, so there must surely have been at least three formations – one Spanish, one Italian and one Walloon.

Montbas divided his regiment into two 200 man squadrons, with Gassion taking command of one and charging the Italians and Walloons, while Montbas charged the Spanish unit. However, as the Spanish deployment in the battle is still the subject of much speculation, we cannot verify exactly which units Montbas was against. It is doubtful whether, instead of a Walloon unit, Montbas was referring to the Burgundian Saint-Amour tercio. In any case, in that sector of the Spanish left flank there do not seem to have been Spanish units that could have been attacked, since the Spanish accounts always refer to the Spanish tercios being inactive throughout the battle and limited to skirmishing with the French musketeers in the front line.

Montbas wrote that the enemy foot was in a shallower depth than his own horse detachment, but had at least three times the frontage of his own detachment. This information is interesting because it allows us to confirm the deployment devised by Fontaine, in which the units had a greater front than depth – either to have more firepower facing the enemy, or because he just wanted to "show", as the Duque de Alburquerque had criticised. Nonetheless, given that Montbas entered the battalion with his horse, killed its commander and disrupted the unit, indicates that the linear formations, supposedly far superior to the "heavy" formations of the tercios, were very vulnerable to horse attacks. It was precisely the fact that they had depth and a high proportion of pikes that enabled these units to defend themselves against horse, as would later become evident in the fighting against the Spanish tercios. We must assume that Fontaine, following Melo's indications, deployed all the units with the aim of being prepared for battle but with the precise objective of not fighting until the arrival of Beck's reinforcements. To do this, Fontaine deployed on a wider front than depth, this would be between 5 and 9 ranks deep, with a broad front. This meant that more shot were able to fire and thus, to weaken the enemy if he advanced.

Despite being dispersed, the foot that the French had defeated put up stiff resistance. Montbas reports that of his squadron of 200 horse only eight rallied, the rest were killed, wounded or broken. Of the second squadron, that under Captain Estournelle, only 56 of the 200 horse were rallied for the next assault.

According to later Spanish historians, the French horse, supported by detachments of musketry, charged the Walloon tercios (La Grange, Bassigny, Meghem, Ligne and Ribacourt) and then charged the German regiments. Flanders accounts state that these units sustained up to three attacks by the French, but were finally defeated and forced to retreat, which they did in orderly fashion. Official Spanish reports after the battle state that they suffered heavy casualties, especially in terms of prisoners taken.

The Walloon regiments fought bravely: six captains of La Grange tercio were killed, and the others were wounded. Four captains of the tercio Bassigny were also killed, together with three of the Meghem tercio. The two sergeant majors of the Ligne and Ribacourt tercios were also amongst the dead.

The accounts do not say anything about whether the German regiments supported the Walloons ahead of them, but that their attack was later so it can be deduced that the second (or third) line of Spanish foot, the German regiments, were deployed too far behind the first line, which would suggest a bad deployment devised by Fontaine.

After forcing the Walloons to retreat, d'Enghien's horse attacked the German regiments. Melo had ridden to them to seek refuge after Alburquerque's horse had broken. He rode through the lines of foot and encouraged them to resist the enemy, reminding them of the oath they had taken on joining the army. According to the Spanish accounts, the soldiers of Rittberg's regiment, closest to Melo, said they would die rather than break their oaths. Rittberg himself fought desperately and when he was taken prisoner he had two sword wounds to his head, another on his left side and a further two in the arm. Four captains of his regiment died and the rest were taken prisoner.

The other German regiments (Rouveroy, Hembise, Guasco and Frangipani) behaved in much the same way, as the battle reports a large number of prisoners in French hands. The German units put up stiff resistance, which would indicate that they had time to reorganise their formation to be more suitable for defence. Additionally, although the accounts do not mention it, that the French horse was supported by foot in order to break the German resistance.

How do you explain how the French were able to defeat the Walloons and Germans? Perhaps, again, the explanation lies simply in the deployment that Fontaine had adopted at the start of the battle, which, as has been said before, was as if the tercios were "on parade rather than ready for battle". It was thus precisely this more linear formation that caused the Walloon and perhaps the German units to lose against the French horse. They either did not have time to change their formation, or did not know how to do so. Thus they faced the French horse and foot with musket fire alone, without being able to defend themselves with a deeper formation – precisely one of the stereotypes of the Spanish tercios, relying on the strength of the pike bodies to repel the charges of horse.

In Guthrie's words, 'it becomes clear that the new style of line warfare had its disadvantages. The old tercios could stand on their own and repulse any horse onslaught without the support of other units. The independent

Pikeman's cuirass, c 1600–1650.
It is completely black and has the following specifications: height 48cm, width 65cm, weight 10kg. Both the belt and the belt buckle mounts are replacements. It is probable that the full assembly contains unrelated parts from different pieces that have been put together a later date. The three straps internally supporting the right and left arms are broken and have been replaced with wire. (Armémuseum, Stockholm, AM.056982)

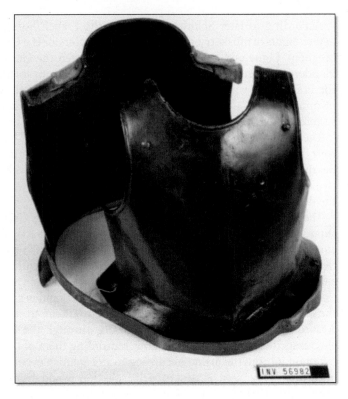

battalions of line warfare could not; once the line was flanked, the whole echelon was lost.'[3]

Perhaps, seeing the defeat of the Walloon and German units, the Italian tercios had time to change their formation into a more compact form, with the shot sheltered under the cover of the pikes. This is corroborated by the fact that all the accounts agree that the Italians were able to retreat in good order and with few casualties. If they were able to do so, it was because they used a more compact formation and not the one originally planned for the battle as Melo and Fontaine had envisaged it.

After the successive collapse of Alburquerque's horse and the Walloon and German foot, Melo rode towards the centre of his deployment, the Italian tercios. The horse of d'Enghien had the same idea. According to French sources, with the collapse of the Walloon and German foot, the Spanish foot ceased any offensive movement. The Spanish accounts consistently state that the Spanish foot did not move from their original position. How can these two versions be reconciled? Maybe we could suggest that at the moment when the two lines of foot were engaged in a fire fight, perhaps the Spanish sent out a number of their shot, as was their usual combat doctrine, and with which they harassed the French front lines. Perhaps this movement by the Spanish shot was interpreted by the French accounts as an offensive movement, but that when the other Spanish units were attacked, these shot were ordered to withdraw

---

3   William P Guthrie, *The Later Thirty Years' War: From the Battle of Wittstock to the Treaty of Westphalia.* Westport USA, Greenwood Press, 2003.

Melo still thought he could win the battle since his centre, the Italian tercios, and the right flank of his foot, the Spanish tercios, were still intact. He moved behind the Italians and tried to rally the various groups of Spanish horse that were still scattered around the battlefield to reform behind the tercios. Having passed the Italian tercios three times, a detachment of French horse spotted Melo and charged directly at him in an attempt to capture him. Perhaps this episode is the same one as recounted above, that Melo was following a horse unit in an attempt to reorganise it, and realising it was a French unit turned back, and was then pursued by the French horse. Melo was forced to take refuge in the squadron of Field Master Visconti. According to some Spanish accounts, Melo encouraged Visconti's men, "I want to die here, with the Italian gentlemen". Visconti is reported to have replied, "We all want to die here for the service of the King, our lord, and of your Excellency". The gentle words used by Melo to refer to the Italians may have been meant to ingratiate himself with them, given that they were in the central position of his deployment, and according to Gualdo Priorato, they had felt insulted by the perceived slight of this positioning.

The composition and formation of the squadron was so mathematically calculated that only Melo and an aide were allowed to pass, his escort being left outside of the formation. Captain Francisco Porta, in command of the musketeer detachment protecting the left flank of the squadron, ordered his men to open fire at point-blank range, killing many of the pursuing Frenchmen and the rest fled.

Gualdo Priorato gives us a different version of this action, although perhaps complementary. When Melo was pursued by the French horse, he took refuge in Ponti's tercio, and although these Italians managed to repulse the French charge, it was at the cost of heavy losses, so Melo ordered them to make an orderly retreat into the woods.

Thus, different Spanish accounts explain the same events, but confusing the protagonists at some point although following the same general narrative. The French launched several coordinated attacks with both horse and foot against the Italian tercios, who were forced to retreat, although they did so still in order and without heavy losses. Gualdo Priorato introduces the comment that, "the three Italian regiments were upset because on that occasion the Spanish wanted both flanks of the vanguard [the front line] for themselves, making them [the Italians] look like cowardly soldiers in battle". This "naive" comment sows doubt about the real behaviour of the Italians in the battle. Was their unhappiness caused by forming up in the centre of the foot instead of the left flank the reason for their retreat? Did they fight with sufficient courage and determination, or did they merely put up token resistance and then retreat? The number of Italian casualties was lower than in the Spanish and Walloon nationalities, and the fact that they retreated "in order" can be interpreted in two different ways. Either they retreated, still "in order" thanks to their training and morale, or because they had hardly fought and were still fresh and without significant casualties...

Furthermore, Gualdo's comment about the Spanish occupying both flanks raises the question of an atypical deployment, since the right flank was for the Spanish, but not the centre or the left flank. Perhaps, by mistake, he means that they were Walloon units, as we have hypothesised the deployment suggestions above. However, Gualdo strongly emphasises that the

Italian tercios were annoyed to be in the centre and not their traditional post on the left flank.

The Italians withdrawal was covered by a small detachment of horse, commanded by Captain Fernando de Noroña, Count of Linares, who faced off against three bodies of French horse who were attacking the Italians. The Spanish horse, although greatly outnumbered, attacked the French on the flank and broke them, then held their ground when the French reformed and charged. These horse held out until the Italian foot took cover in the woods.

Gualdo Priorato gives a similar account. Visconti's tercio was retreating into the forest, being harassed by around 2,000 French horse, when Juan de Liponti, leading 800 horse, charged the French and bought Visconti's men time to reach the forest. Liponti had achieved his goal of covering the retreat of the Italian tercio and ordered his men to retire but only about 150 of his men remained.

All these facts indicate that at this point in the battle there were still units of Alburquerque's horse fighting, so, despite their initial defeat, these horse were still holding out. However, the surprisingly high number of horse indicated by Priorato is perhaps an exaggeration.

A Spanish account recounts the actions of Alburquerque after almost all his horse had been routed. On the right wing and in the place where the Walloon, German and Italian regiments had held out, some parties of Spanish horse, including that of the Duque and his escort, were still fighting. This was not to try to affect the outcome of the battle, but they were fighting for their own lives, since if they fled they would be slaughtered by their pursuers. According to Vincart's account among these groups of horse who were resisting, the majority were officers. This may be a form of poetic licence to indicate that the nobles and officers showed a superior level of courage and honour to their rank and file or perhaps it really was the case that most of the soldiers were already dead or dispersed in flight. With these survivors, Vivero and Villamor attempted to attack a body of French horse facing the horse commanded by the Duque de Albuquerque, but the Spanish horse were repulsed and retreated to join Barón André with what was left of the four reserve units that he had commanded at the start of the battle. The French horse then charged them with such force that André and his force were forced to retreat. Alburquerque, Vivero and Villamor and a few officers were now alone and rode towards the Spanish tercios, who sheltered them from the onslaught of the French horse.

The situation was that the French had defeated the Spanish on the Spanish left wing (the French right). The German horse had defeated the French on the Spanish right (the French left). The Spanish foot was still in its initial deployment positions. The French foot had fallen back a few hundred yards to avoid the fire of the Spanish artillery, and the Spanish foot were passively waiting for the order to advance. The Croat horse of the Spanish army accompanying Isenburg's horse were scattered across the field looting the dead and wounded, swiftly being imitated by the rest of Isenburg's horse breaking formation and dispersing.

While all this was occurring on the flanks and in the centre of the battlefield, Raab's and Schack's Croats, serving on the French side, scoured the Spanish left flank, harassing the retreating squadrons or looting the wounded and dying or the baggage, which was in the rear of the Spanish deployment. There is a direct witness to this: Montbas himself, who records that "our Croats have become rich, because they have probably spent more time taking prisoners and looting than fighting".

La Moussaye describes the climax of the battle in this way. While the Spanish have won on the French left flank and the foot of the tercios remains immobile, the Duc d'Enghien has already defeated the German, Walloon and Italian regiments. It is 7.30 a.m. Faced with this general situation, d'Enghien decided to execute the brilliant manoeuvre that gave him the victory and confirmed him as a great General at just over 20 years of age. The French foot had been crippled by the fire of the fleeing Italian and the still-resisting Spanish tercios; the French guns had been taken and were firing on the French. Isenburg's horse had succeeded against the French left flank. d'Enghien realised that although he had won his flank, the battle was not won, and the decisions that he made would determine the final outcome. He could pursue Alburquerque's horse and the Italians, he could charge the Spanish tercios in front of him, or he could outflank the Spanish foot and attack Isenburg's horse.

There is no agreement in the sources to explain how the battle unfolded at this point, so it is worth looking at the most plausible options. The traditional French version says that d'Enghien made a great flanking movement of almost a kilometre to fight Isenburg's horse. However, here is precisely where a weakness in this account lies: how was the encirclement made when he had to pass close to the Spanish tercios, who could cause casualties on them with their shot, how was it done without being hindered by the wagons of the Spanish baggage? Remembering that Alburquerque complained that these wagons had hindered the reforming movements of his horse.

However, for French historians, d'Enghien's tactical genius shone through at that moment, when he decided to take a risk and continue his advance, pass behind the Spanish foot in the centre of the enemy's deployment, and charge Isenburg's horse. But, apart from the tactical difficulty of such a manoeuvre, this contradicts the version written by Sirot in his memoirs that claims it was his own counter-attack that disrupted Isenburg's horse.

According to those memoirs while d'Enghien and Gassion were fighting against the Walloon, Italian and German tercios (although those successes were not visible even to La Vallière and d'Espenan, let alone Sirot) the French foot line was undecided. The situation did not look good – d'Enghien's horse had "disappeared" behind the Spanish lines, La Ferté's horse were scattered and Isenburg's horse was the master of all of that part of the field and of the artillery. For these reasons de La Vallière gave the order for a general retreat. Again all of this from Sirot's account which also says La Vallière himself rode to Sirot to order him to withdraw, for the "battle was lost".

Sirot does not say who had given such an order, d'Enghien at the time was fighting against the Walloons, Germans and Italians. Sirot sensed that this was the decisive moment of the battle. Some French horse on the left flank had reformed under cover of Sirot's reserve, and the foot of the front line regiments had begun to retreat in the direction of Sirot's reserve. Sirot, aware of his men's dismay, bellowed, "The battle is not lost because Sirot has not yet fought".

The General then rallied the French fugitives, added them into his reserve battalions and ordered them to advance. The French foot regiments in the

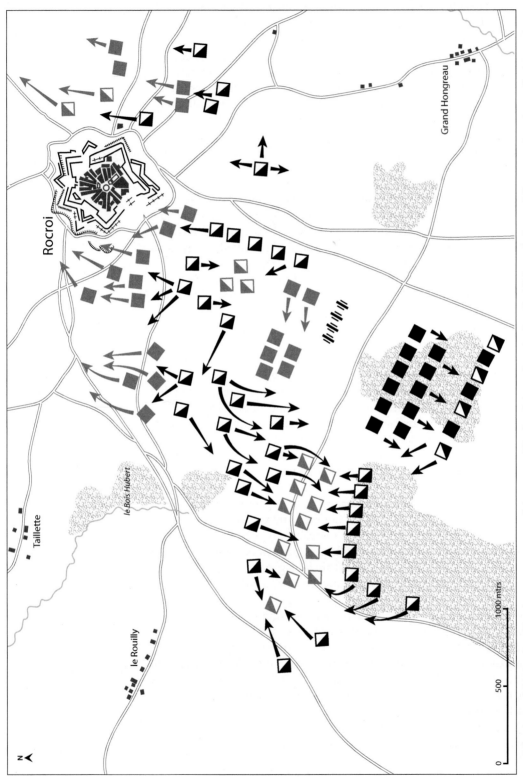

Middle phase of the Battle, 2. The decisive moments of the action. d'Enghien's horse have broken the Walloon, Italian and German units, who are fleeing, and are following up their success by attacking Issembourg's horse. Sirot's reserve joins in the French counter-attack. Inexplicably, the Spanish infantry in the centre has not advanced to consolidate the victory that had seemed imminent just a short time earlier. Small bodies of Spanish horse continue to fight across parts of the field.

centre, Picardie, Piémont, La Marine, Persan and Molondin Suisse, which were withdrawing on La Vallière's orders, seeing the advance of Sirot's troops, halted and joined in the advance. Sirot says that these regiments, 'were very badly beaten but were more than willing to obey the orders of the battle marshal'. This leads to the conclusion that if the tercios had not advanced, these regiments must have been "battered" by the fire of the Spanish musketry, by cannon fire, and/or by the actions of the Alsatian horse, after their having defeated La Ferté's horse.

La Vallière rode to Sirot and ordered him to stop the attack. Whereupon Sirot confronted him and told him that "he did not command his [Sirot's] men and that his order annoyed me very much". Sirot's harsh reprimand made an impression on the officers present and it seemed that they would finally join his attack, but La Vallière stopped them. Thus Sirot could only advance with his own regiments: Harcourt's battalion, the Régiment de Watteville's Suisse, the battalion Royaux plus the Gendarmes, Chârost and Sirot's horse regiments.

Instead, Serres' account says that it was L'Hôpital who ordered Sirot to advance with most of the reserve, and the other units that had been reformed, to support the troops that were still fighting.

Following this autobiographical account, Sirot takes credit for defeating Isenburg's horse and recovering the centre of the battle, as well as recovering the seven guns that the Spanish had captured. All in the face of the passivity of the Spanish tercios, who had received no order to advance: remember that. Melo, who should have given that order was, at the time in a squadron of an Italian tercio, ordering a retreat into the woods.

Sirot claims that after recovering the cannon and reorganising his troops, he was attacked by a "reserve corps" of Spanish horse. We know that there was actually no such reserve, and that this was the various detachments of horse that Isenburg's officers had successfully rallied and reformed. That is, initially the foot and horse of Sirot's reserve charged against Isenburg's scattered horse, and many of these were easy prey, since they were in small groups or too busy plundering the French dead and wounded. But when Isenburg rallied his horse, and with the troops he had mustered stood up to the French, Sirot's troops were hard pushed to advance.

Sirot states that, after "the Spanish horse" initially resisted, he drove them out and "they were finally forced to give in and abandon their foot, consisting of 4,500 Spanish natives in four regiments".

This version of the outcome against the Isenburg horse can be interpreted as complementary to the traditional version of d'Enghien's manoeuvre. The French right wing horse, after getting rid of the Italians, reformed and d'Enghien attacked Isenburg's horse instead of the Spanish foot. Why he did so is difficult to know as is what the various arguments were that swirled through the General's mind to come to this decision.

Perhaps d'Enghien realised that the Spanish tercios were still intact and with only his horse and the supporting foot that had been with them from the beginning of the battle it would not be enough. Perhaps he assessed that the objective of destroying the enemy horse, taking them from behind, was much more feasible and with that success he could attack the Spanish without further complications or interference. Or perhaps he hoped that they would retreat, and he would thus have achieved a tactical and political victory by having thrown back the invaders.

The Battle of Rocroi, Sauveur Le Conte (1659–1694).
The drawing is very precise. In the background, on the top of a plateau, can be seen Rocroi and its bastions and the various camps of the Spanish Army are also easily visible. In the centre the foot of both armies are firing at each other. On the right flank Conte shows the flanking movement of Gassion's horse, while on the left it appears that the Spanish horse is fleeing. On the left flank as well the swamp shows clearly, marking the edge of the battlefield. In somewhat of an artistic licence, the Duc d'Enghien is shown on horseback with his staff. (Musée Condé de Chantilly, Public Domain)

Probably, d'Enghien assumed that he had to destroy Isenburg's horse as a preliminary to gaining complete control of the battlefield. He formed up his horse, amongst which he already counted Gassion's force, which had ensured the complete withdrawal of Alburquerque's horse. The French horse began to manoeuvre to the rear of the Spanish line of battle, avoiding the Spanish baggage train and resisting the temptation to loot it, itself an indication of the high level of discipline of the French horse. They then fell upon the rear of the formations of Isenburg's horse.

French sources claim that d'Enghien's move was effective and he annihilated Isenburg's horse, but Spanish sources claim that there was resistance. The German horse, veterans of years of campaigning against German Protestants and French Catholics, organised themselves with the remnants that they had, supported by a few dozen other horse, mostly officers from Alburquerque's horse.

Lieutenant-General Juan de Vivero observed how two detachments of French foot were advancing to support the attack, and ordered Savary's squadron to charge them. Savary attacked causing a number of French casualties, but without achieving its objective of stopping the foot. Donequel's squadron of horse then prepared to charge, but as Sirot's horse was advancing from the front and d'Enghien's from the rear, the order was rescinded and they settled to resist the French horse.

The Alsatian horse was attacked on all sides, surrounded and massacred. Some managed to break out and flee, others were dismounted and sought refuge in the Spanish tercios still in formation. Isenburg and his escort were surrounded: his groom and his personal trumpeter were wounded and knocked from their horses. Most of his guards were killed and Isenburg received two sword cuts to the head that broke his skull "up to his brains"; another blow cut his nose to his mouth. Nonetheless the veteran General refused to surrender, so a French trooper struck him with the butt of his carbine, breaking his arm and knocking him to the ground. He was then taken prisoner by a trooper of Gassion's regiment.

Now all the horse on the Spanish right flank withdrew, except for some with the battle sergeant-major Jacinto de Vera, who sought the protection of the Spanish tercios, which still remained stationary. It was between 8:00 and 8:30 in the morning.

Sirot reformed his men and launched them against the Spanish tercios, but the attack was unsuccessful, as Sirot himself admits, "with my men alone they were too weak".

He was not discouraged and ordered his men to retreat a few yards and then galloped to the officers of the broken front line regiments and harangued them. He accused them of cowardice but said that, if they returned to the fight, they would win the battle. He convinced them, and as he was rallying them to the attack, the Duc d'Enghien arrived. Sirot informed him of La Vallière's orders, but d'Enghien overruled him [La Vallière] and said that, "he who had said it, had lied".

It was then, according to his version, that d'Enghien with his horse and Sirot with his troops were together able to break the Spanish resistance.

This account of events is probably too simplistic. We have already seen how the Spanish sources report various actions by Isenburg's horse, which although initially scattered, reformed and put up a stiff resistance. And despite Sirot's version, the resistance of the Spanish foot was also very stiff…

All the time that the fighting was going on on both sides of the battle, we have to consider the complete lack of action of the Spanish tercios, as they watch the Walloon, German and Italian soldiers retreat and leave them alone.

Meanwhile, it seems that the veteran Conde de Fontaine was in one of the Spanish tercios, but did not give the order to attack. Perhaps he was still hoping to see the arrival of Beck's soldiers appearing on the plain from the east, and with them to attack the rear of the French horse. We do not know what he was thinking, but we do know what he did – nothing. After so many hours of fighting, Fontaine had given no order for the Spanish tercios to advance – not when Isenburg had defeated La Ferté's horse, not when the French guns had been taken, not when the French foot had been driven back by Spanish artillery fire…

The officers asked Field Master General Fontaine what his orders were. Fontaine, who because of his age and various ailments, had been helped from the saddle by his servants, replied:

> Friends and comrades, my last day is come; I project to die here as
> an honourable gentleman, and without my having had any part in
> this occasion or in this disorder, and so the best thing I can do is to
> die. What you must do is to make your escape, or fight like brave
> men.

Fontaine equipped himself with sword and buckler and placed himself in
the front lines, next to the Count of Villalba, awaiting the French attack.
The officers and soldiers of the tercio, admiring his courage, promised to sell
their lives dearly and die with him if it came to it.

We do not know the exact place and time of Fontaine's death. Vincart
places his death in the first moments of the battle, but without mentioning
any location. This leaves us in doubt as to whether he is referring to the first
moments of the battle or to one of the horse charges by d'Enghien, without
knowing whether he was in the Walloon regiments or in the Spanish tercios.

Aumale points out that Vincart makes Fontaine disappear from the
beginning of the action, and that he does this deliberately to play down the
value of the General's actions. Aumale insists that witnesses to the battle
claim to have seen him fighting with the last tercios. He also records the
tradition that Fontaine was shot by Captain Guimey of the Régiment de
Persan, in the second or third attack of the French columns against the
Spanish tercios, i.e. fighting to the last, as he had himself promised.

After the battle, his body was recovered and his saddle was considered an
important trophy, like the captured colours. Today, the saddle is preserved in
the *Musée de l'Armée* in Paris. Sirot writes that the French troops identified
Fontaine's body and deposited it in the church at Rocroi. Melo requested on
the day of the battle that Fontaine's body be returned. The Duc d'Enghien
ordered the body to be wrapped in a shroud and placed in a coffin. He then
had it transported to Marienbourg in his carriage, "escorted" by all the
captured chaplains, Jesuits and other French and Spanish clergy.

On the other hand, La Moussaye states that, referring to the first attack by
French foot against one of the Spanish tercios:

> The Count of Fontaine firmly awaited them and held his fire until
> the French were fifty paces away. His battalion opened in an instant
> firing from between its rows a volley of eighteen cannons loaded
> with cartridges, followed by a hail of muskets. The fire was so great
> that the French could not withstand it.

In this version, then, the veteran Fontaine was still alive in the last moments
of the battle of the tercios. It is significant that the French honour the
memory of Fontaine, who fell in battle, but do not specify where Melo was.
In this they also agree with the Spanish sources, which also do not say
whether Melo was in that last stand. It is reasonable to consider that, beyond
the question of honour towards the deceased Fontaine, the witnesses to that
event did not lie or were not confused. Fontaine was in a saddle and easily
distinguishable at a distance, so it is almost certain that he could not have
died at the beginning of the fighting.

The question still remains, at what point did Fontaine die? This is another
mystery of the battle – Vincart says that he died in the first moments whereas

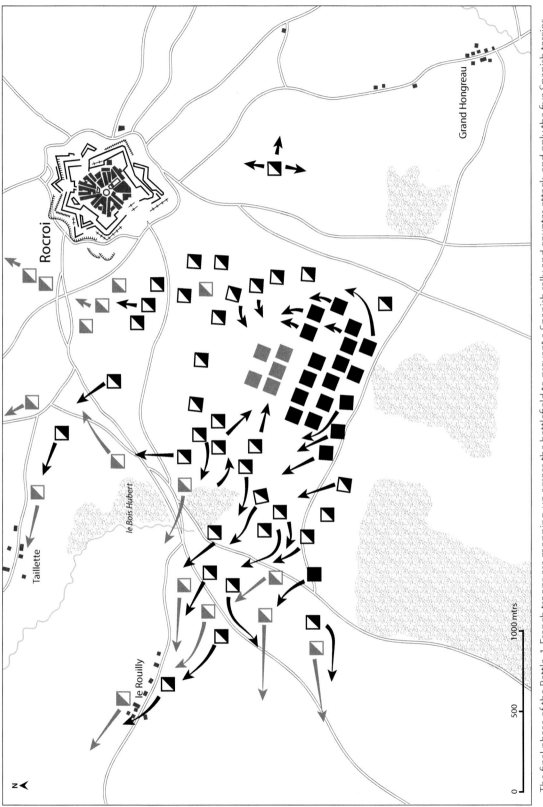

N

Rocroi

Grand Hongreau

le Bois Hubert

Taillette

le Rouilly

0   500   1000 mtrs

The final phase of the Battle, 1. French troops are mopping-up across the battlefield to prevent a Spanish rally and counter-attack, and only the five Spanish tercios remain in order on the field. These five tercios have not withdrawn and, following orders, continue to resist while awaiting the hoped-for arrival of General Beck's army.

123

Flanders historians make him the protagonist of several heroic actions and thus he could not have fallen in the first volleys.

Cánovas tries to find an intermediate explanation between the two postulations. Thus, he states, following the account that, 'Count de Fontaine was killed by a pistol shot in the saddle in which he was being led because of gout, after the battalions around him had been broken up'. This would imply that he did not die in the battle between the Walloon and German tercios but later, perhaps when Fontaine and his entourage were moving towards the Italian or Spanish tercios that were still standing, and he was intercepted by a detachment of French horse and killed there. Cánovas himself accepts that his explanation is intended to be conciliatory, but that it could also be that Fontaine died in combat within one of the Walloon tercios. He insists that his explanation of Fontaine's death is highlighted by the fact that his disappearance in combat deprived the Spanish and Italian tercios of their commanding General to give them the order to advance when the battle was not yet lost. But then, as Cánovas states, it is even stranger that Melo did not give the order to advance, since throughout Vincart's account he suggests that Melo moved along the lines on successive occasions. This account certainly glorifies the defeated General, highlighting his courage, but it also leaves open the possibility that if he was always "so busy", then it is why he did not give the order to attack.

Whether Fontaine had been killed at the beginning of the fighting or at the end of it, still begs the question why *he* did not give the order for the Spanish foot to advance? Why had so many opportunities to attack been lost? Now, when only the five tercios of Spanish foot were left in position, no order was given either. If Fontaine was dead, why did no Spanish field master act on his own initiative and attack the French?

Because discipline in the Spanish tercios was part of their creed, and while they might be mutinous over the payment of their wages at times, they would never mutiny or disobey an order on the battlefield.

All this brings us back to the initial hypothesis about the deployment of the Spanish Army for the battle. Melo and Fontaine had deployed the army with the intention of buying time until Beck's army arrived, therefore, if Fontaine had died at the beginning of the battle, and Melo was somewhere in the front line, the field masters of the five tercios did not advance, following their orders to hold back and stand their ground until Beck's arrival.

There is no single description of the resistance of the Spanish tercios and the end of the battle. The Spanish accounts are confusing and the French accounts try to emphasise the role of d'Enghien and his leading officers, without identifying which Spanish units were resisting. Nonetheless we must assume that between 8.30 and 10:00 in the morning the numerous fighting between the French and the Spanish of the tercios took place.

La Moussaye says that the morale of the Spanish was high, 'their countenance and order indicated that they were prepared to fight to the bitter end'. The Spanish accounts state that the French launched three charges of mixed horse and foot against the five squares of Spanish foot. This was a mistake by d'Enghien, which could have ended in disaster. Having destroyed all of the Spanish horse and the Walloon, Italian and German tercios, he must have felt that victory was at hand, and that he could wipe out the Spanish tercios just as he had done with those of the other nationalities. It was a foolish mistake.

The Spanish held their ground when the French horse and foot charged. The Conde de Fontaine reportedly ordered his men to open fire when the French were about 50 paces away, and his shot fired successive volleys at the enemy advancing against them, then withdrawing to reload and returning to fire again. The pikemen were in position, waiting to engage if the enemy broke through the constant line of fire that the Spanish shot presented. If the Spanish had had horse to advance, the French would not have been able to recover and reorganise.

Moreover, the Spanish still had all their artillery, and they employed them with great expertise. The gunners positioned their guns and loaded with grapeshot. The front ranks of the foot squadrons opened up and the 18 guns spat out their deadly charge of bags of musket balls, firing point-blank at the charging French, causing great havoc.

Three times the French launched the attack, and each time they were thrown back with heavy casualties. The Spanish resisted; to retain their honour, to save their lives, and in the hope that at any moment Beck would appear with his army and save them. The Spanish hopes were not entirely unfounded, for at that moment Beck and his army were close. The Spanish accounts place him at the outskirts of a forest near Rocroi.

Beck, however, had encountered the fugitives from Melo's army, and who had warned him that the battle was lost and that they must save themselves. Beck, afraid that in a few moments the French army would gallop out of the trees and surprise him, ordered his troops to form a covering screen, deploying to meet any threat, and ordered the fugitives to regroup around his colours and drums.

Returning to the narrative thread of the battle... the French, on d'Enghien's orders, had launched three unsuccessful assaults, with Gassion and d'Enhgien's horse and units from L'Hôpital's force, or Sirot's force according to his memoirs.

It was at this point that Sirot brought the French artillery pieces that they had recaptured to the front line: the fate of the Spanish was sealed as the entire French army was ready to crush the tercios.

And so it was. d'Enghien ordered combined horse and foot charges. The tercios on the flank took up defensive positions on three sides, while the other three tercios took up defensive positions to the front and rear.

The French again launched an assault, but were repulsed. However, after a number of successive attempts, they managed to disrupt the tercios. The first to fall were those on the left flank of the Spanish foot, more vulnerable as they were in the open, successively assaulted by d'Enghien's and Gassion's horse, Sirot's reserve, the French guns, and the foot of the French first line. The Spanish, having their squadron formation broken, ran for cover in the squadron immediately to their right, which was momentarily reinforced. But, again, the combined action of the French foot and horse meant that one after another in succession, the tercios were broken, and fewer and fewer Spanish foot joined into the defence of the adjoining tercio.

Traditionally it is said that the first tercios to be defeated were those of Jorge de Castellví and Antonio de Velandia, as they were located on the left side of the deployment, and they were also the least numerous. Velandia was killed, along with a number of his captains. Velandia's tercio, once its field master and most of its officers were dead or wounded along with most of its

ROCROY.

The Battle of Rocroi. Engraving by François Collignon (c.1610–87).
The image of the battle is rather confusing: in the foreground are French soldiers escorting various supply wagons, looking towards the battle, which seems to be in its final stage: in the centre are the Spanish tercios resisting and being attacked from all sides. We see the flanking movement of Gassion, while in the background we can see how many soldiers of the Spanish Army are fleeing. The painter in a single painting has tried to capture the different phases of the battle. (Rijksmuseum, Amsterdam. Public Domain)

musketeers and arquebusiers, retreated to its right, seeking the protection of the next tercio, probably that of Villalba. The pikemen of Velandia's tercio formed a wall on all sides and repulsed the charges of the French horse. When the French horse withdrew to reorganise, the survivors of the tercio moved slowly back to their comrades in the next tercio along. La Moussaye stresses the courage of this whole action.

In one of these moments of the fighting against Velandia's tercio a curious event occurred. Mortally wounded, the Count of Villalba sent an aide to Melo's headquarters asking for the rites of confession before dying. In response, Melo sent his senior chaplain, Carlo Landriano, who on approaching the foot squadron was attacked by a party of Croats. He tried to take refuge among the Spanish, but found himself in the crossfire between the Spanish and the Croats and was wounded by five bullets. Landriano was taken prisoner and taken to the Croat camp, but when he learned that he was there d'Enghien personally interceded and ordered his release.

At one of those moments, Melo and his headquarters were in danger from the attack by the French, and had to enter the tercio of the sergeant-major Juan Pérez de Peralta. However, so as not to break the formation of the squadron – which, let us remember, was designed for a specific number of pikemen – only Melo and his horseman were allowed to pass into the formation with him, leaving the rest of the escort outside, under the protection of the musketeers and the pikes.

Some accounts indicate that the Spanish were grouped into a single squadron, while others claim that there were two cadres. After the death of the field masters Velandia and Villalba, the remnants of their tercios and the soldiers of the tercios of Garcíez and Castellví were grouped together. Aumale says that they formed an "extended rectangle", implying that they were grouped into a single squadron. By contrast, Cánovas wrote that they probably formed in two squadrons, relatively close together, with an interior space – their empty parade ground.

According to Dávila Orejón, a company captain in the tercio of Castellví and a survivor of the battle, the remnants of that tercio and the survivors of the tercio of Garcíez took refuge in the tercio de Alburquerque, and in the other squadron formed by the remnants of the tercios Villalba and Velandia. In various Spanish treatises on the *Arte de Escuadronear* (Art of Squadrons), this formation appears in which all the sides face outwards and allows all-round defence. The usual formations were square squadrons of "terrain" or "people", with an open space inside.

Aumale describes how these last tercios had been joined by the survivors of other units that had been defeated; Burgundians, Italians, officers without men, dismounted horse and wounded soldiers.

d'Enghien ordered an assault. Dozens of musketeers advanced to provide protection. The battalions of Picardy and La Marine on the right, the Royaux, Scots and Swiss in the centre, Piémont and Rambures on the left. d'Enghien with his guards and some detachments of horse, was behind them ready to attack the first breach in the Spanish lines. When the French were close, the Spanish line opened up and fired a point-blank barrage of 18 guns, which shattered the French, then closed up again. La Moussaye wrote that, at that moment if the Spanish had still had their horse, they could have charged the surviving French and won the battle. d'Enghien received a scratch on his thigh, and his breastplate was hit twice, evidence that it was indeed bulletproof.

Maréchal L'Hôpital is the most important figure in the *Verdadere Histoire* after d'Enghien, and takes credit for the victory, recounting that at the end of the battle only two tercios, each of about 1,400 men, were still standing. L'Hôpital attacked one of them, at the head of a battalion of Molondin Suisse, the Régiment de Piémont, and 200 men he had just assembled from the remnants of the Gendarmes and Sully's regiment. The attack was firstly at the front, then from the right and then from the left – the source is not clear enough to clarify whether these were three coordinated attacks or whether it was an initial attack, followed by a withdrawal, then another attack, et cetera. After these three attacks, the *Maréchal* assembled the Régiment de Watteville, the *Compagnies Royaux*, plus some 300 horse, to attack the other Spanish battalion. However as L'Hôpital passed the Spanish, they fired a volley of musketry and he was wounded in his right wrist. He reached the other contingent and gave the order to attack the battalion that had just fired on him. According to this account, it was Sirot who then assumed command for this attack.

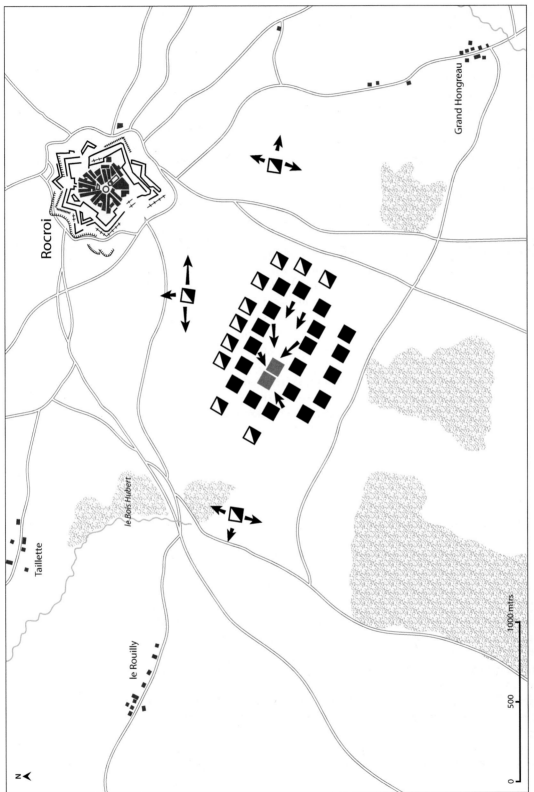

The final phase of the Battle, 2. The combined attacks of the French horse and foot have destroyed the resistance of the Spanish tercios, whose survivors have reformed into two bodies and are still awaiting the arrival of Beck's reinforcements. It is at this point that the Duc d' Enghien offers them an honourable surrender.

Sirot wrote that the final victorious assault was thanks to him, 'I charged them so vigorously that, unable to resist the advance of my troops, they were broken and defeated, leaving two thousand dead along with as many taken prisoner.'

The Spanish accounts say that the French launched five separate attacks against them, all of which were repulsed with heavy losses for the attackers. However, after the intensity of the fighting, the Spanish had exhausted their ammunition. Gualdo Priorato states that the last two volleys were made with only powder, because the supply of bullets was exhausted, and they could only defend themselves with their pikes. This situation was unsustainable and the officers of the last two squadrons, that of the Comte de Garcíez and the one commanded by the sergeant-major Peralta, offered to surrender. The last phase of the battle had come to an end. It was between 9 and 10 and the French had annihilated the Spanish tercios one by one.

According to Vincart, shortly before the surrender of the Spanish tercios, Melo left the tercio of Peralta and fled with his escort to avoid the dishonour of the Governor-General of Flanders falling into enemy hands. The French sources, however, have him leaving the battlefield long before the final attack on the Spanish foot. Some accounts even state that Melo threw his General's baton to the ground to avoid being recognised; something that is inconceivable from the point of view of Spanish honour. An anonymous Spanish account, which has been identified as being written by a soldier who was present, also records rumours that Melo tried to flee in disguise but almost at the start of the battle. The account goes on to state that, a gentleman in his [Melo's] entourage made him realise the error of his ways and Melo was touring the squadrons during the battle, but upon seeing the Italians retreating, he finally fled.

According to Vincart's account, the offer of a truce came from the Duc d'Enghien, advised by Gassion and La Ferté-Seneterre, who warned him of the stiff resistance offered by all the Spanish tercios and especially the two that were still holding out, which seemed like invincible walls. Thus the Duc agreed to propose that they surrender. Garcíez's squadron saw a French Herald approaching, and he urged the Spanish to surrender, with a promise that their lives would be spared. Otherwise he would have his guns loaded with grapeshot and kill them all. The Duc said he would be sorry to have to kill "such good and brave soldiers".

La Moussaye recounts that the Spanish waved their hats to accept the surrender proposal, but when d'Enghien approached to accept the surrender, he was shot and almost killed. Bessé offers the explanation that the Spanish thought that the Prince was about to launch a new attack, so they shot at him. This action was the justification for ordering the French to attack from all sides and massacre the Spanish, leaving none alive. According to the version of La Moussaye, d'Enghien approached his troops with an appeal for clemency and many Spanish officers swarmed to the French General's side for him to protect them,

> His [Enghien's] troops, enraged at the sight of what had happened to their General, attributing it to the bad faith of the Spanish, charged them on all sides without waiting for the order, and avenged by dreadful carnage the danger he had run. The French entered sword

Spanish infantry, early 1640s. Attributed to Nicolaas van Eyck (II), 1645.
A good contemporary view of Spanish foot in action, although it is unlikely van Eyck actually witnessed battle personally. Note the Cross of Burgundy (red on a white field in this example) which typifies Spanish Colours throughout the Century and, indeed, thereafter as well. It is also worth noting that van Eyck depicts the musketeers both with and without rests. At extreme left is a Company Officer in back and breast, although without a helmet, with a very 'bunched up' red scarf around his waist and carrying a half-pike. (Rijksmuseum, Amsterdam. Public Domain)

in hand up to the centre of the Spanish battalion, and in spite of the efforts made by the Duc d'Enghien to restrain their fury, the soldiers gave no quarter, especially the Swiss, who went beyond the French in killing. The Prince went everywhere shouting at them to give quarter. The Spanish officers and also the simple soldiers took refuge around him. Don Jorge de Castellví, field master, was taken prisoner by his own hand. All those who managed to escape the fury of the soldiers hastened on their knees to beg for their lives and gazed at him [d'Enghien] with admiration.

However, this idealised view does not coincide at all with the various Spanish versions, which at least all agree that no unit suffered such a massacre, and neither did the Spanish officers ask for help from the Duc d'Enghien.

After a brief negotiation, the Spanish accepted on the condition that the retained their arms and colours and were repatriated to Fuenterrabía. Terms d'Enghien hastened to grant, although most sources state that it was d'Enghien who offered these generous conditions. The actual capitulation was made by Jorge de Castellví, as the most senior surviving field master. This capitulation is certainly very curious, since not only did the "vanquished" dictate the conditions of surrender, and these were accepted by the supposed "victors", but also these terms were those for the surrender of a fortress: to keep their arms and colours.

Juan Luís Sánchez's studies[4] shows that many of the captains, non-commissioned officers and soldiers of the Garcíez tercio appear in the general muster of the Army of Flanders in November 1643.

At his side, the *escuadron* of the Alburquerque's tercio, commanded by the sergeant-major Juan Pérez de Peralta, refused to surrender. This threatened to complicate Enghien's victory, as it could perhaps prolong the battle until the arrival of Beck's contingent. Sirot was forceful in breaking the resistance: he had managed to get two of the guns from the centre of the deployment that the Spanish had disabled, working again, and he placed them in front of the tercio. They were loaded with grapeshot and were fired into the Spanish foot, causing great gaps in their lines. Now, having little choice, they were forced to surrender.

On this occasion d'Enghien, although these troops had held out longer, was not so generous with his terms. He offered only the guarantee of their lives and possessions, but not that they could retain their arms and their colours. The reason why he was less magnanimous on this occasion is twofold. Firstly, this tercio had not surrendered earlier on more favourable conditions but had continued to fight; and now, although d'Enghien was in a hurry to conclude the battle and was still afraid of Beck's arrival, he could be less generous, since he could crush the last defenders with the whole army if necessary. Nevertheless, d'Enghien wanted to be magnanimous and offered to respect the lives of the Spanish soldiery.

According to Dávila, the field masters Count of Garcíez and Jorge de Castellví passed from their newly surrendered tercios to the last defensive stand of Alburquerque's tercio, but only to meet the same fate. When d'Enghien offered surrender, after discussion with the field masters, Sergeant-Major Peralta and surviving officers agreed to a capitulation. Don Jorge de Castellví, as the most senior field master still alive, officially surrendered on behalf of the tercio.

Other French sources indicate that in order to break the resistance of the last tercio, which was putting up such a fierce resistance, the French massed horse and foot and had to attack simultaneously on their right flank and in the rear. But it was Gassion's horse, attacking from the flank, that finally broke through the tercio's defences. The French horse however, had to fire five or six times at close range to break through the Spanish line.

French sources do not indicate that there were two separate surrenders; they describe the "supposed" massacre of the Spanish survivors by the enraged French and that many Spanish ran to the Duc d'Enghien for help. The Duc was moved to insist that his troops give quarter to the Spanish, and the French officers relayed and repeated the order until they succeeded in stopping the massacre. The field master Castellví was reportedly captured by d'Enghien himself. It should not perhaps be interpreted literally in that d'Enghien captured the field master after a personal combat. It probably

---

4   Juan Luís Sánchez Martín, 'Rocroi, el Triunfo de la Propaganda', *Researching & Dragona*, *3* (1993). Juan Luís Sánchez Martín, 'Rocroi, el Triunfo de la Propaganda', *Researching & Dragona*, *16* (2002).

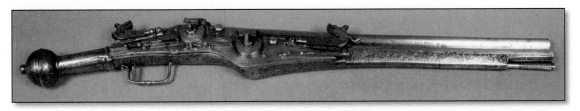

Cavalry pistol, with two wheelocks, German and dating from the early seventeenth century. The pistol is made entirely of iron with front and rear facing wheelocks that have a single common trigger. The upper barrel is round with an octagonal chamber piece 18.8cm long. The lower barrel is completely round. The body is made of iron and is entirely covered with engraving. The pistol measures: length 704mm; calibre 14.5mm; length 486mm; weight 2880 g. (Armémuseum, Stockholm. AM.041980)

means no more than that the field master personally offered the surrender, and this was accepted by the Duc. Castellví was then imprisoned, as indicated by Spanish sources.

d'Enghien ordered his troops to collect together and escort the Spanish prisoners, but Gassion informed him that Beck was on the other side of the forest. However these were merely detachments that he had sent to assist the fugitives from Melo's army in their escape. Beck and his troops had arrived about five miles from Rocroi, around 8 o'clock, when they had contacted the first fugitives, probably from Alburquerque's horse. These had told him that the battle had begun five hours earlier and that the French had been victorious. Cautiously, Beck continued to advance until he reached the outskirts of the woods, then ordered a halt. Faced with an influx of fugitives, he simply gave them shelter, but did not enquire whether the fighting was still going on. In fact at this time the fighting was still undecided and the surviving Spanish squadrons were still holding out. Beck simply organised patrols to find and reorganise the survivors – Melo himself, the Walloons, the Italian and German units…

In the course of these events Isenburg was able to escape from captivity. He was being escorted by some French horse when they came close to a small group of Spanish soldiers, whether they were Beck's scouts or survivors of the battle we do not know, these men recognised Isenburg and went to free him. The leader of the Spanish force was about to kill the soldier holding Isenburg, when Isenburg interceded for his life, claiming that the Frenchman had previously spared his life and had been considerate to him. Isenburg, badly wounded as he was, remained on horseback for nearly 40 kilometres until he reached Charlemont, where he remained and eventually recovered.

We do not know why Beck arrived late for the battle, despite repeated messages from Melo throughout 19 May. Vincart tells us that the first message had been sent around noon on 18 May. The linear distance between Rocroi and Château-Regnault is 20 kilometres.

Did Beck not receive the messages? Did he receive them too late? How long did it take to abandon the siege of that city? Was his march too slow, because of his own mistakes or because of indolence? When did Beck start the march? In the middle of the afternoon between 5 and or 6? Or later in the evening? Did he decide to risk a night march, or did he prefer to start in the early hours of the morning of 19 May?

We have no record of rain at that time in May, but the roads were almost certainly not suitable for the movement of several thousand soldiers.

Commemorative stone on the battlefield. Until this monument was unveiled on Sunday 6 August 1922 there was no marker on the battlefield. The small stone stands on the border between the territories of Rocroi and Sévigny-la-Forêt, on the Rouge-Fontaine road, about 400 metres to the right of the "priest's road", the local road from Rocroi to Sévigny, so-called because it was begun by a priest from Rocroi, during the First (the Napoleonic) Empire. The land on which the stone is erected was donated by Mr Louis Manceaux-Maquart, from Croix-de-Fer, and the location was chosen because, according to local historians, it was the place where the Spanish officers offered their surrender. The monument, made of French Devonian stone, is 1.5 m high, and on the front is the inscription: Victoire du Duc d'Enghien sur les Espagnols. Among the dignitaries who unveiled the monument were: Monsignor Ernest Nevus, Bishop of Arsine; as a representatives of the Duc d'Enghien's family, Prince Site de Bourbon and Count of Villermont; as a representative of the former Governor of Rocroi Noël de Champagne, Monsieur Baré, notary of Rocroi; General Garbit, commander of 4th Infantry Division in Laon, and Monsieur Edmond Petit fils, Deputy of the Province of Ardennes. (Author's photograph)

Additionally, neither Melo's messengers nor Beck's army knew the country: they would not know the roads of the region, and the locals were not predisposed to collaborate – quite the contrary. The rest of the questions posed sadly remain unanswered.

d'Enghien still feared that the Spanish might try to enter the battle again, so, while his regiments were being reorganised and prisoners sent off the battlefield, he ordered *Monsieur* Chevers, *Maréchal des Logis de la Cavalerie*, to scout the road with a detachment of 200 horse. Chevers returned with the information that Beck and the remnants of the Spanish Army were retreating towards Marienbourg, he also brought back two cannon abandoned at the entrance to the forest.

The battlefield secured, the Duc d'Enghien made a triumphal entry into Rocroi, to the sound of bells and amidst the cheers of his men and the inhabitants of the town. In the town the municipal authorities were waiting for him, including Governor Geoffreville and Commander Pierre Noël, who offered him the keys of the town, and d'Enghien in return congratulated the defenders. He spent two days in the town, writing letters about the battle and explaining the day's events.

8

The Results of the Battle

Spanish losses were considerable. However, it is difficult to know even the approximate number; as in any battle, the figures vary depending on who is writing them down. French authors, to make their victory more important, claim that more than 5,000 Spanish died. They claim that the total number of casualties – dead, wounded and prisoners – amounted to more than 15,000: an unmitigated defeat for Spain, an unquestioned success for France. However, it is difficult to know the number and details of the casualties. Various Spanish and French historians have speculated on the numbers. Here are the ones I consider the most reasonable.

The Spanish losses were high: the Army of Flanders had around 7,300 casualties, of whom 3,826 were prisoners. The exact figure and a detailed breakdown from the rank of sergeant up to that of the senior officers is known; of these prisoners about 2,000 were wounded. The dead and wounded were around 4,000, of which, the Spanish tercios suffered around 1,000 dead and 1,500 to 2,000 wounded. The casualties in the units of the other nationalities – Italians, Germans and Walloons – are not known exactly. The French claimed that the Spanish Army lost 8,000 dead. Guthrie gives 3,400 dead and 2,000 prisoners, from the Spanish units alone, and claims that 1,600 Spanish were able to escape. Gualdo Priorato, writing from information given to him by one of the Italian officers who fought in the battle, says that some 4,000 Spanish soldiers died, most of them veteran foot. Aumale completely accepts the exorbitant figures for the Spanish casualties: 7,000–8,000 dead and 6,000–7,000 prisoners, almost all wounded.

The "high-ranking" dead, wounded, and prisoners were indeed numerous: the Italian *Maestres de Campo* Visconti, Orsini, and delli Ponti, and the Barón Hembise. As for the prisoners these included, Rittberg, who was seriously wounded, Baltasar Mercader, lieutenant of *Maestre de Campo General*; Diego de Estrada, Lieutenant-General of the Artillery, the Conde de Beaumont, the Conde de Roeux, the Barón de Saventhem, the Conde de Montecuccoli, Francisco de La Cueva and Manuel de León. However, there was no annihilation or massacre of the tercios; in his research in the French and Spanish archives, José Luís Sánchez Martín states that, of the 95 documented Spanish captains of foot present at the battle of Rocroi, only four were listed as killed.

Generally, French sources indicate that the Army of Flanders had between 6,000 and 8,000 dead, with around 6,000 to 7,000 prisoners. In respect of the wounded, the most serious would be finished off on the battlefield. It should be remembered that while the French and Dutch generally gave mercy to the Nationalities in the Spanish Army, they did not give quarter to the native Spanish. They were well aware of the difficulty that Spain had to replace losses of Spanish troops; but the less seriously wounded were taken with the unwounded to their places of imprisonment, although given the lack of health care, many ended up dying. With regard to the officers, the French sources claim that all the officers were "taken prisoner or killed", detailing that 200 to 500 officers and 200 to 600 NCO *reformados* were captured.

The prisoners were grouped first by nationality, and then divided into officers, NCOs and 'rank and file'. The groups of prisoners went first to the main cities of Champagne (Reims and Rethel), then later, following a policy of dispersion to limit escape attempts, they were distributed throughout France (Rouen, Caen, Alençon, Le Mans, Amboise, Loches, Nantes, Niort, Nevers, Moulins and Clermont). The burden of feeding the prisoners fell on the municipalities, who demanded compensation – this was always promised but rarely arrived. The Spanish prisoners did not collaborate or cooperate and it was common for them to create altercations and to escape.

Despite the bitterness of the conflict between Spain and France, prisoner exchanges were agreed between them, as Spain had done in previous decades with the Dutch and the English. These prisoner exchanges began sporadically and gradually became general, creating an exchange system based on the military rank of the prisoners. One of the problems was to agree a standardisation of the various ranks, because they were not the same in the two armies. This would happen in the negotiations after the Spanish defeat of Rocroi.

While they were imprisoned, the Governor of Flanders sent money to the cities to co-sponsor the maintenance of the prisoners. Baltasar Mercader was in charge of paying for the food for months.

Of the 3,895 prisoners, including 578 officers; it is traditionally claimed that some 2,000 of them were handed over at Fuenterrabía at the end of July 1643. However, research by Palau and Mirecki suggests that there were not that many, nor were they soldiers captured at Rocroi, but rather from the operations in Roussillon and Catalonia. Mazarin delayed the exchange of the Rocroi prisoners as long as possible, and when the French were defeated at Tuttlingen on 24 November 1643, he gave priority to exchanging French prisoners with the Bavarians, Imperials and Lorrainers. It was not until the defeat of Lérida on 15 May 1644, in which the Spanish took 4,000 French prisoners, that Mazarin accelerated the exchange of Spanish prisoners. In 1646, France still had 1,500 prisoners from Rocroi, and it seems that even in 1661, according to Palau and Mirecki[1], there were still 120 Spanish officers and non-commissioned officers in the little village of Pont-de-l'Arche.

As for materiel, 18 field guns and 6 siege pieces, 60 standards, 170 colours, 14 trumpets, and all of the baggage were lost in the battle. The General paymaster of the Army of Flanders estimated that they had lost 40,688 *escudos* in the chests hidden in the baggage, more than a month's salary for the entire army.

---

1   José Palau Cuñat & José Luís de Mirecki Quintero, *Rocroy. Cuando la Honra Española se Pagaba con Sangre.* (Madrid, Actas, 2016).

French horse and foot at the Battle of Kempen. Engraver unknown, 1642. The battle was fought on 17 January 1642 and was a victory by a French Army commanded by the Comte de Guébriant over the Imperial Army of General Lamboy. (Rijksmuseum, Amsterdam. Public Domain)

With all these important losses, for Marc Blancpain,

'the proud preponderance of Spain in Europe had found its grave at the end of a slow agony of death: and that morning in Rocroi had marked, at the same time , the victorious culmination of the efforts pursued, also for half a century, by the young Bourbon dynasty'.[2]

But Spain did not lose its hegemony in Rocroi nor were the tercios annihilated, although they did suffer significant casualties, especially Castellví's Tercio, which suffered the most casualties, both in officers and soldiers.

The Rocroi myth has also served to generate both a heroic and a defeatist mysticism among the Spanish units. Thus, the Tercio commanded by the Conde de Villalba had so many casualties that henceforward it was known as *El Sangriento* ('The Blood Tercio'). This name is still retained by its descendant unit, Regiment No. 9, officially called "Soria". However, the nickname appeared for the first time after the battle of Les Avins (20 May 1635), when all 15 company captains were casualties: 8 died and the other 7 were taken prisoner.

Equally famous is the legend that when a French officer wanted to know the number of enemy troops present at the battle, a haughty Spanish officer simply replied, "Count the dead". Spanish researcher José Luís Sánchez

---

2   Marc Blancpain, *Le Mardi de Rocroi*. (Vanves, Éditions Hachette, 1985).

"The Cornets, Guidons and Colours taken from the enemy in the battle of Rocroi brought in to Notre Dame by the Cent Suisse", by Nicolas Cochin (c.1643). This engraving shows the triumphal entry into the Cathedral of Notre Dame in Paris of the standards and colours taken from the Spanish at the Battle of Rocroi. Research has made it possible to identify some of the colours to Spanish tercios that fought in the battle: Albuquerque's Spanish tercio, the Italian tercios of Strozzi, Visconti and Jorge de Castellví, and Frangipani's German regiment. Some standards and colours and objects from the battle were deposited in the Château de Chantilly, in the Galerie des Batailles, commonly called "Les Trophées de Rocroy". (Rijksmuseum, RP-P-OB-81.524)

Martín, ascertained that the phrase was taken from *Mercurio Overo Historia de' Correnti Tempi*.[3] In this book, after narrating the combat of Avigliana on 10 July 1630, Siri explains a conversation, probably apocryphal, between the Duc de Montmorency and Martín of Aragon, *Maestre de Campo* of the Tercio of Lombardy. Siri indicates that Aragon was a prisoner, but the Spanish accounts state that he was not present at the battle. Siri says that when the Duc questioned the Spaniard about the number of the defeated, the *Maestre de Campo* supposedly replied, "The soldiers of my Nation do not know what it is to retreat. You need do no more than count the dead or prisoners". Later, when describing the battle of Rocroi, French sources rescued this phrase and used it in their version of the day's events, acknowledging the courage of the Spanish while magnifying their defeat and d'Enghien's success.

The French had 4,000 casualties, half of them dead, highlighted by the death of the Compte de Noailles. Some French sources minimise these losses, claiming that they were few. In a letter, Melo stated that the French had 2,000 dead and 1,500 wounded, and that they had suffered more dead than the Spanish. The Duque de Alburquerque stated that the French victory had cost them dearly in blood, 'out of every 10 dead, 6 were French'.

Perhaps it may be said that these claims have no credibility because they are from the Spanish and they were defeated, but it should be remembered that the Alburquerque's account is very objective and critical in narrating the general facts, and is only subjective when it extols his own merits. The truth of Alburquerque's claim is perhaps confirmed by the fact that d'Enghien had to rest his army for several weeks before returning to the attack, and that his subsequent actions were very limited. Aumale lists the principal French casualties: the field marshals Ayen, Altenove and d'Arcambal, 18 captains and almost all the Guards of the Duc d'Enghien. Among the wounded were

---

3   Vittorio Siri, *Mercurio Overo Historia de' Correnti Tempi*, Venice 1642.

L'Hôpital, La Ferté-Seneterre, the *Mestres de Camp* Beauvau, Persan and La Trousse, and captains François de Barthou, Vicomte de Montbas, of Cardinal Richelieu's regiment, and Pédamont, Captain-Sergeant-Major of the Régiment de Picardy.

With the victory in hand, d'Enghien took the opportunity to announce the death of Louis XIII to the army, after which he and his men fell to their knees to sing the *Te Deum* to thank God for the victory. The captured Spanish standards and colours were immediately sent to Paris to be presented to the King.

On June 28, Monsieur de Chevers, leading an escort of 100 Swiss Guards, presented the trophies captured in battle to Louis XIV and his mother, the Regent Anne of Austria. Later these trophies were transferred from the Palace of the Louvre to be laid up in Notre Dame Cathedral.

9

Repercussions

The high number of casualties in the ranks of the Army of Flanders, especially of the Spanish veterans, was a severe blow to the military and political strategy of the Spanish Monarchy. After an exhaustive analysis of subsequent events, though, it was perhaps not as decisive as has traditionally been believed, nor can it be considered, *per se*, as the beginning of the decline of the military model of the tercios or of the Spanish Monarchy itself.

Thus, at the political-military level, Spain was able to continue fighting on all active fronts (Flanders, Italy and in the Iberian Peninsula itself), with numbers of both victories and defeats in future years.

As for the specific theatre of operations in Flanders, General Melo escaped with a good part of his horse, but with only about 3,000 foot. In a letter written by a secretary of Melo, it was stated that the troops under Beck and the Count of Fuensaldaña numbered about 10,000, who had not entered the battle. With the survivors of the battle and the garrison troops in Flanders, around 9,000 men could be gathered to fight, so the disaster of the battle was not as bad as might have been thought. The secretary lamented the loss of many experienced commanders and officers, which he considered "irreparable". The death of Fontaine was particularly deeply felt, although he was blamed for the defeat, he was honoured by his heroic end. Also lamented was the loss of the *Maestres de Campo* Velandia and Villalba, as well as the capture of the Conde de Garcíez, the lieutenant of *Maestre de Campo General* Baltasar Mercader, Colonel Count Rittberg, Count Montecucolli, and many others.

With the survivors and prisoners freed from Rocroi, as well as the new levies recruited urgently over the following weeks, Melo was able to rebuild an important part of his field army. In fact, Melo asked the King for permission to recruit only 2,000 soldiers, proof that, after recovering those released, the Spanish army had not suffered an exaggerated imbalance in its offensive capacity. The musters of the Army of Flanders actually show an increase in the strength of the army between 7 November 1643 and 1 July 1644.

Another testimony to the relatively small impact of the defeat is that, according to the musters lists, most of the Spanish captains of foot who fought at Rocroi were already back in Flanders before the autumn of 1643, and almost all of them were rewarded with command of a company of horse.

Further proof that the defeat of Rocroi did not cause a cataclysm for the defence of Flanders was that Felipe IV did not send the 2,000 Spanish committed in June 1643 to Flanders, but instead sent them to the Army of Aragon, to fight in Catalonia. In December 1643, a fleet of four ships with the regiment of horse of Carlos de Padilla, who had fought in the battle of Rocroi, set sail from the port of Dunkirk bound for Spain. Thus the "defeated and annihilated" Army of Flanders was actually able to spare some of its troops to reinforce the front in Spain.

On the French side, d'Enghien's victory was not as decisive as is believed either. With 4,000 casualties, the French troops were so battered that they were unable to take advantage of the victory. According to the Duque de Albuquerque, 5,000 men were missing from the muster taken by Condé of his army on 15 June. Aware of his heavy losses and that Beck had rallied the survivors of Rocroi alongside his own troops from Luxembourg, d'Enghien ordered the withdrawal towards Guise, leaving the Regiment of Aubeterre guarding Rocroi. He spent two weeks regrouping his forces and resting them, given the heavy casualties at Rocroi. Meanwhile, he sent the inexhaustible Gassion, at the head of 1,500 horse, to ride the roads to Brussels and sow terror in the Spanish regions of Flanders.

d'Enghien had in mind to advance towards Brussels, but feared that the Spanish would ask the Imperial Armies for help. If Emperor Ferdinand III sent troops from the Rhine, these troops could reach Luxembourg after passing the stronghold of Thionville. The direct consequence of the battle of Rocroi was that the French were able to advance and open the siege of Thionville on 16 June. Thionville held out for almost two months, despite having a small garrison, surrendering on 10 August after having cost the French more than 3,000 casualties. d'Enghien could not undertake the invasion of the Spanish Flanders, nor could France reinforce the Catalan rebels or invade Franche-Comté. In September, d'Enghien was forced to send 4,000 foot and 1,300 horse, under Lieutenant-General Josias de Rantzau, to reinforce the Army of the Rhine, under *Maréchal* Guébriant.

Meanwhile, the Spanish Army quickly rallied and went on the offensive, and the Conde de Fuensaldaña entered the Boulonnais forcing the Duc d'Angoulême to withdraw. The Dutch tried to take advantage of Rocroi's defeat and attacked northern Flanders, only to be repulsed by Andrea Cantelmo's army.

However, the main effect of the battle of Rocroi was the success of French propaganda in fabricating a "great" defeat of the Spanish tercios; and, in fact, this version of events has been maintained ever since. The date of the battle of Rocroi is considered to be the beginning of the definitive decline of the dominance of the tercios, and of Spain, to the benefit of France. The account of the battle written by François Goyon, Marquis de La Moussaye, became the official version of the battle and the starting point for later studies, and also for the creation of the Rocroi myth of d'Enghien's military genius and the superiority of French armies.

But La Moussaye's account contains important inaccuracies compared to other sources (both Spanish – Melo, Alburquerque, Vincart, and pro-French – Galeazzo Gualdo Priorato and Sirot). La Moussaye exaggerated the number of Spanish casualties, stating that there were more than 8,000 dead and 7,000 prisoners, but the archives and other sources of the period indicate that it was only half of those numbers. However, the general premise of La Moussaye has been maintained throughout the centuries. Not in vain did he write with a vibrant pen, as well as a panegyric, of the success

Battle of Rocroi, Sébastien de Beaulieu (1612?-1674). (Paris 1643) (Wikimedia Commons)

of Rocroi and the genius of d'Enghien, soon to be Prince de Condé, and the protection that Providence provided him:

> Seeing that victory was now assured, the Duc d'Enghien fell to his knees on the battlefield and ordered all his men to do the same, to give thanks to God for such a great success. In fact, France had good reason to thank God, it had not won such an important and glorious battle for many centuries.

In his work on d'Enghien, Pierre Costé wrote:

> Nearly all of Spain's infantry perished on this occasion, and in subsequent campaigns the enormity of this loss, from which Spain never recovered, was well seen.[1]

Along the same lines, Henri Martin demonstrates this view in his *Histoire…*,

> The Spanish armies could never recover from this terrible blow: the moral damage was much more pronounced than the mere material loss, already difficult to repair for an empire in decline. The fame of military superiority that the Spanish had enjoyed passed decisively to the French.[2]

---

1   Pierre Costé, *Histoire de Louis de Bourbon.* Cologne, 1695.
2   Henri Martin, *Histoire de France Depuis les Temps les Plus Reculés Jusqu'en 1789, tome 14.* Paris, Furné, 1846.

This firm belief has been maintained over the centuries, and until today. In the words of Marc Blancpain, 'this victory appeared bright as the fires of a dawn: the dawn of new times.'[3]

The Duc d'Enghien had achieved a tactical success – the Spanish defeat and the liberation of Rocroi – and a strategic one in that he had defeated the Spanish invasion. But the French monarchy also needed a political success, which would strengthen the new King, Louis XIV, his mother, the Spanish Anne of Austria, and reinforce French national support and morale, after several years of war without any visible successes.

The battle was taken advantage of by the Queen Regent and Cardinal Mazarin, given the reaction of the high French nobility after the death of King Louis XIII and Cardinal Richelieu. The nobility was conspiring to recover their power, trying to undermine the authority of the Queen Regent, both because she was Spanish and because she was a woman, and of Mazarin, because of his Italian origin and the power he had accumulated in imitation of his predecessor Richelieu. The regency thus gave maximum publicity to the victory over the Spanish and the "great victory" was manufactured. The number of enemy casualties was exaggerated to 8,000 dead and 7,000 prisoners. The Duc d'Enghien himself participated in the process; his personal fame and reputation increased, along with that of his family, the House of Condé. This latter was particularly important after the mediocre military performance of his father, whom Richelieu had described as a person of no political and military capacity.

Rocroi was presented as a strategic victory that marked the end of the supremacy of the Spanish foot; but such an affirmation must be qualified, since the Spanish tercios had already been defeated a number of times[4]. In the other way, after the battle of Rocroi, the Spanish managed to defeat the French in various battles – notably at the Battle of Valenciennes (16 July 1656), when a Spanish Army of 12,000 foot and 8,000 horse defeated a French force of 17,000 foot and 8,000 horse. For all these reasons, Wilson[5] affirms that Rocroi's victory was not as decisive as he was led to believe, "but hardly indicative of Spanish collapse (…) Rocroi's real significance was the French avoidance of a defeat that might have destabilised Anne's regency and obliged the Country to make peace."

Modern Spanish historiography considers that it was from the Battle of *Las Dunas* (or the Battle of The Dunes or The Battle of Dunkirk), on 14 June 1658, in which 8,000 Spanish foot and 6,000 horse were defeated by 6,000 Anglo-French foot and 9,000 horse. The Spanish tercios thereafter showed a weakness that became permanent and on the battlefield they were frequently, although not always, defeated. Although in the defence of fortress (Flanders, Italy, Catalonia) they showed an extraordinary operational capacity against much stronger forces. In any case, it was after the

---

3   Marc Blancpain, *Le Mardi de Rocroi*. Vanves, Éditions Hachette, 1985.
4   Ceresole Alba (15 April 1544), the island of Djerba (May-July 1560), Heiligerlee (23 May 1568), Tunis (July-September 1574), Fontaine Française (5 June 1595), Turnhout (24 January 1597), Nieuwpoort (2 July 1600), Barcelona (26 January 1640).
5   Peter Wilson, *Europe's Tragedy. A History of the Thirty Years War.* (Harvard, Belknap Press, 2011)

Battle of *Las Dunas* that the decline of the tercios and of Spanish tactics was evident, but not in Rocroi.

The Battle of *Las Dunas* has, however, been even more widely ignored by historians. Why? The answer is simple: if the Spanish decline is evident after this battle, then the battle of Rocroi could not have been so important. In fact, Spain was able to maintain, despite the battle of Rocroi, its presence in Flanders, Catalonia and Italy, during the 1640s and 1650s; and it was only after so many years of war against France, in so many theatres of operations and on distant battlefields, that it was finally exhausted, but only as far back as 1658…

Following the supposed French supremacy after Rocroi's, in the framework of the Thirty Years' War, the French were defeated by the Imperials and Bavarians, and a small contingent of Spanish, on 24 November 1643, in Tuttlingen. The coalition of Imperial, Bavarian and Lorraine troops, under the command of General Franz von Mercy, together with some companies of horse from Flanders under the command of Juan de Vivero, annihilated the French and Weimar forces led by *Maréchal* Josias von Rantzau. Of the 15,000 Franco-German troops, 4,000 were killed or wounded and almost 7,000 taken prisoner, including 8 generals, 9 colonels and 260 officers, with 10 guns and all of the wagons, ammunition and provisions. Only 4,500 men escaped the defeat and France lost all its conquests made since 1638. The French Court downplayed the defeat, which has gone completely unnoticed in the annals of French history.

As for Spain, the war on so many fronts (Flanders against The Netherlands and France, Spain, against the Portuguese and the Catalan rebels supported by the French, and Italy, against France and its Italian allies) was unsustainable. In Flanders, Spain lost Gravelines in 1644, Hulst in 1645, and in 1646 d'Enghien captured Dunkirk, whose corsairs had held the Dutch and French in check. Nonetheless the French military successes hid the enormous fiscal pressure required to keep their armies fighting in Flanders, Germany and Spain, and the noble opposition, organised in the Fronde, threatened armed rebellion, which finally broke out in 1648 and would last until 1652.

This distraction allowed Spain to recover the initiative in Flanders and especially in Catalonia, where the rebels had only continued resisting thanks to French support. In 1651 the bastard son of Felipe IV, Juan José of Austria, began the siege of Barcelona, the capital of the rebellion, which surrendered the following year, coinciding with the Spanish reconquest of Gravelines, Mardick and Dunkirk.

These successes caused euphoria in Spain and instead of negotiating an advantageous peace then, Felipe IV ordered the continuing the war. However the tables had turned in France, which had left its instability behind. The Royalist victory against the Fronde, beginning in 1653, allowed France to slowly recover lost ground. On 14 June 1658, the Anglo-French army, under the command of Viscount Turenne, resoundingly defeated the Spanish forces led by Juan José de Austria and the Duc d'Enghien himself, who had changed sides, after his failed leadership of the noble revolt of the Fronde, at the Battle of *Las Dunas*. This was the strategic victory that forced Spain to negotiate a peace, as she was exhausted after so many years of war. At the Peace of the Pyrenees in 1659, Spain ceded to France Roussillon and Artois, and various cities in Hainaut, Flanders and Luxembourg.

10

Analysis of the Battle

In light of the events of the battle of Rocroi, it may be too easy to expose the mistakes and successes made by the contending sides, without any nuance. The truth is that their decisions must always be placed in the context of the heat of battle, that is, the decision of a General should not be judged by the data that we know with hindsight, but by the information available to the commander at the time. That is why, at first glance, it can be easy to argue that Melo was hasty and should have waited for Beck, or delayed the fight until Beck's forces joined his army, since we now know that around between 8 and 9, Beck's fresh troops had reached the outskirts of Rocroi. However, in 1643, Melo was only aware that he had given the order to Beck to join him as soon as possible, and that by mid-morning that army should arrive, but he did not know exactly when.

In his explanatory report, the Duque de Alburquerque places the blame for the defeat on Melo and Fontaine, and especially the latter, who, after his death during the battle, preserved a halo of heroism, but who could not defend himself against Alburquerque's accusations. The Duque affirmed that if his advice to attack on the afternoon of 18 May, when the French were advancing through the gorge, had been followed, the Spanish Army would have been successful. Had they fortified themselves as he suggested, d'Enghien's army would not have dared to attack. Moreover, on 19 May, if Fontaine had deployed the army as Albuquerque suggested, the French would not have been able to outflank them and again the Spanish Army would have been victorious. Albuquerque elaborated that Fontaine had not reinforced the wings of horse with detachments of foot, as he had asked him to. Nor had he ordered a general advance when the two wings of Spanish horse had defeated their opponents, leaving the French foot alone and without support. In short, Alburquerque lamented that his advice had not been followed, and therefore the battle had been lost.

In the first place, it is necessary to analyse the preparations for the campaign. On the one hand, Melo acted prudently in trying to hide his invasion plans about the tactical or strategic objective of the campaign. Whether the plan was for the capture of a certain city or of a province? Whether it was for the destruction of the enemy field army, et cetera? However this, perhaps excessive, caution was taken to the extreme. On a strategic level, the consequences manifested themselves in the fact that the generals, field marshals and the general staff were not aware of the plans, causing deep discomfort, which would only increase more throughout the campaign.

This discomfort of the high command with Melo was caused by the discontent generated by the appointments for the commands for the campaign of 1643. The veteran officers of Flanders were unhappy with the appointment of the Duque de Alburquerque as General of the Horse, and Álvaro de Melo's promotion as General of the Artillery. The first was appointed for being a nobleman of high birth without military experience; the second, for being his brother – although Álvaro had a lot of experience, because he was the senior *Maestre de Campo* in the Army of Flanders. In this same line of errors in the appointment of senior officers, the figure of Fontaine should be highlighted. Fontaine was a veteran and a respected officer, but he was an expert in the Dutch theatre of operations and his appointment in the French scenario was due to Melo's need for an experienced man of prestige as an adviser. By contrast he placed Andrea Cantelmo in command of the secondary army against The Netherlands, although he had experience against the French.

Also noteworthy is the disunity in the Spanish high command. The appointment of Alburquerque as General of the Horse sowed discontent among the ranks of the Spanish high command. Although Melo really did nothing more than follow the guidelines of Olivares, who was convinced that the higher nobility should participate more in state and military affairs, and that therefore their destiny was to serve in the generalship, even if they had no previous experience. Alburquerque's promotion angered Cantelmo, Bucquoy and others, causing a chasm between the professional generals and the 'upstart' nobility. If Melo had been more diplomatic, he could have resolved these differences but he could not, or he did not know how to.

To go deeper… Did Melo not realise that by taking the position of "General of the Horse" from Bucquoy, he would be doing a great disservice to all the native nobility of Flanders? Moreover, if he had at least handed over command to a professional officer, perhaps there would have been less anger – but he handed over command to the Duque de Albuquerque! How could a man like Melo, so diplomatic and political, make such a mistake? The most plausible answer is perhaps that Melo was carrying out the orders he had received from Madrid?

On a military level, the lack of knowledge of the objective of the campaign meant that the appropriate supplies for that campaign, including siege guns and ammunition, were not stockpiled, nor were they concentrated at the right time and place, for example, Namur, Charleroi or Mariembourg. If the Spanish had had more siege pieces, and taken due precautions, for example, moving the guns towards a simulated target to mislead any spies, Melo would have overcome Rocroi's defences, his reports indicated that the walls were weak, capturing the city and forcing the French to besiege them or fight a desperate battle.

Once the campaign began, the continuous marches and counter-marches were exceedingly tiring for the troops. Although these confused the French as to both the location of the Spanish Army and the objective of the campaign, they undermined the confidence of the Spanish high command, and the rank and file, in their commanding General.

When the field army finally reached Rocroi, the lack of adequate supplies was revealed in all its harshness. Melo ordered frontal assaults that caused many casualties, and perhaps his excessive confidence in the military skills

LES HEVREVX COMMENCEMENTS DV REGNE DE LOVIS XIII.
1644
SOVS LA GENEREVSE CONDVITE DV DVC D'ENGVIEN.

ROCROY

LA BATAILLE DE ROCROY

Battle of Rocroi, engraver unknown. 1643 or 1644. (Wikimedia Commons)

of his men, in addition to the lack of siege artillery, made him believe that the walls could be stormed with only courage and determination.

It must be said that Melo was so confident that the French would react too late that he did not send patrols to scout the territory beyond the Les Pothées forest. That is, if the diversionary movements made by his army, and especially by Isenburg, were successful in preventing d'Enghien from discovering the Spanish objective, then Melo became complacent and made no effort to find the size and location of the French relief army.

Moreover, he was so convinced that no relief army could come in time, and that three or four days would be enough to take the city that he did not protect his camp with defensive works.

Apart from the above, Melo did not know how to take advantage of his experienced horse. If Isenburg's horse had achieved a great feat by confusing the enemy army and making a great ride to surround Rocroi, then Melo did not use them properly to scout the region and locate the French relief army that he knew was coming soon. He did none of that, but kept Isenburg's and Albuquerque's horse in the siege lines, guarding the gates and walls, and only sent out small parties to reconnoitre. If Melo had acted differently, he would have prevented Gassion's *coup de main* from getting a relief party into the besieged town. Above all, Melo did not send horse or foot detachments to watch and protect the gorge that emerged onto the Rocroi plain. Surely, if access *had* been cut off, when d'Enghien held his council of war, L'Hôpital's counsel, of avoiding pitched battle, would have prevailed; the French would have withdrawn and Melo would have captured Rocroi. The battle as we know it would not therefore have taken place. Without a doubt, the French would have looked for an opportunity to recover Rocroi and force a battle, but this is a hypothetical situation that we cannot analyse…

None of the above precautions, which seem to be logical, were applied by Melo. The only possible explanation is his absolute, and excessive, confidence in the experience and numerical and qualitative superiority of his troops. However, this does not exempt him from using all of the resources and actions necessary to achieve a victory. He should have defended the access to the forest and to the gorge, and if the French had continued forward, he should have prevented their access to the plain and subsequent deployment. In fact, the French commanders were afraid that the Spanish would prepare an ambush for them in these dangerous areas, and were amazed to find that they were allowed to deploy on the plain without being attacked.

The episode on the hill, a strategic position that the French also observed, when Alburquerque insisted that it be occupied but was ignored, is highly indicative of Melo's overconfidence and disregard for tactical detail.

Nor did Melo order any large-scale attack on *Maréchal* La Ferté-Senneterre's horse, when on the afternoon of 18 May, they stumbled across the marshes and were highly vulnerable to any counter-attack. If Melo had taken advantage of that moment, with the French horse dispersed and the bulk of the French army tired by the successive marches and only recently deployed, he could have destroyed a large number of the enemy. Perhaps this may have persuaded d'Enghien not to engage in battle, or if he had done so, he would have had an even smaller and demoralised army.

The next day, when the battle began, the errors of Melo and Fontaine also manifested themselves. The annihilation of the detachment of musketeers in the forest, without Melo ordering their reinforcement… This action, moreover, shows the lack of caution with which Gassion acted: he should have sent scouts to locate the Spanish detachment sheltered in the forest.

Melo's main concern on 19 May was to prevent the French from reinforcing Rocroi. The deployment of the army in such an extended line, served both to show its strength and to occupy as much ground as possible to prevent the French from outflanking the Spanish deployment, as they had managed to do on the evening of 18 May. In the writings of Melo and Vincart, the expression "rescue the city" is mentioned on several occasions as the supposed objective of the French, or rather it was Melo's main concern. Perhaps Melo wanted to avoid the relief of the town on 19 May, and to present battle on the 20, counting by then on the support of Beck's experience and his men.

Melo did not act as a Commanding General and remain in a central position on the battlefield, stay at the side of his Field Master General Fontaine, and issue the appropriate orders as events unfolded. He in fact did none of that. Instead, following the panegyric account of his secretary Juan Antonio Vincart, Melo was at all the most violent points, in a clear exercise of publicising the value of General Melo, and thereby acting as a field marshal, but not as a Captain-General. In fact, and quite correctly, Aumale questions Vincart's account of the real role of Melo, who was supposedly present at all the decisive moments of the battle. Aumale asks, ironically, that *on serait frappé du nombre de kilomètres auquel on arrival faire* (we would be struck by the number of kilometres that he managed to cover).

At this point, one must question whether the decision made by Olivares to appoint Melo as Governor of Flanders, and Captain-General of the Army, was correct or not. His appointment was due to his service as a courtier and a diplomat, and a faithful supporter of the *Valido* Olivares. Thus, Melo was a member of the Cardinal-Infante's entourage and had first-hand knowledge of the military strategy followed by the Prince in Flanders, but that does not mean that Melo was a great General. In fact, a great doubt hangs over whether Melo had the personal conviction to be a great General. The Governor-General had several military successes in the campaign of 1642 culminating in the great victory of Honnecourt, but this was largely due to the participation of Beck. It would not be strange, however, if Melo now overestimated his own military capabilities and allowed the French to approach Rocroi unimpeded, trusting that Beck and his men would arrive in time to help him destroy the French army.

Neither Melo nor Fontaine acted as was expected of them, regardless of how they deployed the army – whether in three or four lines, whether with a longer frontage or with more depth. Presumably, Melo gave instructions to Fontaine that Beck's 5,000 men would arrive in a few hours, so they had to delay the battle or hold out until reinforcements arrived and with that superiority, defeat the French. Fontaine lengthened the front of the units and made the diplomatic mistake of placing the Italians in the centre, instead of on the left flank, perhaps to reward the Walloon tercios. All of these possible errors were perhaps caused by the initial assumption that in a short time they would have 5,000 fresh soldiers.

The main errors, and if it can be said, major, were the absence of orders to advance the foot when such aggressive action was needed. When the French fought against the musketeers in the forest, no reinforcements were sent. When Alburquerque's horse was attacked, neither reinforcements nor an advance by the foot was ordered. When Isenburg's horse swept away La Ferté's horse, no advance of the foot was ordered. When the French guns were overrun, the order to attack was not given. When the French foot halted and wavered, the tercios were not ordered to attack. Finally, the French right flank was allowed to successively attack the Walloon tercios, the German regiments and the Italian tercios without an order being given to the other echelons of the Spanish line to advance in support of the attacked units.

Alburquerque wrote in his letter,

In short, the French have clearly said that if we had attacked them the afternoon before, when I said, that we would have broken them; that if they found us fortified, they would have left; and that if in the morning we had changed the position we were in at night, we would have broken them. And Gassion, the Governor of the French horse, said that when he came to scout out our deployment in the morning, and finding us deployed as the day before, he had said to Duc d'Enghien: We charge, they are all ours.

Melo and Fontaine allowed the units of Spanish foot, without the support of the horse, to be attacked on the flank piecemeal and without mutual support, while simply waiting for Beck's reinforcements. All without planning any offensive action at the many times when they had the opportunity to.

This is how Alburquerque summarises it in his letter:

> Well, the horse went out to fight against the horse and foot of the enemy, who came mixed and united, and our infantry remained [quiet], without us helping each other.

In the field of hypotheses, what would have happened if Alburquerque had resisted? What if the Spanish foot had attacked? What if the horse of Isenburg had not scattered and had kept their order, as the horse of d'Enghien and Gassion did? And, in the worst-case scenario, if Melo had ordered the Spanish tercios to withdraw, as he did with the Italian tercios, could a defensive battle have been fought in the woods to the east of Rocroi? Could Melo have retreated with half an army and put up a fight the next day, reinforced with Beck's detachment?

In short, Melo failed in his immediate objective: the conquest of Rocroi. He failed to provide adequate means and he failed to take the town. On learning of the arrival of the French army, he should have focused on the initial objective; to capture Rocroi, and to do so he should have obstructed the passage of d'Enghien's army in the gorge. At best, he would have destroyed the French army; at worst, he would have caused heavy casualties and forced it to retreat. He could then have captured Rocroi the next day -remember, they had plenty of fascines ready for use. After capturing Rocroi, and with the French demoralised, he could have captured another town or attempted a pitched battle.

If Melo wanted to defeat the French in a battle on the Rocroi plain, he should have at least attempted some skirmishing in the gorge to inflict casualties and damage their morale. Moreover, when La Ferté-Seneterre attacked the Spanish right flank, a great opportunity presented itself, and he should have at least taken the opportunity to destroy that detachment, and then have proceeded to the rest of the French army.

When the battle finally took place on 19 May, if Melo really intended to fight, he should have used the full strength and experience of his Spanish tercios, which he did not. And if he was planning a defensive battle to wait for General Beck's troops, he should have organised his forces better to present a defensive battle and to gain time until the arrival of Beck's detachment – Melo failed again.

In contrast, the Spanish strategic objectives of the 1643 campaign were achieved. The French did not launch any offensive in Burgundy and the actions they undertook in Flanders, the conquest of Thionville, were costly in terms of men and resources and without any major success. Despite the human losses at Rocroi, the Spanish were able to quickly rebuild their army and launch attacks on the Dutch, whom they contained and forced to sign a truce.

With regard to the French victory, first and foremost the French intelligence service should be highlighted. Melo spent the whole campaign trying

Probably French troops, c1635. Engraving by Jacques Callot. The army is either drawn up for parade or, more likely, is illustrated as manoeuvring into line of battle. (Rijksmuseum, Amsterdam. Public Domain)

to conceal his decisions, or rather, he never expressed them to his General Staff, for fear that Dutch and French spies would report his intentions. This is an important reason why the Spanish Army was so ill equipped for the actions it had to undertake.

The enigmatic role played by the deserter, or spy, who informed d'Enghien of the early arrival of Beck's detachment has not been dealt with in the historiography. Perhaps he was indeed a spy that the French had managed to place in the Spanish ranks. It was not complete paranoia that Melo feared his plans would be discovered by the French, and his concerns proved fully justified precisely because of this spy.

Although the French did not know the details or Melo's plan of campaign, they did manage to call together various detachments which had been scattered across northern France and assemble them at various points – Vervins, Aubenton, Bossus-lès-Rumigny – as they approached the border, managing to match and even surpass the numbers of the Spanish Army.

It is worth looking to the planning of the battle by the Duc d'Enghien. He won a victory on the battlefield, but despite this victory, and despite what has been written about him by many eulogists, some of his decisions are, to say the least, questionable. First, he withheld the information from his troops and officials about the death of the King. He did not respect the advice of his most veteran generals and simply followed his own opinion – remember that he was only 20 years old and had very limited military experience. If he had not won the battle, d'Enghien would have been branded as crazy irresponsible, and disrespectful to the wisdom of his advisers. However because he won, all of these "errors" were classified as examples of his superior strategic initiative.

Enghien's arrogant attitude earned him the hostility of many of his generals, who expressed their disagreement in different ways in the following hours. *Maréchal* L'Hôpital's bitter opposition to engaging in battle and his inactivity during it. The disorderly attack on La Ferté-Senneterre during the afternoon of 18, frustrating d'Enghien's initial idea of engaging in battle that day. The unexplained withdrawal order given by La Vallière, acting on his own initiative because d'Enghien was fighting on the French right flank, beyond the Spanish lines.

Like Melo, d'Enghien acted more like a field marshal or the commander of a regiment than as a commander-in-chief. d'Enghien was determined to achieve glory in battle, and rather than remain with La Vallière and Sirot, he decided to assume personal command of the second line of Gassion's wing. From a strategic point of view, it was irresponsible, because he would lose the "vision" of the battle as a whole, and would only know the course of the combat in his sector. In addition, it was a tactical error, since the veteran Gassion was fully capable of commanding the right flank alone. For his brilliant actions, d'Enghien promised to ask Louis XIV for a *Maréchal*'s baton, which Gassion received a few months later. Thus, the fact that d'Enghien decided to be on that wing and at the head of combat troops was due entirely to his desire to gain personal glory, while relying on Gassion's talents to carry out the actual command.

d'Enghien left it to La Ferté to attack on his flank and he was unaware for much of the battle that those horse had been broken by Isenburg's attack. He was not present at the command position, next to La Vallière and d'Espenan, to order the French foot attack to retrieve the guns. Neither could he give La Vallière the controversial order to withdraw, nor did he order Sirot to ready the reserve. All this because he was behind the Spanish lines, fighting alongside of his horse and not commanding the army.

Was d'Enghien's decision to go from one side to the other of the battlefield behind the Spanish lines the right one? Given the outcome, the answer is yes, but again there are caveats. Firstly, it was unwise that the commander-in-chief of an army separated from the bulk of his army and away from a central or his anticipated position. Secondly, to ride through the enemy lines, with the obstacles of baggage and the chaos of battle, and under fire from Spanish musketeers, does not seem reasonable either. It must be said that if d'Enghien had been defeated, many of the decisions taken that now seem "brilliant" would have been described as "absurd, reckless and unwise".

On the other hand, the decision to attack Isenburg's horse instead of the Spanish tercios seems very reasonable, considering that the tercios were fresh and were going to be much more difficult to destroy than the Italian, Walloon and German units. We cannot know whether, from d'Enghien's position, he knew whether Isenburg's horse were formed or were scattered, whether he knew they had defeated La Ferté or whether he assumed they were still fighting; I am inclined to think the latter. d'Enghien threw his horse against Isenburg's rear perhaps in the belief that this would support La Ferté's troops, thus clearing the flank so that he could attack the foot unhindered.

d'Enghien, given his arrogant character and extreme lust for glory, disregarded the advice of his veteran generals, and had the support of only a few officers, such as Gassion, who was probably also involved in planning the overall strategy for the battle. In addition, Gassion and his scouts provided valuable information about Rocroi and its defences, to ascertain how long the City could hold out. Additionally, and especially, they provided intelligence about the terrain surrounding the village – the woods, gorge, the Houppe marsh and the plain. Knowledge of the topography of the region was undoubtedly essential to d'Enghien's plans.

If one had to make a brief summary of the battle of Rocroi, one could say that it was a battle between horse, where the French defeated the Spanish, and then, supported by foot, eliminated the Spanish foot units. The Spanish tercios were never able to demonstrate their potential, because neither Melo nor Fontaine gave them the order to attack, and thus they could only show their defensive tactics, although delaying the French victory for hours.

Regarding the Spanish horse, Melo lamented that it was poorly organised in *trozos*, and praised the French regimental system, noting that with the "regimental" model there were more officers and NCOs to command the squadrons. After the battle, Melo wrote that the survivors from the foot complained that the horse had not done their duty and had deserted them. The complaints reached the point that the Governor did not gather the survivors together, for fear that the horse and foot would fight each other.

However, the hypothesis that the French horse was manifestly superior to the Spanish horse should not be accepted without a more detailed analysis. La Ferté's French horse was defeated by Isenburg's Spanish horse, but d'Enghien and Gassion's horse did manage to defeat Alburquerque's horse. If the French horse was superior, why was it victorious on one flank but not the other? Isenburg was a veteran General, whereas Alburquerque was not? Perhaps the precautions taken by the former were entirely different from those ordered by the latter. What is certain is that Isenburg attacked when he observed a weakness in La Ferté's charge, while d'Enghien attacked when he observed weakness in Alburquerque's horse. Those who were more aggressive, won; those who were more unprepared, were defeated.

It should also be remembered that the Albuquerque horse, after being initially disorganised, put up fierce resistance with small detachments, proving that at company level, effectiveness and courage were at a very high level. The same was true of Isenburg's horse, who courageously withstood the attacks of Sirot's more numerous reserve.

However, both Melo and Vincart lamented the poor organisation of the Spanish horse, and gave as an example to follow the organisation of the French horse. A French regiment had a colonel, a lieutenant-colonel and a sergeant-major, and each company had its own captain and subaltern officers. These numerous officers manage to keep their squadrons in close formation and rally them back when they were dispersed. On the other hand, the lack of officers in the *trozos* made it much more difficult to reorganise the Spanish detachments after a charge or when they were dispersed.

In contrast, the Spanish had "Commissaries General of the Horse" as superior officers, but their appointment was for only six months, after which time they had to return to their usual ranks, which is why many

Battle of Lens, 20 August 1648, Jean-Pierre Franque (1774–1860), between 1835 and 1837. The painter intentionally highlights the figure of Louis de Bourbon, Prince de Condé, deservedly famous and termed Le Grande Condé. Without a doubt, the white horse, the Prince's luxurious attire and the horse's ornaments stand out. Condé wears his characteristic black hat with white plumes, a symbol of his Royal blood, and the blue sash, and catches the eye of his officers pointing their swords at the enemy. The French, led by Condé, won a resounding victory over the Spanish. However, the military success was not accompanied by a political one, since in France the bloody, noble revolt of the Fronde broke out, which paralysed the Country for several years. (Palace of Versailles, Galerie de Batailles MV 2726. Public Domain via Wikipedia Commons)

horse captains or *trozo* commanders would not obey these provisional commissaries.

Melo proposed that the Spanish horse in Flanders should be organised into regiments of 10 companies, but this proposal was not followed. After the defeat of Lens on 20 August 1648, in which the Duc d'Enghien himself defeated Leopold Wilhelm, Governor of Flanders, the regimental model was adopted, being called "tercios de caballería", composed of five or six companies.

Another French superiority in battle was the cooperation between horse and foot: indeed, their horse squadrons attacked mixed with the regiments of foot. This tactic is acknowledged to have originated in the reign of Henri IV of France, and was used from the early seventeenth century by several countries, although it reached its peak during the German campaigns of Gustav II Adolph of Sweden. The Spanish were no strangers to its use: indeed, Beck used horse and foot in his assault on the French flank at the

Battle of Honnecourt. The superiority of this combination was clear, hence Alburquerque's call for the presence of foot alongside his squadrons of horse. The annihilation of the Spanish musketeer detachment in the forest was undoubtedly due to the joint action of d'Enghien's foot and horse.

In addition, another advantage of this mixed disposition was that, in case of defeat or disorganisation of the horse's squadron, the horse withdrew behind the foot and reorganised safely, and then returned to fight.

In view of the final result and the French accounts, one gets the impression that the battle was in some ways a triumphal walkover for the French, as d'Enghien's genius had it all figured out – nothing could be further from the truth. Although Gassion and d'Enghien's horse disrupted Alburquerque's horse, they continued to hold, in small groups, delaying the French advance. Likewise the French attacks, although they managed to put the Walloons, Germans and French to flight, came at a high price. Furthermore, and to cap the supposed "total defeat" of the Spanish tercios, and by extension the Army of Flanders, if d'Enghien managed to annihilate the tercios, why did he not advance directly towards Brussels, given that he had "a clear road"? Why did he settle for conquering Thionville after a protracted siege and then conclude the campaign? The answer is simple: the Army of Flanders had not been destroyed, nor had the Spanish tercios 'ceased to be invincible in the face of the overwhelming technical and qualitative superiority of the French regiments'.

d'Enghien's idea of attacking Isenburg's horse from the rear was brilliantly and masterfully executed. However, the success achieved in the battle so far led him to underestimate the resilience of the Spanish tercios, and thus he made the mistake of launching three bloody and unsuccessful attacks with only his horse and accompanying foot. Only the arrival of whole French army and reserves, with the remaining cannon, allowed him to inflict the heavy casualties on the Spanish that forced their surrender.

The real French success at Rocroi is the belief created over the following centuries that "French linear tactics" were superior to those of the "monolithic Spanish tercios", when in truth this was not the case. French superiority, according to this point of view, was overwhelming. It is clear from reading the sources of *both* sides that this was not the case: the combined French horse and foot defeated the Walloon and German tercios, but they were no match for the Italians, or the Spanish tercios, whose musketeers and arquebusiers held the French at bay for two hours.

According to Peter Wilson[1], the French victory was due to a combination of factors, such as having a united high command, which was superior to the Spanish and a better regimental organisation of the horse. The Spanish were unfortunate that their high commanders fell in battle and Melo was unable to capitalise on his initial successes, failing to send his powerful foot into combat.

---

1   Peter Wilson, *Europe's Tragedy. A History of the Thirty Years War.* Harvard: Belknap Press, 2011.

French horse processing through Paris displaying the Spanish and cornets and guidons captured at Rocroi. Engraving, Nicolas Cochin, 1643. (Rijksmuseum, Amsterdam. Public Domain)

Guards of the *Cent Suisses* carrying colours captured at Rocroi in procession through Paris. Engraving, Nicolas Cochin, 1643. (Rijksmuseum, Amsterdam. Public Domain)

Colour Plate Commentaries by Stephen Ede Borrett

1. Spanish Army of Flanders, Gentleman Cavalry Trooper

Reconstruction based on a series of paintings showing the clothing of Spanish soldiers of the period by many of the most famous artists of the era, such as Jusepe, Rizi and Fray Juan Andrés. The trooper is armed with a sword and shown holding one of a pair of wheelock pistols. Unlike the foot, powder and shot were not usually carried on the body (as they would be later when cartouche boxes were commonplace) but at the saddlebow where the pistol holsters were positioned. His primary armour is the near ubiquitous 'buffe coat', which was flexible and lighter than metal armour but could withstand or turn most blows from an edged weapon. He displays his loyalty in the red military scarf widely used throughout all Habsburg Armies.

2. Spanish Army of Flanders, veteran pikeman

Based on images of Spanish soldiers from the 1630s, but especially a pikeman shown by the little-known Spanish artist Félix Castello (Madrid, 1595-1651). The pikeman's clothing is fashionably of the period and he wears decorated breeches but a plain, functional coat. The coat looks as if it is made of leather, although it would not be of the heavy protective leather of a 'buffe coat', nonetheless this would have been a highly effective and practical coat on campaign, the sort of design that might be favoured by a veteran. Gauntlets are commonly shown on many contemporary illustrations but feature very rarely in documents and thus must have been a private purchase. The armour and a sword carried from a baldric are usual for most armies of the early seventeenth century. It is worth noting that by the mid seventeenth century, most European Armies were moving towards some sort of uniformity, deliberate or otherwise, the Spanish Army deliberately resisted putting any uniformity onto its foot until well into the second half of the Century. It was common for Spanish soldiers to wear a red ribbon on their arm, to signify they belonged to the Army of Flanders.

3. Spanish Army of Italy, veteran musketeer

Again, the figures are based on the appearance of soldiers by contemporary Spanish painters, and the same comment applies to his clothing and a lack of uniform. The musketeer is shown in typical Spanish military clothing of the mid century. His coat is worn below a form of cassock with slit sleeves left to hang loose. The breeches (*gregüescos*) are fairly baggy, in a fashion that was already falling into disuse in favour of the tighter form worn by the pikeman in illustration 2. His stockings are often misinterpreted as boots – in fact he wears the usual stockings but with a second pair over the top and pulled high, giving the impression to modern eyes (although it is doubted if the same was thought at the time) of 'bucket-top boots'. Below the cassock the musketeer may be carrying his powder and shot in a bag at his right-hand side above the visible flask, making it easy to access. His sword is, as with many veterans, a privately purchased extravagance. Note the match lit at both ends, a strange convention but one that all contemporary manuals refer to – in this case, the musketeer is almost at the point of needing to use a new length of match, which would have been looped around his belt.

4. Croat Trooper

This figure is based on numerous depictions of the Croat Cavalry in the paintings of Pieter Snayers. He is dressed in a long coat in a style adopted from the Balkan lands, and which would continue in use by Croats as a distinctive item for a number of decades. The narrow trousers with short boots are again distinctive of the Balkan territories – albeit that many of the men in these units may not have been originally from that region. His hat is again distinctively 'Croat', but would become widely imitated by others (cf for example the illustration of the musketeers of the Garde Françaises shown in the *Maréchal de Bataille*, Paris 1647). He wears the famous *kroatka*, a 'tie' that became fashionable during the later Thirty Years' War amongst both horse and even senior officers and which survived until the end of the 18th century (the neck scarf today known as a cravat is its continued legacy). He is armed with a curved sabre slung from a narrow shoulder belt, a carbine slung at the other hip (note the small pouch for bullets) and a warhammer has changed little in form over the previous two centuries.

5. French Royal Guard cavalry, trooper

This trooper is reconstructed around armour of Thirty Years' War in the Musée de l'Armée in Paris. The trooper's head is well protected by a helmet, an unusual form of late burgonet incorporating elements of the zischägge. He wears the usual cavalry 'buffe-coat' but even so has added to its appearance by the use of open sleeves, which he may have had the ability to close when necessary. His use of a deep gorget in place of the back and breast had been pioneered by Gustav II Adolph, who had medical reasons for doing so; in this example, the gorget is etched, but note the 'frilled' edge of the red lining. He carries an expensive wheelock carbine from a baldric and a sword from an elegant, decorated waist belt.

6. French 'Swiss Pikeman'

The figure is based on the 'Swiss' Pikeman's armour, dated to c1620s-30, which is on display at the Musée de l'Armée in Paris. The whole suit is highly unusual and was almost certainly never actually intended for field use, which does not of course mean that it was not so used, especially if the armour was intended for the *Compagnie Générale*. His breeches are in the fashionable style of the 1640s but their red colour, and the red colour of his coat which shows through beneath the armour, is coincidental as the *Gardes Suisses* were not uniformed in red until 1662 (although individual companies may have been) and the Swiss Foot possibly not until 1672.

7. and 8. French Pikeman and Musketeer

These figures show a pikeman and musketeer from the 1630s and early 1640s, and there is little that can be said beyond the obvious about their clothing. The reconstructions again use armour and weaponry on display at the Musée de l'Armée de l'Armée in Paris. Also used for the figures are the 1645 engravings of Petrus Rucholle, as well as images of French soldiers on paintings of the 1630s in the house of Cardinal de Reschiller at Versailles, and the engravings of Jacques Callot. Like the Spanish Army, the French Army was not yet uniformed although many regiments certainly already boasted uniform colour coats.

Appendix I

Order of Battle of the French Army

Army of Picardie. Louis II of Bourbon

Refer to the map on page 103

A1. Right wing Horse, 1st line. Henri de Saint-Nectaire. 10 squadrons
    1 – Régiment de Raab Croate
    2 – Régiment de Schack Croate
    3 – Gardes du Duc
    4 and 5 – Royaux (former Cardinal-Duc and Dragons du Cardinal)
    6 and 7 – de Mestre de Camp Général
    8 – Régiment de Lenoncourt
    9 – Régiment de Coislin (or Coeslin)
    10 – Régiment de Sully

A2. Right wing Horse, 2nd line. François de L'Hôpital. 5 squadrons
    11 – Régiment de Roquelaure (or Roclore)
    12 – Régiment de Maineville (or Menneville)
    13 – Régiment de Sillard (or Zillard or Sillart) Weymarien
    14 – Régiment de l'Echelle (or Leschelle) Weymarien
    15 – Régiment de Vamberg (or Vümberg or von Bergh) Croate

B1. Centre Foot, 1st line. Roger de Bossòst. 8 regiments/battalions
    16 – Régiment de Picardie
    17 – Régiment de La Marine
    18 – Régiment de Persan
    19 and 20 – Régiment de Molondin Suisse
    21 – Régiments de Biscaras and de Bourdonné
    22 – Régiment de Rambures (or Rambure)
    23 – Régiment de Piémont

B2. Centre Foot, 2nd line. Chevalier La Valière. 7 regiments
    24 – Régiment de La Prée-Vervins
    25 – Régiment de Vidame d'Amiens
    26 – Régiment de Watteville Suisse

27 – Régiment Écossais
28 – Régiment de Roll Suisse
29 – Régiments de Brézé and de Langeron (or Lantern)
30 – Régiments de Guiche and de Bussy

C1. Left wing Horse, 1st line. Jean de Gassion. 8 squadrons
31 – Régiment de La Clavière
32 – Régiment de Beauveau Liégeois
33 and 34 – Régiment de La Ferté-Senneterre
35 and 36 – Régiment de Guiche
37 and 38 – Régiment de Fusiliers à Cheval de Son Eminence

C2. Left wing Horse, 2nd line. Louis de Bourbon. 5 squadrons
39 – Régiment de Netaf (or Nothaf/Notaf or Vaubecourt) Weymarien
40 – Regiment (Unknown)
41 – Régiment de Marolles (or Marolle)
42 – Régiment de Hendicourt (or Heudicourt)
43 – Régiment de Harcourt

D. Reserve. Barón de Sirot. 4 Regiments of Horse and 3 Regiments/battalions of Foot
44 – Régiment de cavalerie Hongrois Sirot
45 – Régiment mixte d'infanterie : d'Harcourt, d'Aubeterre and de Gesvres
46 – Régiment de cavalerie Gendarmes
47 – Régiment d'infanterie Watteville Suisse
48 – Régiment de cavalerie Gendarmes
49 – Régiment d'infanterie Royaux
50 – Régiment de cavalerie Chârost

E. Artillery. Henri de Chivré, Marquis de la Barre. 12 guns
Additionally Général Susane[1] records several regiments as having been present at Rocroi that are not referenced on the battle plans:
Régiment d'infanterie Quincé
Régiment d'infanterie Montclar
Régiment d'infanterie Espenan
Régiment d'infanterie La Mailleraie
Régiment de cavalerie Conti
Régiment de cavalerie Vatimont
Régiment de cavalerie Lignon
Régiment de cavalerie Grancey

---

1   *Histoire de l'Infanterie Française*: Louis Susane. 8 volumes, Librairie Militaire de J Corréard, Paris 1849–1853. *Histoire de la Cavalerie Française*: Le Général Susane. 3 volumes, Librairie J Hetzel & Co, Paris 1874.

Appendix II

Order of Battle of The Spanish Army

Army of Flanders. Francisco de Melo

Refer to the map on page 103

1 – 500 musketeers sheltering inside the forest

A. Left wing, Horse of Flanders and Hainaut. Francisco de la Cueva
2 – 1st line. Juan Pérez de Vivero: *trozos* Gaspar Bonifacio, Juan de Borja y Aragón, Césare Toralto, Antonio de Butrón y Mújica, Antonio López de Ulloa y Virgilio Orsini.
3 – 2nd line. Pedro de Villamor: *trozos* Ottavio Morone, Juan Antonio Barraquina, Rodrigo de Rojas, Ernesto Bentivoglio, João Mascarenhas, Barón de Gramont.
4 – Reserve? Barón d'André: 4 squadrons. Antonio Vicentino, Carlo Colombo, Conde d'Umego, Barón d'André.

B1. Centre Foot, 1st line. Paul-Bernhard de Fontaine
5 – Spanish Tercio Villalba
6 – Spanish Tercio Garcíez
7 – Spanish Tercio Alburquerque
8 – Italian Tercio Strozzi
9 – Italian Tercio Ponti
10 – Walloon Tercio Bassigny (or Bassigniesor or Beaucignies)
11 – Walloon Tercio Meghem

B2. Centre Foot, 2nd line. Paul-Bernhard de Fontaine
12 – Spanish Tercio Velandia
13 – Spanish Tercio de Castellví (Sardinian and Spanish)
14 – Italian Tercio Visconti
15 – Burgundian Tercio Saint-Amour
16 – Walloon Tercio La Grange (or Granges)
17 – Walloon Tercio Ribacourt
18 – Walloon Tercio Prince de Ligne

C. Right wing, Horse of Alsace. Ernst von Isenburg

19 – 1st line: Ernst von Isenburg: *Trozos* Conde de Bucquoy, Conde de Linares, Barón de Bicht, Pierre de Broucq, Carlos de Padilla and Charles-Guillaume de Doneckel (or Dunkel).

20 – 2nd line. Jacinto de Vera: *Trozos* Jacinto de Vera, Warlusel, Henin, Louis de Savary, and Croat Ystuan – some sources indicate a squadron of Vichet.

D. Reserve

21 – German Regiment Frangipani
22 – German Regiment d'Hembise (or Ambise)
23 – German Regiment Rittberg
24 – German Regiment Rouveroy
25 – German Regiment Guasco
26 – Barón de André?: 4 squadrons. Antonio Vicentino, Carlo Colombo, Conde de Umego, Barón d'André and Conde de Meghem.

E. Artillery. Álvaro de Melo. 18 guns

Bibliography

Books

Albe de la Cuesta, Julio, *Arcabuces, Mosquetes y Fusiles. Guerras Galanas, Románticas, al Francés y Otras Victorias y Derrotas*, (Madrid, Ollero y Ramos, 2013)

Albe de la Cuesta, Julio, '*De Pavía a Rocroi. Los Tercios de Infantería Española en los Siglos XVI y XVII*', (Madrid, Desperta Ferro Ediciones, 2017)

Aldea Vaquero, Quintín: *España y Europa en el Siglo XVII. Correspondencia de Saavedra Fajardo*, (Madrid, CSIC, 1986–2008), 3 volumes.

Barado, Francisco: *Museo Militar. Historia del Ejército Español*, (Barcelona, Establecimiento Tipográfico de Evaristo Ullastres, 1883–1886)

Belloso Martín, Carlos: *La Antemuralla de la Monarquía*. (Madrid, Ministerio de Defensa, 2010)

Bessé, Henri: *Relation des Campagnes de Rocroi et de Fribourg en 1643 et 1644*. (Paris, Delangle, 1826)

Black, Jeremy: *Atlasilustrado de la Guerra: del Renacimiento a la Revolución, 1492–1792*, (Madrid Akal, 2003) pp.75–77

Blancpain, Marc, *Le Mardi de Rocroi*. (Vanves, Éditions Hachette, 1985)

Cano Arjona, José Antonio, *La Batalla de Rocroi: Alcance y Consecuencias*. (Granada, Universidad de Granada, 2016)

Cánovas Del Castillo, Antonio, *Estudios del Reinado de Felipe IV*, (Madrid, Imprenta de A. Pérez Dubrull, 1888), volume 2

Cánovas Del Castillo, Antonio, *Bosquejo histórico de la casa de Austria en España*. (Madrid, Victoriano Suárez, 1911)

Chartrand, René, *The Armies and Wars of the Sun King 1643–1715 : The Guard of Louis XIV*. (Warwick, Helion & Co, 2019)

Chartrand, René, *The Armies and Wars of the Sun King 1643–1715 :. The Infantry of Louis XIV*. (Warwick, Helion & Co, 2020)

Chartrand, René, *The Armies and Wars of the Sun King 1643–1715 : The Horse of Louis XIV*. (Warwick, Helion & Co, 2020)

Claramunt Soto, Álex & San Clemente de Mingo, Tomás: *Rocroi y la Pérdida del Rosellón, Ocaso y Gloria de Los Tercios*. (Saragossa, HRM, 2014)

Contamine, Felipepe (ed.), *Histoire militaire de la France*, tome 1. (Paris, Presses Universitaires de France, 1992)

Corvisier, André, *Les Généraux de Louis XIV et Leur Origine Sociale*. Amiens, Yvert et Cie, 1959.

Costé, Pierre: *Histoire de Louis de Bourbon*. (Cologne, 1695)

De La Cueva Y Benavides, Pedro Alfonso, *Espejo Poético en que se Miran Las Heroicas Hazañas, y Gloriosas, Vitorias, Ejecutadas, y Conseguidas por el Excelentísimo Señor don Francisco Fernández de la Cueva, Duque de Alburquerque*, (Granada, Imprenta Real, 1662)

Dávila Orejón, Francisco: *Política y Mecánica Militar Para Sargento Mayor de Tercio*. (Brussels, 1684)

De Sotto Y Abach Langton, Serafín María, Conde de Clonard, *Historia Orgánica de las Armas de Infantería y Caballería,* (Madrid, D.B. González, 1851–1853), volume 2–4

D'Orléans, Henri, Duc d'Aumale, *La Journée de Rocroy (19 mai 1643).* (Paris, Champion, 1890)

D'Orléans, Henri, Duc d'Aumale, *Histoire des Princes de Condé,* (Paris, Calmann Levy, 1895), tome 4.

Dubet, Anne & Ruiz Ibáñez, José Javier (coords.): *Las Monarquías Española y Francesa (siglos XVI-XVIII) ¿Dos Modelos Políticos?* (Madrid, Casa de Velázquez, 2010)

Elliott, John H., *Richelieu and Olivares.* (Cambridge, Cambridge University Press, 1984)

Elliott, John H., *El Conde-Duque de Olivares: el Político en Una Época de Decadencia,* (Barcelona, Crítica, 1991)

Esteban Ribas, Alberto Raúl, *La Batalla de Gravelinas.* (Madrid, Almena, 2010)

Esteban Ribas, Alberto Raúl, *La Batalla de Kinsale: la Expedición de Juan del Águila a Irlanda, 1601–1602.* (Zaragoza, HRM, 2013)

Esteban Ribas, Alberto Raúl, *La Batalla de Tuttlingen.* (Madrid, Almena, 2014)

Esteban Ribas, Alberto Raúl, *The Battle of Nördlingen.* (Warwick, Helion & Co, 2021)

Fernández Duro, Cesáreo, *Francisco Fernández de la Cueva, Duque de Alburquerque. Informe en Desagravio de tan Ilustre Procer.* (Madrid Imprenta y Fundición de Manuel Tello, 1884)

Martínez Ruiz, Enrique (coord.): *Presencia Germánica en la Milicia* Española, (Madrid, Ministerio de Defensa, 2015)

Gerrer, Bernhard, Petit, Patrice and Sánchez Martín, Juan Luís, *Rocroi 1643. Vérités et Controverses sur une Bataille de Légende.* (Rocroi, Office de Tourisme de Rocroi, 2007)

Gimémez Martín, Juan, *Tercios de Flandes,* (Madrid, Falcata, 2004)

Gonzáles de León, Fernando, *The Road to Rocroi: Class, Culture and Command in the Spanish Army of Flanders, 1567–1659.* Leiden, Brill, 2009.

Priorato, Galeazzo Gualdo, *Historia di Leopoldo Cesare,* (Vienna, Gio. Battista Hacque, 1674)

Guthrie, William. P., *The Later Thirty Years' War: From the Battle of Wittstock to the Treaty of Westphalia.* (Westport, USA, Greenwood Press, 2003)

Hildesheimer, Françoise, *Richelieu.* (Paris, Flammarion, 2004)

Iselin, Bernhard, *Les Batailles qui ont Fait la France – Collection en 1000 Images.* (Paris, Editions Du Pont Royal, 1965)

Israel, Jonathan, *Conflicts of empires. Spain, the Low Countries and the Struggle for World Supremacy, 1585–1713,* (London, A & C Black, 1997)

Lépine, Jean-Baptiste, *Histoire de la Ville de Rocroi: Depuis son Origine Jusqu'en 1850: Avec une Notice Historique et Statistiue sur Chaque Commune de son Canton, et une Galerie Biographique des Hommes Célèbres ou Dignes de Souvenirs qui l'ont Habité,* (Rethel, Chez Lépine, 1860), pp.147–173

Létouf, Claude de, Baron de Sirot, *Mémoires et la Vie de Messire Claude de Letouf, chevalier, Baron de Sirot.* (Paris, Chez Claude Barbin, 1683)

Lonchy, Henri, *La Rivalité de la France et de l'Espagne aux Pays-bas (1635–1700),* (Brussels, Hayez, 1896)

Lynn, John A., *Giant of the Grand Siècle. The French Army, 1610–1715.* (Cambridge, Cambridge University Press, 2009)

Maffi, Davide, *En Defensa del Imperio. Los Ejércitos de Felipe IV y la Lucha por la Hegemonía Europea (1635–1659).* (Madrid, Actas, 2013)

Martin, Henri, *Histoire de France Depuis les Temps les Plus Reculés Jusqu'en 1789,* (Paris, Furné, 1846) tome 14 pp.7–12.

Martínes Laínez, Fernando & Sánchez de Loca, José María, *Tercios de España, la Infantería Legendaria.* (Madrid, EDAF, 2006)

Monlezun, Jules-Frédéric, *Bataille de Rocroi.* (Paris, J. Dumaine, 1877)

Mongrédien, Georges: *Le Grand Condé.* (Paris, Hachette, 1959)

Mugnai, Bruno, *Wars and Soldiers in the Early Reign of Louis XIV. The Armies of Spain 1659–1688.* (Warwick, Helion & Co, 2021)

Pacheco Fernández, Agustín: *Rocroi, el Último Tercio.* (Madrid, Galland Books, 2011)

Palau Cuñat, José & de Mirecki Quintero, José Luís, *Rocroy. Cuando la Honra Española se Pagaba con Sangre.* (Madrid, Actas, 2016)

Parker, Geoffrey, *La Crisis de la Monarquía de Felipe IV.* (Barcelona, Crítica, 2006)

Parker, Geoffrey, *The Army of Flanders and the Spanish Road 1567–1659: The Logistics of Spanish Victory and Defeat in the Low Countries' Wars.* (Cambridge, Cambridge University Press, 1972)

Parker, Geoffrey, *El Éxito Nunca es Definitivo.* (Madrid, Taurus, 2001) pp.140–142.

Parker, Geoffrey, *La Guerra de los 30 Años.* (Madrid, Antonio Machado Libros, 2003)

Parrott, David, *Richelieu's Army. War, Government and Society in France, 1624–42.* (Cambridge, Cambridge University Press, 2001)

Périni, Édouard Hardy, *Batailles Françaises (1643–1671),* (Paris, Ernest Flammarion, 1900) tome 4

Picouet, Pierre, *Les Tercios Espagnols 1600–1660.* (Paris, LRT Editions, 2010)

Picouet, Pierre, *The Armies of Philip IV of Spain 1621–1665: The Fight for European Supremacy.* (Helion & Co, Warwick, 2019)

Pujo, Bernhard, *Le Grand Condé.* (Paris, Éditions Albin Michel, 1995)

Quatrefages, René, *Los Tercios.* (Madrid, Ministerio de Defensa, 2015)

Ragel, Luís-Felipe, *El Sombrero de Rocroi.* (Madrid, Edición Cálamo, 2001)

Rodríguez Villa, Antonio, *El Duque de Alburquerque en la Batalla de Rocroy: Impugnación á un Artículo del Duque de Aumale Sobre Esta Batalla y Noticia Biográfica de Aquel Personaje.* (Madrid, Imprenta D.G. Hernando, 1884)

Segura García, Germán and Vázquez Bravo, Hugo, *Atlas Ilustrado de los Tercios Españoles en Flandes.* (Susaeta, Madrid, Susaeta, 2017)

Stradling, Robert, *Felipe IV y el Gobierno de España, 1621–1665.* (Madrid, Catedra, 1989)

Thion, Stéphane, *Rocroi 1643 : The Victory of Youth.* (Paris, Histoire et Collections, 2013)

Thion, Stéphane, *French Armies of the Thirty Wears' War.* (Auzielle, LRT Editions, 2008)

VVAA, *Memorial Histórico Español,* volume 17. (Madrid: Imprenta Nacional, 1863)

Wilson, Peter, *Europe's Tragedy. A History of the Thirty Years War.* (Harvard, Belknap Press, 2011)

Articles

Albe de la Cuesta, Julio, 'La Batalla de Rocroi, 19 de mayo de 1643' in *Desperta Ferro: Historia Moderna,* 9 (2014), pp.44–51.

Alvar Ezquerra, Alfredo: 'Va a Estallar Una Guerra: ¿Dónde? ¿Cuándo?' in *Desperta Ferro: Historia Moderna,* Especial I (2012), pp.6–9.

Black, Jeremy: 'Military Revolutions and Early Modern Europe: the Case of Spain', in García Hernán, Enrique and Maffi, Davide: *Guerra y Sociedad en la Monarquía Hispánica: Política, Estrategia y Cultura en la Europa Moderna,* (Madrid, Laberinto, 2006) volume 1 pp.17–30

Borreguero Beltrán, Cristina, 'De la Erosión a la Extinción de los Tercios Españoles', in García Hernán, Enrique and Maffi, Davide: *Guerra y Sociedad en la Monarquía Hispánica: Política, Estrategia y Cultura en la Europa Moderna,* (Madrid, Laberinto, 2006) volume 1 pp.445–484

Borreguero Beltrán, Cristina and Retortillo Atienza, Asunción, ' La Sua Professionefu di soldato. Italianos en el Ejército de los Austrias', in Torres Sánchez, Rafael (coord.), *Studium, Magisterium et Amicitia: Homenaje al Profesor Agustín González Enciso,* (Pamplona, Ediciones Eunate, 2018), pp.187–200

Camarero Pascual, Raquel, 'La Guerra de Recuperación de Cataluña y la Necesidad de Establecer Prioridades en la Monarquía Hispánica (1640–1643)', in García Hernán, Enrique & Maffi, Davide: *Guerra y Sociedad en la Monarquía Hispánica: Política, Estrategia y Cultura en la Europa Moderna,* (Madrid, Laberinto, 2006), volume 1, pp.323–358.

Chauviré, Frédéric, "Le Problème de l'Allure dans les Charges de Cavalerie du XVIe au XVIIIe Siècle", in *Revue Historique des Armées,* 249 (2007), pp.16–27.

Corvisier, André, 'La Mort du Soldat Depuis la Fin du Moyen Age', in *Revue Historique,* 254 (Paris 1975), pp.3–30.

De La Vega Viguera, Enrique, 'Juicio Sobre la Infantería Española en la Batalla de Rocroi', in *Boletín de la Real Academia Sevillana de Buenas Letras,* 23 (1995), pp.239–250

De Mesa Gallego, Eduardo, 'El Mito de la Batalla de Rocroi, 19 de Mayo de 1643', in *Historia Abierta. Colegio Oficial de Doctores y Licenciados en Filosofía y Letras y en Ciencias,* 256 (2015), pp.14–17

D'Orléans, Henri, Duc d'Aumale, 'La Prémiere Campagne de Condé', in *Revue des Deux Mondes,* 56 (1883), pp.481–514.

Drevillon, Hervé, 'L'Héroïsme à l'Épreuve de l'Absolutisme. L'exemple du *Maréchal* de Gassion (1609–1647)", in *Politix,* 15 (2002), pp.15–38.

Echevarría Bagcigalupe, Miguel Angel, 'El Ejército de Flandes en la Etapa Final del Régimen Español', in García Hernán, Enrique and Maffi, Davide: *Guerra y Sociedad en la Monarquía Hispánica: Política, Estrategia y Cultura en la Europa Moderna,* (Madrid, Laberint, 2006), volume 1, pp.553–578.

Felipo Orts, Amparo: "Monarquías Rivales. Francia (1610–1661) y España (1598–1665)", in Floristán, Alfredo (coord.), *Historia Moderna universal.* (Barcelona, Ariel, 2015), pp.351–371.

García García, Bernhardo José, 'La Guerra de los Treinta Años y Otros Conflictos Asociados', in Floristán, Alfredo (coord.), *Historia Moderna Universal.* (Barcelona, Ariel, 2015), pp.373–398.

Gonzáles de León, Fernando, 'La Administración del Conde-Duque de Olivares y la Justicia Militar en el Ejército de Flandes (1567–1643)', in *Investigaciones Históricas: Época Moderna y Contemporánea,* 13 (1993), pp.107–130.

Gózar Gutiérrez, Ramón, & Muñoz Rodrígues, Julio David, 'El Reino en Armas. Movilización Social y "Conservación" de la Monarquía a Finales del XVII', in García Hernán, Enrique and Maffi, Davide, *Guerra y Sociedad en la Monarquía Hispánica: Política, Estrategia y Cultura en la Europa Moderna,* (Madrid, Laberinto, Madrid, 2006) volume 1 pp.435–458.

Guillaume, Henri-Louis-Gustave, Baron Guillaume, 'Fontaine (Paul-Bernhard, Comte de)', en *Biographie Nationale,* (Brussels, Académie Royale des Sciences, 1883), tome 7 pp.188–191.

Israel, Jonathan, 'Olivares, the Cardinal-infante and Spain's strategy in the Low Countries (1635–1643): the Road to Rocroi', in Kagan, R.L. & Parker, Geoffrey (eds), *Spain, Europe and the Atlantic World. Essays in Honour of John H. Elliott.* (Cambridge, Cambridge University Press, 1995)

Iung, Théodore: 'Les errata historiques militaires. Campagne de 1643', in *Revue Militaire,* January (1870), pp.87–116.

Jiménez Estrella, Antonio, 'Pavie (1525) et Rocroi (1643): Impact Politique et Idéologique de Deux Batailles Contre 'el Francés'', in Ariane Boltanski, Yann Lagadec and Franck Mercier (dir.): *La Bataille: du Fait d'Armes au Combat Idéologique, XIe–XIXe siècle.* (Rennes, Presses Universitaires de Rennes, 2015)

Jiménez Moreno, Antonio: 'Opciones Estratégicas de la Monarquía Hispánica a Comienzos de la Guerra Contra Francia', in *Chronica Nova, 38* (2012), pp.177–202.

Maffi, Davide, 'Las Guerras de los Austrias', in Ribot García, Luís Antonio (coord.), *Historia Militar de España. Edad Moderna (II). Escenario Europeo.* (Madrid, Ministerio de Defensa, 2013) pp.79–118.

Maffi, Davide, 'Un Bastione Incerto? l'Esercito de Lombardiatra Filippo IV e Carlo II (1630–1700)' in García Hernán, Enrique y Maffi, Davide: *Guerra y Sociedad en la Monarquía Hispánica: Política, Estrategia y Cultura en la Europa Moderna*, (Madrid, Laberinto, 2006), volume 1, pp.501–536.

Martínes Laínez, Fernando, 'Los Tercios Españoles: la Fiel Infantería del Imperio de los Austrias'. *Historia y vida*, 450 (2005), pp.68–79.

Novoa, Matías de, 'Historia de Felipe IV, Rey de España'. *Colección de Documentos Inéditos Para la Historia de España* (CODOIN), (Madrid, 1878–1886) volumes 69, 77, 80 & 86.

Parrott, David, 'France's War Against the Habsburgs, 1624–1659: the Politics of Military Failure'. GARCÍA HERNÁN, Enrique & MAFFI, Davide (eds.): *Guerra y Sociedad en La Monarquía Hispánica: Politica, Estrategia y Cultura en la Europa Moderna (1500–1700)*, (Madrid, Laberinto, 2006, pp.31–48) volume 1

Picouet, Pierre, 'The Battle of Rocroi', *Arquebusier: The Journal of the Pike and Shot Society*, XXXI/I. London, The Pike and Shot Society, 2008, pp.2–20.

Quesada Sanz, Fernando, 'Fulgor y Ocaso de los Tercios. Los Mitos de Rocroi'. *La Aventura de la Historia*, 97 (November 2006), pp.60–71.

Rodríguez Hernándesz, Antonio José, 'La Caballería Hispánica. Un Arma en Alza' in *Desperta Ferro: Historia Moderna*, Especial XIX (2019), pp.44–48.

Rodríguez Hernándesz, Antonio José, 'Los Prisioneros de Guerra en la Monarquía Hispánica del Siglo XVII: Una Aproximación'. *Revista Universitaria de Historia Militar (RUHM)*, vol. 9, 18 (2020), pp.17–42.

Rodríguez Villa, Antonio, 'La Batalla de Rocroy', in *Boletín de la Real Academia de la Historia,* volume 44 (1904), pp.507–515.

Sánchez Martín, Juan Luís, 'Rocroi, el Triunfo de la Propaganda', in *Researching & Dragona*, 3 (1993).

Sánchez Martín, Juan Luís, 'Rocroi, el Triunfo de la Propaganda', in *Researching & Dragona*, 16 (2002).

Sanzsalazar, Jahel: 'Encarar el Miedo. Don Francisco Fernández de la Cueva, VIII Duque de Alburquerque (1616–1676)', in *Philostrato. Revista de Historia y Arte*, 7 (2020), pp.61–98.

Stratigos, Nicolas, 'Rocroi : Le Triomphe du Duc d'Enghien', *Vae Victis 11*, Paris, 1996.

Stradling, Robert, 'Catastrophe and Recovery : the Defeat of Spain, 1639–43', *History,* volume 64, 211 (1979), pp.205–219.

Vincart, Juan Antonio, 'Relación de los Sucesos de las Armas de S. M. C. el Rey D. Felipe IV Nuestro Señor, Gobernadas por el Excelentísimo Sr. D. Francisco de Melo, de la Campaña del Año de 1643', *Colección de Documentos Inéditos Para la Historia de España* (CODOIN) (Madrid: Imprenta de Miguel Ginesta, 1879) volume 75